WHO FIGHTS? WHO CARES?

War and Humanitarian Action in Africa

JUSTICE AFRICA &
INTERAFRICA GROUP

Africa World Press, Inc.

P.O. Box 1892
Trenton, NJ 08607

P.O. Box 48
Asmara, ERITREA

Africa World Press, Inc.

P.O. Box 1892
Trenton, NJ 08607

P.O. Box 48
Asmara, ERITREA

Cover design: Debbie Hird
Book design: Wanjiku Ngugi

Library of Congress Cataloging-in-Publication Data

Who fights? who cares? : war and humanitarian action in Africa / edited by Alex de Waal.
     p. cm.
Includes bibliographical references and index.
   ISBN 0-86543-863-3 -- ISBN 0-86543-864-1 (pbk.)
  1. Africa, Sub-Saharan--Politics and government--1960- 2.Protracted conflicts (military science)--Africa, Sub-Saharan. 3. Intervention (International law) 4. Humanitarian assistance--Africa, Sub-Saharan.
I. de Waal, Alexander.
  DT352.8 .W52 2000
  967.03'2--dc21

00-010130

DEDICATION

This book is dedicated to the million or more victims of genocide in Rwanda and the Great Lakes region, and to those who survived and are struggling to deal with the consequences of genocide and build a peaceful, stable and just order in Africa.

As a symbol for those who cherish justice and peace, this book is specifically dedicated to the memory of Lt.-Col. Wilson Rutayisire, popularly known as Shaban, former Director of Information at ORINFOR, a lifelong pan-Africanist and liberation fighter, who met an untimely death in the Democratic Republic of Congo on 5 June 2000.

CONTENTS

ACKNOWLEDGEMENTS

The chapters in this volume were initially prepared for the consultation 'humanitarian and political challenges in Africa' held in Kigali, Rwanda, 12-14 October 1999. The consultation was convened by InterAfrica Group and Justice Africa and hosted by the Pan African Movement. The consultation was made possible by the generous support of the Swedish and Norwegian governments and the Economic Commission for Africa. The papers for the consultation were based on a wide range of contributions, written and verbal. They were kept anonymous because this was the best means of obtaining pertinent and incisive analysis, especially of controversial issues. The editorial committee consisted of Alex de Waal, Abdul Mohamed and Tajudeen Abdul-Raheem. In addition, Susanne Zistel provided immense editorial and organisational support that made the consultation and book possible. They do not represent the views of any individual, institution, or government, and should not be taken as firm viewpoints or statements of doctrine or policy, but instead as attempts to stimulate thought.

Acronyms

AFDL	Alliance of Democratic Forces for the Liberation of Congo-Zaire
DRC	Democratic Republic of the Congo (formerly Zaire)
ECOMOG	ECOWAS Military Observer Group
ECOWAS	Economic Community of West African States
EPLF	Eritrean People's Liberation Front
EPRDF	Ethiopian People's Revolutionary Democratic Front
ICRC	International Committee of the Red Cross
IGAD	InterGovernmental Authority on Development
IDP	Internally Displaced Person
IHL	International humanitarian law
IMF	International Monetary Fund
IRIN	Integrated Regional Information System
MSF	Medecins Sans Frontieres
NGO	Non-governmental organisation
NIF	National Islamic Front (Sudan)
NRA	National Resistance Army (Uganda)
NRM	National Resistance Movement (Uganda)
OAU	Organisation of African Unity
OLF	Oromo Liberation Front
RPF	Rwandese Patriotic Front
SADC	Southern African Development Community
SPLA	Sudan People's Liberation Army
TPLF	Tigray People's Liberation Front
UN	United Nations
UNAMIR	UN Assistance Mission in Rwanda
UNDP	UN Development Programme
UNHCR	UN High Commissioner for Refugees
UNICEF	UN Children's Fund
UNOSOM	UN Operation in Somalia
WFP	World Food Programme

Foreword

Major General Paul Kagame
President of Rwanda

The contributions to this book represent an important and timely discussion on humanitarian and political challenge in Africa at the turn of the Millennium. The issues covered include: the persistence of war in Africa; genocide and its implications; structures for regional peace and security; interventions and sanctions; democratic political process and the fight against famine; humanitarian capacities and institutions; international humanitarian law; and humanitarian accountability. These are subjects that need to be discussed deeply, frankly and with open minds.

I shall focus my remarks on Rwanda as a case to highlight the humanitarian and political challenges in Africa. I will also take the liberty to pose questions, which, hopefully, can provoke further discourse on matters that touch the lives of many millions of people in Africa.

The context of this discussion is the plight of the African people. We can decide to be intensely academic and sophisticated, but the bottom line remains the dire consequences of extreme poverty; the hopelessness of the survivors of the genocide; the social wreckage that comes with armed conflicts; the political and economic marginalization that has characterized much of Africa for too long; the condition of women and children who cannot find their rightful place in an environment crowded with vested interests; serious human rights abuses inspired and executed by states and non-state actors against undefended citizens; environmental degradation that further takes away the livelihood of already impoverished African people; and the pandemic of HIV-AIDS that threatens to wipe out our modest achievements.

As we consider these themes we must constantly attempt to find out how our discussions can help to change the condition of the African people. Since 1959, Rwandese people have gone through a period of turmoil and relentless human rights abuses that culminated in the 1994 genocide. All the themes covered in this book run through this period, during which the state machinery became an instrument of violence against sections of the population. Denied the right to citizenship, Rwandese became some of the earliest refugees on the African continent. Discrimination on the basis of ethnicity and region became more entrenched and widespread. Political exclusion became the guiding principle in theory and practice. Social and economic benefits became more and more exclusive privileges of a narrow circle of those who were in power. Unwilling to involve the Rwandese people in the enterprise of governing, the state became more dependent on external sources of support in order to survive.

Therefore, the humanitarian and political crisis was deepening as the regimes of the day and the international community failed to respond. It is against this background that the Rwandese Patriotic Front (RPF) waged an armed struggle, having exhausted all possible peaceful means to redress the unresolved problems.

The Government of National Unity, established in 1994, was a step further in this struggle to reconcile and unite the Rwandese people; to eradicate the culture of impunity in our society; to create a new political dispensation based on inclusion; to establish conditions for social and economic transformation; to guarantee security for all Rwandese people and their property; and to promote cooperation and economic integration in our region.

It is the commitment to our people that has enabled the government and people of Rwanda to stabilize the situation and move forward. Let me use Rwanda's case to state the following points.

First, only by creating viable political mechanisms in which African people participate as engines and beneficiaries of change, can we sustain the struggle against humanitarianism and political crises. Political manipulation can only alienate our people, thus creating conditions for the recurrence of conflict and its consequences.

Second, resolving the political issues entails dealing with the problem of how resources are generated and distributed. Very often, in their attempt to appropriate national resources, Africa's ruling elite creates and manipulates divisions among the people to serve their vested interests. We have heard, many times, how economics determines politics.

Third, the 'new humanitarianism' has created a situation in which international relief agencies and NGOs dominate the humanitarian landscape. But how disinterested and apolitical are these agencies and NGOs? How effective are they in empowering the African people to take charge of their destiny? Between 1994 and early 1997 the international community, through these agencies and NGOs, spent over 3 billion US dollars in maintaining refugee camps that were controlled by the perpetrators of genocide. When we closed the refugee camps and repatriated our people, the outcry from the same international community was that this was a 'forced repatriation' and therefore 'against' international humanitarian law.

Fourth, occasionally humanitarianism becomes a pretext for blatant military intervention as exemplified by 'Operation Turquoise', the French unilateral intervention in Rwanda in 1994. It is important to note that the same United Nations that had abandoned Rwanda during the genocide was very willing to give a Chapter VII mandate to this force.

Fifth, genocide in Rwanda occurred when there had been sufficient early warning to the international community. What was lacking was the will and resolve to act timely and decisively to prevent or stop the genocide. Across the continent of Africa, there is constantly early warning but limited engagement from Africa and beyond to deal with the humanitarian crises.

Sixth, the events in Bosnia, Kosovo and East Timor highlight the double standards of the international community. We are yet to witness a similar level of interest and engagement in Africa. All are aware that the Lusaka Peace Agreement, which deals with the interest of the Congolese people, as well as the legitimate security interests of Congo's neighbours, like Rwanda, has not attracted significant interest from the international community.

Last, but not least, there seems to be a persistent inability to have lessons learned from previous experiences of conflict situations and efforts to deal with them. For example, in the case of Rwanda before, during and after the genocide, the weaknesses of the international system were evident. What corrective measures should be instituted to apply regional or international instruments in time to prevent humanitarian crises?

To be able to deal with the humanitarian and political crises generated by conflict, there has to be a deliberate attempt to empower the people; to build and strengthen institutions, while at the same time acting together at a regional and international level to complement local efforts.

I recognize the Pan African Movement's motto, 'Don't agonise, organise!' This book, reflecting the consultation held in Kigali, Rwanda, in October 1999, can be an important step to organize African people in tackling the challenges that they face. That is why we, the Africans, must own the debate about our destiny. This alone, though, would not suffice. We must democratize the practice.

INTRODUCTION

Africa's conflicts are diverse, complex and intractable, and it is difficult to generalise about them. One feature these conflicts have in common is that they tend to erupt in countries with limited scope for action by citizens to call their leaders to account, and they tend to intensify authoritarian and militaristic government. Disturbingly often they originate with, or develop, an ethnic element, which at its extreme can result in genocide. Too often, conflict and ethnic violence create their own spiral of grievance and reprisal, which can catch entire countries and even whole regions in a cycle of war and genocide. Escaping this 'war trap' is one of the most difficult challenges for whole swathes of Africa today.

A second feature of contemporary African conflicts is that they usually result in humanitarian crises, including mass displacement and famine. In the longer term, war has been a prime cause of the evisceration of African governments' capacity for sustaining food security systems, leading to widespread vulnerability to famine and the intensification of poverty. Meanwhile, in the short term, the humanitarian dimension to conflict has been the entry point for much international concern and action in Africa, ranging from relief provision to military intervention. These kinds of international engagement have their own consequences for Africa's position in the international order, and have contributed to Africa remaining relatively marginal and powerless.

This book stems from a recognition that the debates on conflict and humanitarianism in Africa have been dominated by concepts and discourses that originate in Europe and North America. It is not too strong to speak of an 'ideology' of conflict resolution, humanitarianism, and governance that is 'owned' by international institutions, western governments, and their associated think-tanks and universities. Despite lip-service to the need for African 'partnership' and even 'ownership' of these discourses, the reality remains that the African input has been disappointingly modest.

The challenge for an African input into international doctrines and practices of peace and security, and humanitarian action, has never been greater. Increasingly, responsibility for regional peace and security, including the task of military intervention, is falling upon regional and subregional organisations. Since the crises in Somalia and the Great Lakes, the Permanent Five at the UN Security Council are increasingly unwilling authorise interventions in Africa. Instead, operations such as the Nigerian-led ECOMOG interventions in Liberia and Sierra Leone are heralded as the model for the future. But the delegation of responsibility for action from UN to regional level does not solve the fundamental problems, it merely displaces them onto new actors. Hence the challenge for Africa to develop its own doctrines and practices to meet the realities of the 21st century.

Recent years have seen some very important developments in this regard. A notable case is the OAU resolution that forcible transfer of power is unacceptable, and the wider acknowledgment that war in any country or between any countries is a legitimate concern of the wider African and global international community. Other initiatives such as the Africa Leadership Forum, and the revival of the Conference on Security, Stability, Development and Cooperation in Africa mark a broadening of the continent's structures for peace and security. Most important have been the ECOWAS decision to intervene in Liberia and sustain that intervention over a long period and the SADC intervention in Lesotho. Despite their evident shortcomings, these actions represent an African assumption of responsibility for urgent political action to resolve crises on the continent, in the context of multi-lateral institutions and international law.

Africa's assumption of responsibility for humanitarian action has lagged behind. At a national level, governments have made great strides in developing food security policies, but the political will for implementing urgent measures has often been lacking. Equally seriously, African institutions have a notable lack of capacity for humanitarian engagement during conflict. Why is it always the ICRC, Medecins Sans Frontieres, Oxfam and CARE that are seen taking the lead in humanitarian crises in Africa? And why is it that UN agencies which are supposed to be equally owned by all sovereign states across the globe seem to be chiefly beholden European and North American agendas? Africans are no less generous than other citizens of the world, and in fact by far the greatest burden of caring for the victims of Africa's humanitarian crises falls upon Africans, especially the unrecognised heroes of every African famine and mass exodus, namely ordinary citizens who share their resources with their stricken brethren. But the humanitarian capacities of the OAU and subregional organisations are notable by their absence, and pan-African humanitarian NGOs are weak or non-existent. Is this simply a problem of resources? Or does it represent a wider failure of African civil and political systems?

This book derives from an initiative by African civil society organisations and the OAU to convene a forum in which these challenges can be discussed in a frank and open manner. The chapters in this book cover a range of political and humanitarian questions.

1. Why does war persist in Africa? This chapter develops a simple but provocative thesis, namely that war tends to generate more war. Without downplaying the importance of a range of political, social and economic causes for conflict, the chapter focuses on the vicious cycle whereby conflict escalates, spreads and re-ignites, creating a 'war trap' from which it may be difficult to escape.

2. What are the causes and implications of genocide? The 1994 Genocide of the Rwandese Tutsis was a profoundly shocking crime, and an episode whose consequences continue to reverberate throughout central Africa and beyond. This chapter examines this

genocide, in the context of other genocides in Africa and elsewhere, and tries to draw some preliminary conclusions about the nature and implications of genocide in Africa.

3. What are the prospects for regional peace and security in Africa? The last decade has demonstrated that regional peace and security must be a concern for every African country. Meanwhile, responsibility for African peace and security is increasingly delegated to African intergovernmental organisations. But a robust peace and security order demands far more from African governments and civil society.

4. What doctrines and mechanisms for coercive diplomacy (interventions and sanctions) should be considered in Africa? Interventions in Liberia, Sierra Leone and Lesotho, among others, have demonstrated the pressing need for African doctrines and methodologies of intervention. The use of economic sanctions in a poor and economically vulnerable continent also needs careful consideration.

5. What political processes can help prevent famine? The policy debates on food security have belatedly begun to focus on 'governance' as a component of famine prevention. This chapter elaborates on the democratic mechanisms that may be effective in helping to ensure that effective food security measures are developed and implemented.

6. What institutions and capacities can be effective in preventing and relieving humanitarian crises? African national and international capacities for humanitarian action remain disappointing. One of the reasons is that the policy and regulatory frameworks are oriented towards either government action or towards international agencies. Other frameworks and models need to be considered, some of which are discussed in this chapter.

7. What is the position of international humanitarian law? This chapter argues that, despite some significant shortcomings, the Geneva Conventions and other basic documents of international humanitarian law provide a very firm foundation for guiding and

regulating humanitarian action during conflict in Africa. A focus on the proper interpretation and implementation of existing laws should be the priority, rather than the development of new doctrines of 'humanitarian principles' and similar initiatives.

8. What mechanisms for humanitarian accountability can be developed? In the last decade, international humanitarian agencies have paid much lip service to the need for accountability. Africans have been conspicuously marginal in these debates. This chapter presents some proposals for how principles of accountability could be made real in the African context.

This is not an academic book. Neither is it a policymaker's collection of bland proposals. Some of the chapters promote controversial views. They are envisaged as the starting point for a frank evaluation of the challenges faced by Africa today.

A general theme of the book is that Africa's problems are complex and deep-rooted, but not insoluble or unique. A common thread runs through the chapters: solutions to the myriad challenges have been found in different places at different times, and by taking a broad-minded, wide-perspective approach to the situation today, solutions can be identified. Above all, African contributions to the debate on conflict and humanitarianism are essential if solutions are to be identified and become a reality.

1

THE PERSISTENCE OF WAR IN AFRICA

INTRODUCTION

A decade ago, as the Cold War ended and Apartheid capitulated, there were high hopes that Africa's wars would be rapidly resolved. For decades, external factors had provoked or stoked most of the armed conflicts across the region. It followed that the sudden unipolar geopolitical order brought a dazzling chance to bring these conflicts to an end. Ten years later, the outlook is less sanguine. While the pessimist view that wars will proliferate and the continent will descend into wholesale anarchy has not been borne out, there is no sign of wars becoming significantly less common. Despite their poverty, African governments have an apparently infinite capacity to wage war. Academic and pseudo-academic Afropessimism has never been more fashionable.[1] Critics are pointing to a range of factors allegedly inherent in African political structures that make the continent especially prone to war. Many African states are said to be 'criminalised',[2] governed by the 'politics of the belly'.[3] 'Neo-medievalism' is said to on the rise, with many countries dominated by 'warlords' or 'post-adjustment rulers' whose political strategies involve systematic violence.[4] Mercenaries have never had such a good press. According to these views, there are inherent characteristics (academics prefer to avoid words such as 'defects', but that is what they mean) in African societies that render them uniquely prone to war. Moreover, the academic-humanitarian industry that has sprung up on the subjects of 'protracted internal conflicts' and 'complex emergencies' is premissed on the specificity of African warfare. Supposely, when wars duly occur, they do not resemble the conventional wars familiar from European or north American history, but instead are highly irregular wars involving a combustible mix of ethnic politics and plunder.

Is this diagnosis, admittedly caricatured, remotely correct? Certainly it is true that if Clausewitz were to be asked to study contemporary African wars, there is little that he would recognise. Perhaps only the massive and bloody trench warfare and tank battles between the huge regular armies of Eritrea and Ethiopia would resemble his analysis of war as the 'conduct of politics intermixed with other means.' Other conflicts, from the confrontation between the mujahidiin of the Sudan Government and the guerrillas of the Sudan People's Liberation Army (SPLA), to the 'sobels' (soldier-rebels) of Sierra Leone, would be anathema to Clausewitz. But does the reason for this lie in the Clausewitzean analysis of warfare per se, or in the arch-realist theory of international relations implicit in his work? Arguably it is the latter. War in Africa is undoubtedly the conduct of politics intermixed with other means. But, in contrast to nineteenth century Europe, it is not, or not always, the pursuit of political interest in the international arena by relatively autonomous states. African states are notorious for their lack of autonomy from wider society; they are deeply embedded in networks of social, economic and political interest. The subunits of African countries—in particular regional or ethnic groups—often act autonomously and at the expense of the state, almost as if they were mini-states themselves. If we revise our theory of state and state interest to take account of these realities, the Clausewitzean maxim still holds good. The variety and irregularity of much warfare in Africa reflects the varied and complex socio-political terrain upon which armies are mobilised and wars are fought, and the nature of political process and political ambition in many parts of the continent.

Closer analysis makes it difficult to generalise about African wars. They cover the entire spectrum from solidly 'conventional' (Ethiopia versus Eritrea) to mass mobilisation on ethnic lines (Hutu extremism in Rwanda) to forms of predatory insurrection in which it may be difficult to distinguish soldier from rebel (Sierra Leone), with many variants in between. There are armies based on ethnicity or clan (some with ethnic ideologies), others mobilised in pursuit of religious extremism, still others with ranks partly filled by child soldiers, and others apparently organised mainly as business ventures. The complete or partial collapse of states in Somalia, Liberia and Zaire/D.R. Congo has also brought particular variants of warfare. Seek a variant of warfare, and it can probably be found in Africa today. The one thing that the continent seems to have in common is simply that wars are common.

This chapter begins with a simple hypothesis. It is that there have been wars in Africa in the 1990s because there were wars in Africa in the 1980s and 1970s. In earlier decades there were certain reasons for warfare, primarily anti-colonial liberation struggles and Cold War rivalries, along with some anomalies left over from the decolonisation period (Eritrea, Western Sahara, 'Greater Somalia' and arguably Southern Sudan). For some pastoralist groups, resistance to the post-colonial state was merely a continuation of resistance to the colonial state and its impositions. Our hypothesis, at root, is that the wars of the 1990s have erupted or continued because there were wars before or wars in neighbouring countries. Wars beget wars.

This 'wars cause wars' hypothesis has a weak and a strong version. The weak version is that wars tend to occur where there have been wars before. It makes no supposition about what causes wars. In this form, the argument is uninteresting. It is quite compatible with the argument that wars arise from 'root causes' such as ethnic diversity within artificial boundaries-because those root causes persist over time and can cause repeated conflicts. If ethnic diversity caused a war in a country in (say) 1975, then it is quite possible that it will continue to cause wars in 1985, 1995 and 2005.

The strong version of the hypothesis is that there is something in the nature of war itself that causes war to break out again, and it is the very fact of war, not its root cause, that is most important. This is what will be examined in this chapter. The legacy of earlier wars includes 'unfinished business' from incomplete or incompletely implemented peace deals, a recent tradition of the pursuit of political aims by military means, and the presence of military entrepreneurs with arms, followers and backers at their disposal. Also, wars tend to spill over borders, as neighbours become entangled with one another's conflicts. This creates 'conflict systems' in areas of the continent such as the Horn, the Great Lakes and parts of west Africa. Add to this two other factors: the logic of war itself, which tends to escalate and prolong, and the weakness of many African states, which renders them vulnerable to conflict.

The first section of this chapter examines this strong version of the hypothesis that war begets war, empirically, focussing on internal war. It concludes that this cannot be a complete explanation of war, but it is an important dimension, and in fact is arguably the most important factor in continuing war in the African continent.

WHY IS THERE WAR IN AFRICA?
Since the 1970s the number of wars in Africa has remained roughly constant. During the 1990s there have been more than a dozen new or protracted internal conflicts in Africa: this analysis is concerned with sixteen. The categorisation is fairly rough-and-ready: analysis of war is not an exact science, so simplifications are in order. Pre-existing wars that have been settled (such as Mozambique, Chad, Western Sahara and the Eritrean and Ethiopian struggles against the Mengistu regime) and coups d'etat have been excluded. Island wars (e.g. the Comoros) have not been included. Border skirmishes are excluded. However, border conflicts that have escalated are included as possible causal factors for subsequent internal wars in either country (Uganda-Tanzania, 1979; Mauritania-Senegal, 1989-90). 'War before' refers to a prior civil war or serious border dispute in the same country within ten years of the descent into civil war. 'War next door' means an ongoing conflict at the time the war broke out.

Table: Wars in Africa, 1989-1999

Country	War before	War next door	Other
Angola	Yes	Zaire/Congo	
Burundi	(1970s)	Rwanda	
Congo-Brazzaville	No	Zaire/Congo	
Djibouti	No	All neighbours	
Guinea Bissau	(1970s)	Casamance, Senegal	
Liberia	No	No	Exception
Mali	(1960s)	Algeria, Mauritania	
Rwanda	(1960s)	Uganda	
Senegal (Casamance)	border wars	border wars	
Sierra Leone	No	Liberia	
Somalia	Yes	Ethiopia	
Sudan	Yes	Ethiopia, Uganda, Chad	
Ugandan insurrections	Yes	Sudan, D. R. Congo	
Zaire/D. R. Congo	(1960s, 70s)	Rwanda, Angola	

In addition we have two border disputes that have become wars and also had wider repercussions involving mass expulsions of civilians.

Countries	War before	War next door
Mauritania-Senegal	yes (Mauritania)	Western Sahara
Ethiopia-Eritrea	yes (both)	Sudan, Somalia

This is an extremely crude tabulation which makes no attempt at tracing causal links. Some of the correlations are clearly spurious. For example there is no discernable direct link between the war in Sudan and the Ethio-Eritrean border conflict.

Nonetheless the correlations are impressive. Of sixteen cases, seven have had recent wars before and a further five have suffered prior wars within twenty years. Only one case had no neighbouring war, though in a further two cases (the two border wars) the causal link is tenuous or non-existent. There is only one case, Liberia, that is clearly an exception. The complementary hypothesis also holds true: sub-Saharan African countries that have been at peace, and that are surrounded by peaceful countries, generally stay at peace.

This analysis points us to two important elements in African wars. In Africa, wars are generally persistent, and they are readily transmissable from one country to its neighbours. (Indeed, investigation of wars in other continents leads to the same conclusion.) This obliges us to examine the genealogy of war, the logic of war whereby it continues and spreads, and is difficult to resolve, and the vulnerability of African countries to war.

The hypothesis of 'wars before or next door' should also generate some false negatives, i.e. cases where one would have expected wars but they did not happen. Cases in point include Mozambique, Chad, Nigeria ('wars before') and Kenya, Tanzania, Zambia, Malawi and Guinea ('wars next door'). Any general attempt to explain wars in Africa will have to examine these cases also, accounting for their recovery from, or resistance to the war contagion.

Finally, wars in Africa are closely linked to external factors, from outside the African continent. This was more evidently the case during the previous generation of African wars, when anti-colonial struggles and proxy conflicts arising from the Cold War were common, but it remains true in the late 1990s. The influence of foreign powers, notably the US and France, is important.

THE GENEALOGY OF WAR

Almost every war in Africa can trace its genealogy to a conflict in the 1960s or '70s, or even before (Southern Sudan has been intermittently at war since 1955). The major exception to this is Liberia and its own offspring, Sierra Leone. Every other major conflict in Africa today can only be understood by looking at its history.

The wars of these earlier decades had numerous consequences. One is simply the amount of weaponry in Africa and the numbers of men trained in its use.

A second consequence reflected the tendency of African rulers and their adversaries to fall back on ethnic mobilisation in one form or another at some point. As a result, in most war-affected countries, ethnicity has become militarised, and ethnic divisions have become sharpened. In some instances there are specific events that proved a turning point in militarised ethnicity. For example the Somali government's near-genocidal counter-offensive against the Somali National Movement in mid-1988, which led to the flight of most of the population of northern Somalia to refugee camps in Ethiopia where they were mobilised on a clan basis to continue the insurrection, was the most critical turning point in the militarisation of clan in Somalia. In Sudan, the government's recruitment of ethnic militias in 1983-86 began a process of ethnic conflict that reverberates fifteen years later. In the case of Uganda, the colonial government's preference for recruiting soldiers from the north of the country had important consequences.

Many ethnic or regional polities in Africa have traditions of self-government, and some have previously conducted relations with neighbouring polities in a manner roughly similar to interstate relations. In realist international theory, states are seen as pursuing their interest in an anarchic international environment. Some ethnic or regional polities aspire to do the same, usually as a defensive reaction to their marginalisation or repression. The spectacle of quasi-independent fiefdoms arising within the boundaries of one country, enjoying a high degree of political and military autonomy, has given rise to theories of state collapse, warlordism and 'neo-medievalism.' In Somalia, for example, one can see clan-based and regional polities pursuing their interests in a broadly 'anarchic' national environment. (Though the tendency for Somali factions to fissure should counsel against taking this model too far.)

A third consequence is that wars impoverished the countries in which they were fought. Agricultural and pastoral sectors were the worst hit, mineral extraction, logging and smuggling often the least. In Europe and America, wars have often seen the extension or entrenchment of the bureaucratic state, as it seeks to mobilise people and material throughout society. In such cases, the loss of capital, income and people in war may have been matched by a wider social mobilisation that could assist with post-war reconstruction. In Africa this has been less common. One reason is that Africa's wars have been largely internal, so that state mobilisation has been confined to certain regions or ethnicities. Another reason is that most governments were highly dependent on external military support and economic or humanitarian aid for their war effort and indeed their very survival. Often, anti-government forces were in a similar situation. Use of domestic resources has in some cases extended no further than selling diamonds or oil (Angola), logging (Liberia) or livestock raiding and looting (many cases). Support from diasporas has also been important, for example in the Eritrean People's Liberation Front (EPLF), Somali National Movement (SNM), and Rwandese Patriotic Front (RPF). There are very few cases of wars being fought primarily on the basis of internal resource mobilisation: the Tigray People's Liberation Front (TPLF) in Ethiopia and the National Resistance Army (NRA) in Uganda are among these exceptional cases. As a result, war has usually heightened dependency and left states weak.

The withdrawal of geo-strategic interest in Africa at the end of the 1980s has forced African governments and insurgents to draw on their own rather meagre resources to prosecute war. Only in Angola, because of mineral wealth, can the two sides buy lavishly over a prolonged period. The reduced capacities of states and insurgents have had far-reaching implications for the conduct of war. It encourages self-mobilising or self-financing war strategies, which entail a reduction of central control over armies. In turn this makes it harder to end wars, and easier for those discontented with a peace deal to restart them.

However, this break with the past should not be overstated. We need to be aware that many of the previous generation of wars in Africa were 'dirty wars', in which colonial, racist or Cold War powers used irregular insurgency or counter-insurgency methods. (This was particularly true of the South Africans, Rhodesians, Portuguese, French, and Americans and slightly less so of the British, while the Soviet Union and its allies preferred to build conventional armies.) The military technologies developed in these 'dirty wars', seen at their most extreme in the use of terror and conspicuous destruction by Renamo in Mozambique, were well-adapted to conditions of scarcity and weak central authority.[5] They were essentially cheap methods of destabilisation.

These social technologies for military mobilisation and the maintenance of discipline have endured and developed in the years subsequently. The Rhodesian Central Intelligence Organisation recruited the first Renamo 'pseudo-terrorists' and trained them with 'dirty war' techniques of sowing fear and distrust. They were encouraged to loot and rape, to invoke magical sanctions, and to try to divide communities along ethnic lines. Later these techniques were perfected by South African military intelligence, which itself

8

was working hard to play on ethnicity as a means to divide and rule at home. The recruitment of children as shock troops and the targetted use of massacres and mutilations were further developed. One technique, used to a much greater extent in Angola, was the indiscriminate use of anti-personnel land mines as a means of spreading terror and preventing people from using their land.

At the other end of the continent, another Western-sponsored state was simultaneously developing effective methods of fighting war on the cheap. Under President Jaafar Nimeiri, Sudan was the linchpin of US policy in north-east Africa. The growing insurgency in Southern Sudan in the early 1980s was centred on Chevron's oil concessions, whose first response was to propose bringing in foreign mercenaries. Nimeiri's response was essentially to propose Sudanese mercenaries instead, and from the outset, a key element of Sudanese counter-insurgency was the militia force, ethnically mobilised and dedicated to plunder. Militias proved an extremely cheap way of combatting the SPLA, while sowing deep ethnic divisions in the South and reducing vast swathes of countryside to severe famine.[6] Like the Rhodesian and South African-sponsored 'Contra' incursions in Mozambique, this was a deniable war, at least at first. Later, Sudanese military methods adopted a parallel track of destabilisation warfare, brought to the Arab world by the CIA-trained international brigades of the Afghan mujahidiin.

In almost every African war, a comparable set of genealogies can be traced. Soviet doctrines of massed conventional armies proved enormously destructive but less enduring: they are inherently much more demanding in terms of organisational capacity, equipment, training and expense. The liberation warfare tradition, adapted from Maoist principles, has proved more successful. Direct links can be traced from Frelimo to Uganda's NRA to Rwanda's RPF and elements in the civil war in Zaire/D.R. Congo. Another strand runs from the Algerian war of liberation to the Eritrean Liberation Front, the EPLF and, adapted, to the TPLF in Ethiopia. In all these cases, there was much learning from experience and the development of indigenous doctrines for mobilisation, organisation and strategy. In the NRA-RPF case, a counter-doctrine of ethnic massacre can also be seen, practised by the movements' enemies.

The war with no genealogy was Liberia. But in the case of Charles Taylor, Liberia suffered from a supreme military entrepreneur, who was able to adapt and apply 'dirty war' methods to dramatic effect. The speed with which the destabilisation in Liberia intensified into an all-out war, which in turn brought war to Sierra Leone, is a testament to the effectiveness of these kinds of social-military technology.[7]

These genealogical links are very strong. African war cannot be theorised without an appreciation of this range of military methods and the small but extremely influential groups of military men who have been trained in these techniques and further developed them. Africa's military entrepreneurs and their methods will be the core of the analysis of 'agents of transmission' of wars in Section IV below.

Conflicts involving pastoralists demand special mention. Pastoral societies appear to be more prone to conflict, including fighting between different pastoral communities, disputes with settled agricultural communities, and conflict with the state. For many herding communities, resort to force is a common and customary response to stress. Pastoralists are commonly well-armed in self-defence, and may resort to raiding or armed enforcement of movement through certain locations during times of drought or other stress. Farmers commonly encroach upon territory that pastoralists consider their grazing grounds or migration routes, and herders often respond with force. Most significantly, governments tend to encourage or force pastoralists to settle, they often impose restrictions on their movements and expropriate pastures for commercial farming or ranching, or they impose what herders see as punitive taxation. Pastoralists are often in a state of quasi-insurrection against the state.

This should not be seen as contradicting the earlier more general arguments about the origins of wars. Most conflicts involving pastoralists also fit the general pattern: they are continuations of earlier wars or spill-overs from nearby conflicts.

THE LOGIC OF WAR

Clausewitz argued that limited war has an inherent tendency towards total or absolute war. The conventional wars of the 19th and early 20th century proved that he was correct: these wars tended to become prolonged and to escalate, far beyond the initial anticipations of the belligerents. What is unthinkable at the outset of a war becomes thinkable, do-able and even subjectively necessary as the war develops. Constraints on war fall away as war continues.

Africa's wars exhibit the same tendencies, though the different nature of the continent's societies, economies and states means that 'total war' appears very different to European World Wars, Iran-Iraq or the Vietnam war. In the developed world, 'total war' entails the abandonment of restraint, the exercise of military technology to its limits, combined with the redirection of civilian industry to military production, and the use of propaganda for mass mobilisation. This may apply to the Eritrea-Ethiopia conflict, but in most of contemporary Africa, 'total war' entails the abandonment of restraint in applying various low-technology social technologies for war, and war becoming a way of life for certain groups.

Internal war is commonly the struggle for state power. African states usually have a 'winner takes all' structure in which the head of state has power over the political, social and economic life of the country. Whoever controls the symbols of sovereignty also has access to external resources, which, although relatively modest compared to those available during the Cold War, are still impressive. Authority over aid budgets, national currencies, commercial contracts, land law, etc, provides disproportionate power. Even when the state has collapsed, as in the case of Somalia or Liberia, the anticipation of these privileges sharpens the political and military struggle for control over the state. Compromise is therefore inherently unattractive.

A second main engine of conflict is struggle for greater autonomy for an ethnic group or region, including claims for self-determination and even secession. Some African states have been successful at managing diversity within a unitary sovereign state, but others have been spectacular failures. While the stated war aims of regional movements are often couched in terms of an equitable share of power and resources, the unstated aims on both sides usually tend towards the extremes—complete suppression of the revolt and a return to a unitary framework, as against seizure of state power, or failing that, secession.

It is common to note that the rationale for starting a war changes as the war continues. Initial war aims may be modest, but they tend to escalate rapidly.[8] This is true of both internal and some inter-state wars in Africa: they may start over a relatively minor issue but after a while both sides demand nothing less than the total capitulation or destruction of the other. The rapid escalation of the Eritrea-Ethiopia dispute from a minor border skirmish into all-out conventional warfare including aerial bombardment of cities is a striking case. Although each side accused the other of having prepared for a major war, the evidence points to mutual miscalculation being the major reason for the descent into armed conflict.

It is also commonplace to notice that as wars continue, the methods employed become more extreme. This is clearly the case for the use of material technology: commanders become more ready to use artillery against cities and landmines against civilians. It is also the case for social technologies.

One of the aspects of the logic of war that tends to prolongation is the element of uncertainty. During a war, accidents or misinterpretations of signals by the other side can lead to an escalation or prolongation or the rejection of a peace offer. Where there are centralised ar mies, it is possible to set up a channel of communication through a third party to ensure that these dangers are minimised. But social technologies of war that entail the decentralisation of authority to militia leaders or soldier-businessmen make it harder to avoid such incidents. A political-military leader in Africa may have to establish central control over disparate armed forces or achieve consensus among his lieutenants before he can meaningfully negotiate. A case of this was the first Sudanese civil war. In the late 1960s it was difficult to negotiate with the Anyanya insurgents because they were so disparate, and it was only after Joseph Lagu managed to centralise command (because he was the sole conduit for arms supplies from Israel) that a peaceful settlement could be negotiated. The fractiousness of Somali militias is another case in point: whenever a peace deal appears to be on the cards in Mogadishu, one of the contending factions is liable to split, with a dissident commander walking out with his own forces.

It is important to note that political or religious extremism tends to develop during wars rather than previously existing and providing a reason for war. In Sudan, Islamic extremism played only a minor role in the 1983 mutinies that sparked the civil war. On the contrary it was the ongoing war that played a major role in radicalising the Islamists to the point of seizing power in a coup in

1989 and declaring jihad in 1992. The role of Christian fundamentalism on the opposition side is even more striking. At its inception
the SPLA was secular and strongly anti-clerical, but as the war has
progressed, a combination of internal transformations in Southern
Sudan (including widespread conversion to Christianity) and the
readiness of Christian extremists to support what they see as an
anti-Moslem struggle, if necessary by supplying arms, has made
political Christian extremism into a growing force.[9]

The somewhat bizarre syncretic religious cults that sprouted in
Mozambique and Uganda, which mobilised certain constituencies
for armed rebellion, have also been spawned in conditions of prolonged war and suffering. They clearly represent a politics of des-
peration.

Nationalism and ethnic exclusivism, while pre-dating the armed
conflicts in central Africa, have reached their most extreme mani-
festations during war. Appeal to ethnic sentiment is the simplest
and sometimes the most effective means of mobilising an army
and paying for it. The extremist philosophy of Hutu Power existed
in Rwanda from the 1950s, but it was during the civil war of 1990-
93 that it was cultivated into a genocidal force.[10] Other forms of
ethnic chauvinism have also deepened and become more violent in
a cycle of warfare in the region. In west Africa, military entrepreneurs such as Charles Taylor and Foday Sankoh appear to have
had some success in deliberately creating and deepening political
ethnicity as part of their strategy for mobilising for war; these ethnic dynamics have subsequently taken on their own grim logic.

It appears therefore that most wars have started over issues other
than ideology: the ideological elements have been introduced later.
Once these elements have been introduced, it becomes much harder
for wars to be resolved. Even if the political-military leader who
first introduced the ideological element, perhaps in a tactical way,
is ready for compromise, any ideological mobilisation is likely to
spawn its extremists who will not be ready for any settlement short
of outright victory, even if that entails the complete physical eradi-
cation of the opposition and its constituency.

Economics is another factor. The relationship between resources
and warfare is complex and has its own dynamics. One of the aims
of wars is to control resources. Some wars started in part as business ventures, and in many cases military entrepreneurs have made

partnerships with their commercial counterparts to help in financing their war efforts, as well as enabling them to grow wealthy themselves. In a country such as Angola, the extraordinary wealth that is available in the form of oil and diamonds has enabled the belligerents to finance a war that has brought almost every other form of economic activity to a halt. The fact that sovereign power brings with it immense power to control economic resources, especially external aid, currencies and minerals, sharpens political-military competition across the continent.

The conduct of warfare is also strongly determined by the nature and availability of resources. Command and control of military forces depends on a mixture coercive capacity, ideology/loyalty, and control over the resources necessary to sustain an army. During the Cold War, most armies—both government and insurgents—had external patrons that made it possible to sustain centralised armies on the basis of centralised resourcing. The decline in external patronage and the fiscal crises afflicting many states have made this more difficult. Instead, armies have become more self-reliant, and as a result, more prone to fragmentation. In Somalia this was taken to the extreme.

Somalia illustrates the logic of military fragmentation, and also its limits. The ultimate prize in the Somali conflict is control over a sovereign government, and all the privileges that entails. Like many African countries, the Somali state was a 'winner takes all' state: there were no benefits to being in opposition. But since 1991 no one faction has been powerful enough to impose itself. One of the reasons for this is that each faction is essentially a voluntary coalition of self-supporting units with their own leadership structures. As soon as achieving power is within grasp, there is enough personal ambition, suspicion and jealousy among coalition members to break the alliance apart. Unable to seize state power, the factions then turn their attention to fighting over key strategic resources, such as ports, airports, important markets, and major agricultural areas. If they are unable to achieve a stable dispensation at this level—either domination by one faction or a compromise settlement—the fighting then goes to a lower level, over local resources such as pastures, wells, small town markets, etc. The Somali militias rapidly went through this fragmentation process during 1991 and 1992, with the focus of conflict shifting from major factions fighting over the state, to interfactional fighting over regional resources, to subfactions fighting over local resources.

This process has its limits. When the conflicts are over local resources, local mechanisms of conflict resolution are potentially workable, especially if the ambitions of factional leaders can be restrained. In Somaliland (ex-north-west Somalia) the process of fragmentation reached its limit in early 1992 and was then reversed, by a succession of inter-clan conferences that resulted in the creation of a government for the territory. The economic foundation of this dispensation is a consensus among the businessmen of Somaliland over their common commercial interests (primarily in the livestock trade and remittance incomes). A similar process of consolidation has occurred in north-east Somalia ('Puntland') but has yet to occur in the south, where resource conflicts are much more substantial. But even here, the logic of resource war is likely to reach its limits, particularly if there is attention to settling the resource questions before trying to set up a national government, rather than vice versa.

The logic of resource conflict in Angola and D.R. Congo has the important difference with Somalia that mineral resources are central. Whoever controls these commands sufficient funds to maintain a centralised army with enormous firepower, and to sustain presidential ambitions.

Not all wars are indefinitely prolonged. As in the case of the developed world, there are also limited wars in Africa. A limited war is most likely to occur when there is an inter-state conflict between two well-established governments without either already being prone to an internal war. Cases that hardly went beyond skirmishing include the clashes between Mali and Burkina Faso (1963, '74, '85), Nigeria and Cameroon (1997), and Senegal and Guinea Bissau (1988-90). Across the world, border conflicts of this nature are not uncommon, from Peru/Ecuador to Armenia/Azerbaijan to Pakistan/India. Such conflicts are particularly common where countries are facing difficult transitions from authoritarian to pluralist or democratic government.[11]

Border conflicts in Africa have a dangerous potential for escalation. There is a temptation for one or either side to engage in the internal destabilisation of the other, which is rendered easier because of cross-border ethnic commonalities, the likelihood that there is already some violent dissent in the other country, and the weakness of most African states. The Somali-Ethiopia war of 1977-78, the Tanzania-Uganda war of 1979, the prolonged Libya-Chad wars and the Mauritania-Senegal confrontation of 1979-80 are cases in point.

WHY DO WARS SPREAD?

The previous section has tried to explain why African wars tend to prolong themselves and escalate within a country. This section will examine how they spread from one country to its neighbours. Wars are contagious. They do not respect borders. Several reasons are apparent.

First, many of Africa's borders are recent and artificial, and thus a source of political tension. They are porous, as many of those living near the border can pass as citizens of both countries. Porous borders make it relatively easy to smuggle arms and people from one country to another. This is a standing provocation for one country to interfere with its neighbour. Border zones are often politically complex and sensitive. Not only smugglers, but political entrepreneurs of various kinds, need borders. One country's insurgents, resident within a neighbour's borders, may also be so badly behaved that they bring disorder and war to the neighbour. They may find it easier to mobilise among members of the same ethnic group who live across the border in the next country. Or they may introduce militant ideologies into their host countries.

Second, in extreme cases, insurgent forces will take refuge in neighbouring countries. Refugee camps are ideal places for military mobilisation. During the Cold War, UNHCR and western NGOs fed and protected many anti-communist insurgents (in Thailand, Afganistan, Somalia and central America). Southern African liberation movements tried to use refugee camps for similar purposes, but with less success, especially after the South African military's tendency of attacking refugee camps forced UNHCR and South Africa to negotiate over the principle of demilitarising camps. However, the South African precedent appears to have been forgotten in the 1990s, and instead the tradition of giving indiscriminate assistance to impoverished people encamped across a border has continued, even though the camps are often heavily militarised.

The assistance to the former Rwandese government in camps in Zaire is a case in point. This is an exaggerated version of the 'porous border' factor, a standing invitation for cross-border military action, as well as a profound destabilisation of the host country.

Third, states may be unable to control armed factions on their territories. In some cases, a state's capacity to police faraway regions is inadequate and an insurgent force from a neighbouring state may set up camp there with total impunity. The Sudan government was simply unable to control Chadian factions on its western borders in the late 1980s and early 1990s. With no state power at all, Somalia cannot control Islamic extremist groups on its territory bent on destabilising Ethiopia. Variants of this occur when the armed faction is in some way related to the host state, for example the RPF grew from inside the ruling NRA in Uganda.

A fourth variant is that military entrepreneurs may see advantages in taking the war to a neighbouring state. This may be to control resources, set up a safe haven, put a friendly government in power, or simply to destabilise a potentially hostile power. Thus the Liberian civil war was brought to Sierra Leone, where it developed its own logic. The RPF invasion of Rwanda was also an act of military entrepreneurship, as was (arguably) the RPF's later decision to take the war in Zaire beyond the cordon sanitaire along its border all the way to Kinshasa.

A possible fifth aspect is copycat wars and coups. The example of a successful coup or insurrection in one country can encourage soldiers in a neighbouring country to try the same. A coup in Nigeria may inspire potential putchists in Ghana.

Finally, the logic of retaliation and escalation works across borders. If one state is hosting or sponsoring an insurgent in the territory of another, the latter is likely to respond in kind. The deadly logic of escalation sets in. This logic has applied to Sudan and its neighbours. Sudanese support for the Lord's Resistance Army and other Ugandan insurgents was instrumental in changing Ugandan Government attitudes towards the SPLA from merely allowing (or not preventing) SPLA use of its territory, to active support. The same logic has brought both governments into the 1998-9 war in the D.R. Congo. Sudanese support for jihadist groups fighting the Eritrean Government and the Oromo Liberation Front and Ittihad al Islami fighting the Ethiopian Government led these two countries to retaliate by giving bases and support to the Sudanese opposition. Exactly the same process led the Rwandese Government to support anti-Mobutu forces, and invade Zaire in 1996.

There are some notable exceptions, such as Kenya. Kenya's foreign policy, with regard to its immediate neighbours, has been one of calculated self-interest, stopping short of outright military engagement. The partial exception to this has been close links with certain Somali factions in the immediate aftermath of the fall of Siad Barre. This exception proves the rule, first in that the other Somali factions were in no position to respond by destabilising Kenya, and second in that the policy was later reassessed. Kenya is perhaps the most 'realist' of states in north-east Africa in terms of international relations, and its policies have so far minimised the impact of the civil wars that have so damaged its neighbours. Another case is Zambia, which has so far succeeded in staying out of the wars in Angola and D.R. Congo. But the extreme pressures on the Zambian government to become engaged illustrate the difficulty of remaining an exception to the rule that wars do not respect borders.

WHY DO WARS RECUR?

If a country has been at war before it is likely to succumb to war again. One important reason is that no peace settlement will satisfy all. There is always 'unfinished business' after a settlement. Some dissatisfied elements on one side or the other will believe that a better deal could have been achieved with a slightly longer struggle or a different strategy, or they will believe that the deal has been 'sold out' by ambitious or corrupt leaders. Such dissatisfied elements are potentially dangerous military entrepreneurs. Their dissatisfactions may erupt quickly after a settlement, or they may nurse their grievances for many years. War remains within easy reach of those who have the skill, means and will to organise violence.

The dangers are exacerbated by several factors. First, there is likely to be war in a next door country, and hence a potential sponsor for any armed dissident, or at least a safe refuge. There are relatively few cases in which associated wars in neighbouring countries are settled simultaneously.

Second, the regional-political fragmentation that accompanies internal war brings certain advantages to regional or ethnic blocs and their leaders. During a civil war, an ethnically-based force— or to be specific, its leaders—may enjoy more autonomy than during peacetime. Heads of movements are like mini-heads of state, with their own armies. Such autonomy may be lost after a peace settlement.

Third, guns are usually readily available in any post-conflict society, and where they are not, people still have the networks by which they can acquire them. No country seems to be so poor that it cannot afford to import arms. The proliferation of small arms has recently received much attention as a contributor to violence and conflict. The availability of arms certainly plays a role. But, a factor that is probably more important is the proliferation of trained soldiers: in post-war societies there is no shortage of trained men able to form the core of an insurgent or mutinous group. Moreover, for men who have been engaged in war, fighting is a legitimate form of political activity. In some cases, liberation fronts have even developed ideologies that stress how armed struggle can be politically liberating. This predisposes to resuming war.

Fourth, the most common reason for a recurrence of war is failed disarmament, demobilisation and reintegration of former combatants. The reasons for these failures may include politically inept handling of absorption or discharge, lack of economic opportunities, non-payment of salaries or other frustrations, removal of commanders from political office, or a violent government crackdown in response to a protest by frustrated demobbees. It only takes one mutiny, badly handed, for a war to recur. Most processes of disarmament and demobilisation result in episodes of violent resistance including mutiny. There do not seem to be any exceptions to this rule. Even in the case of Ethiopia in 1991, where the army was completely defeated and there were no mutinies, there was serious violence for several years. Ethiopia suffered a big upsurge in violent crime, caused largely by unemployed demobbees, and some elements in the former army joined the OLF and launched a short-lived insurrection, while others were hosted by the SPLA and tried to re-invade Ethiopia from Southern Sudan. In Eritrea too, the demobilisation of former EPLF combatants did not always go smoothly. For those planning disarmament and demobilisation programmes, the question is not if there will be an episode of violent resistance, but when it will happen, how big it will be, and how it will be handled.

Lastly, in a post-war society, political violence retains its legitimacy. In a country where the current government has come to power by use of force, and are enjoying the privileges of legitimate sovereignty, it will always be attractive for other military entrepreneurs to follow the same path. The OAU principle of outlawing unconstitutional transfer of power is an important step against the entrenched legitimacy of organised violence.

A post-war society is therefore ideal terrain for an ambitious military entrepreneur. Cases of re-started wars including Angola, Somalia and Sudan demonstrate this. Counter-examples include Nigeria and Mozambique: in both cases it is likely that the economic satisfaction of potential military entrepreneurs was vital to the successful peace.

WHAT OF ROOT CAUSES?
Most analysis of war in Africa focusses upon the 'root causes' of conflict, arguing that conflicts can only be resolved when the root causes are addressed. Thus for example, it is argued that the war in Southern Sudan can only be understood in the context of decades of marginalisation and oppression of Southern Sudanese by a succession of governments in Khartoum, which have betrayed promises of federation, autonomy and self-determination. These arguments have much force. First, they reflect historical realities. Second, the people engaged in fighting the war strongly believe in their historical grievances, and will not be ready to settle unless the problems are comprehensively addressed.

But what is the 'root cause' of the war in Angola? Historically, the war began as an anti-colonial struggle against the Portugese empire. That empire ceased to exist in 1974, and the war took on a different character, related to the proxy conflict of the Cold War superpowers. In 1991, the Soviet Union ceased to exist and Apartheid was coming to an end. But the war has continued. What could be the 'root cause' of the war today?

Is it simply a struggle for power between competing elites? In some wars, 'root causes' appear to be more important than in others. In some cases, the root cause (colonial rule, Apartheid) is a grave injustice, inflicting huge suffering that is comparable to the suffering caused by the armed struggle to redress the basic wrong. In others, the root cause (e.g. exclusion of certain groups from state power, use of force in a border dispute) is certainly an injustice, but appears relatively mild compared to the havoc and suffering caused by full-scale armed conflict.

Some of the root causes cited by analysts of war in Africa include the following:

•Ethnicity, including both the domination of the state by one ethnic group to the exclusion of others and competition between different ethnic groups for power and resources.

•Artificial boundaries, which cut across ethnic groups, creating cross-border tensions and internal power imbalances.

•Resource scarcity, leading to armed conflict among certain groups (often especially pastoralists) over resources essential for survival. Often this is combined with arguments about environmental decline and alleged overpopulation.

•Economic dependency and underdevelopment, truncating the growth of a mature democratic politics.

•Alien models of statehood imposed by colonial powers. Post-colonial African states rested on shaky legitimacy: the independence generation of leaders rejected (initially at least) more traditional forms of legitimation, and sought to move into the positions formerly occupied by the colonial rulers.

The main argument of this chapter should not be taken as dismissing the importance of the root causes of Africa's wars. On the contrary, each war must be understood in its specific historical context. As stated above, many of those who fight are fighting for a cause, rooted in the history of their country, and will agree to settle for peace only when these historical grievances are redressed.

A focus on root causes, to the exclusion of the dynamics of war itself, is very incomplete and has several dangers.

1. A focus on real or supposed root causes can justify either continuing a war, or starting a war. It is common to see that in post-colonial wars, as the conflict continues and escalates, the alleged reasons for the war become deeper and more profound.

2. Root causes can be notoriously difficult to resolve. The different sides in a war have very different interpretations of the root cause, and focus on them can help drive them further apart.

3. Most supposed root causes for war are in fact root causes for conflict. Conflict can be non-military, confined to the political sphere. Historically, African peoples have had few options other than violence when faced with oppressive rule including colonialism and military dictatorship. But this is less the case today. There are more opportunities for the political resolution of disputes that could potentially spark war.

4. It is easy to assume that a settlement that addresses the supposed political roots of a war is a comprehensive settlement, whereas factors associated with the mechanics of war, and in particular the provisions for disarmament, demobilisation and reintegration of former combatants, can be just as important if not more so.

It follows that it is important to bear in mind both root causes and the dynamics of war.

WAR AND THE VIABILITY OF STATES

There is no doubt that at the time of the end of the Cold War, there were far-reaching changes in the nature of state power and the conduct of warfare in Africa. The aid-supported states that had been characteristic of the Cold War period, particularly where there was strategic competition between the super-powers, found themselves in crisis. Certain trends already present became accentuated:

Governmental authority no longer held sway over large rural areas of many countries; local political structures might establish greater de facto authority.

•Armies began to support themselves through licit and illicit commercial activities.

22

•Ethnically, regionally or commercially based militias began to proliferate.

•Local politics began to focus on issues of identity rather than political ideology.

•Population displacement (ethnic cleansing) became a favoured tactic in conflict.

•Unpleasant military methods such as using child soldiers and conspicuous atrocity were used in several conflicts.

The extent of this crisis needs no restating. Between the appalling nadirs of the wars in Ethiopia, Eritrea, Sudan, Somalia, Angola and Chad (all in the years 1986-89) and the Genocide of the Rwandese Tutsis in 1994 and its aftermath, African history is a list of massive tragedies, with relatively few hopeful interludes—many of which were quickly dashed. One of the most far-reaching implications of this time of crisis was the intellectual demoralisation of many Africans: far too many believed that the only possible solutions to their problems c ame from outside the continent.

It is interesting to note that the other great Cold War theatres have also suffered their crises, some of them in rather similar forms. The period 1989-96 saw many conflicts in the former Soviet Union and its peripheries. This list makes Africa's record pale by comparison: Former Yugoslavia, Albania, Trans-Dniestr, Abkhazia, South Ossetia, Georgia, Chechnya, Nagorno-Karabakh, Tajikistan, Afghanistan. These conflicts flared, frightening many Europeans and Americans who feared that these intense ethnic conflicts would spread like brushfire across the world, and then subsided.

These developments have elicited contrasting interpretations. One interpretation is various strands of Afro-pessimism, including 'the coming anarchy', 'neo-medievalism' and the like, which leave the concepts of sovereignty and legitimacy are radically relativised. According to this view, African states fall into two categories. One category is 'failed states' where the only authority lies with warlords, and where the international community must come to the rescue. The second is 'post-adjustment rulers', who are seeking to rule like internationally-recognised warlords, undermining the rule of law and bureaucratic order at home and abroad in their search for wealth and power. Such views hold that wars in Africa hold to an internal logic of self-perpetuation. As state authority collapses, war becomes a way of life—in fact, a highly adaptive means of survival and profit for certain groups—and therefore feeds on itself. Dwindling formal economies and environmental crises combined to create a self-perpetuating downward spiral of uncontrollable violence.

Attractive though this theory may be to detached observers, reality is a bit more complicated. A second interpretation recognises that these developments have been a reality in some parts of Africa, but seeks to locate their origin, not in a universal African tendency towards disorder, but specific historical circumstances. This view argues that certain African states have suffered a breakdown in legitimate political authority because of a combination of deliberate strategy by cold-war authoritarian rulers and the collapse of unsustainable government structures. The cases in point are Zaire/D.R. Congo, Somalia, Liberia, Sierra Leone, Sudan, and (in a somewhat different manner) Angola. This has resulted in differing political landscapes of 'warlordism', militia proliferation, and war economies. In circumstances where central power has been illegitimate and abusive, regional or ethnic mobilisation for resistance can be credible and effective. Recreating a viable state from a range of entities including ethnic and regional militias is not easy, but it is usually what citizens want, and the benefits of establishing a working state are such that it is usually achieved. This approach gains credence from previous instances of state collapse in Africa, such as Chad and Uganda, where credible national authorities have been reconstituted. Rebuilding states in Somalia, Liberia, D.R. Congo and Angola will require different strategies in each case, with careful attention to the issue of political control of resources.

Moreover, if we examine some of the unanticipated consequences of the current round of wars in Africa, we can see that— in some cases at least—they are leading to the consolidation rather than the collapse of states. In Ethiopia and Eritrea, both governments have gained more internal legitimacy and support during the conflict, and the mobilisation for war has strengthened the centralised bureaucratic control of each state. In the case of the war in Congo it is remarkable that, despite the massive involvement of neighbouring states, the contest is for the control of the state, not its dismemberment or dismantling. In short, the state in Africa is here to stay. Now and again, a particular state may undergo a severe crisis that leads to its collapse, but such instances are the outcome of particular circumstances rather than a general and irreversible trend.

HEGEMONIC PROJECTS IN THE 1990s
The 1990s have seen a number of continental or sub-regional hegemonic projects. Had any of these proved successful, they would have provided a possible foundation for a new order for peace and security in Africa (though not necessarily democracy and human rights). None have done so.

THE HUMANITARIAN INTERNATIONAL IN AFRICA
The first such hegemonic project was the idea of international humanitarian intervention.[12] This was an hegemonic project with a difference: its ideology was not territorial conquest or the projection of political and military power, but the projection of a particular set of values. This was not an attempt by the UN to usurp the powers of major states, or a project for recolonisation. Instead it was an attempt by major states to use the UN and other 'humanitarian' institutions to impose particular supposed solutions on Africa. Most senior staff of the humanitarian international would vigorously dispute the claim that they had hegemonic ambitions. Their motives were probably not recognisably imperial. But the perception—based on practical experience—of many Africans has been that the humanitarian international is practicing a new form of imperial control. They have not forgotten that 19th century imperialism was spearheaded by philanthropists too.

This aggressive multilateral interventionist policy was spearheaded by the United Nations and large humanitarian agencies-though the driving forces were the US Government (initially) and the the French and Belgian governments (more consistently). The experiment did not last. At the time of writing, the prospects of future large scale international humanitarian intervention in Africa, instigated by a western power, are remote. But it is remarkable that very similar 'humanitarian' rationalisations have since been cited by NATO for its intervention in Kosovo.

Extra-continental factors cannot be ignored in any analysis of the nature of African warfare. The involvement of colonial powers and super-powers was critical in starting numerous wars, supplying weaponry and expertise and developing military doctrines over decades. Western-imposed economic policies, notably structural adjustment, have also been important in creating the economic context in which governments and insurgents have relied on militias and 'dirty war' methods. The prominent role of humanitarian agencies has also dictated some war strategies, which have been premissed on the availability of relief food for war zones. In the early 1990s, the fashion for humanitarian intervention, and its operationalisation in Somalia, influenced African wars. Some belligerents tried to entice foreign military intervention, others sought ways of pursuing their aims despite the presence of foreign troops. In the case of Somalia, the intervention poured resources into the country to enable the fighting to continue, while heightening faction leaders' expectations that a future Somali state would enjoy international patronage and would therefore be a prize worth fighting for.

POLITICAL ISLAM AND WAR IN SUDAN

The civil war in Sudan is exceedingly complicated and defies easy categorisation. It has witnessed an important innovation in a modernised form of Jihad, Islamic holy war, which developed ambitions for regional hegemony in the early 1990s, reaching its maximum in 1995 at the time of the attempted assassination of Egyptian President Hosni Mubarak. While terrorist actions such as this garnered most attention, the political philosophy of the ruling National Islamic Front (NIF) had evolved into a far-reaching programmes of social transformation. This passed under various names: the most ambitious version was the Comprehensive Call (*al Da'awa al Shamla*), one of the most far-reaching cases of nationwide political engineering ever attempted in Africa.

Although religion was a relatively minor ingredient in the outbreak of the Sudanese civil war, its importance has increased over the years. The NIF's seizure of power in 1989 and the promulgation of the Comprehensive Call in 1991 and Jihad in 1992 marked important steps down this path. The NIF's extremist Islam is an almost wholly alien phenomenon to western secular or Christian audiences (not least because the NIF, in its English language statements, restricts itself to rather anodyne claims). It is nothing less than an attempt to redefine the nature of a state. This involves collapsing conventional secular distinctions between state and civil society, private and public, secular and religious, charitable and commercial, and civil and military. Dr Hassan al Turabi, leader of the NIF, has written eloquently about his vision.[13]

> [A]n Islamic state is not primordia; the primary institution in Islam is the ummah [community of all believers]. The phrase 'Islamic state' itself is a misnomer. The state is only the political dimension of the collective endeavor of Muslims.

Many Islamist institutions can be formally autonomous from the state, but part of an extended Islamist network of like-minded entities. Even the collection and disbursement of taxes can be done through non-state institutions, in accordance with the principles of the *zakat* (Islamic tithe). This gives a flexibility and strength to the NIF rule that was lacking in monolithically centralist Communist systems.

In other respects, NIF rule in Sudan is conventionally centralist, with ultimate power vested in a relatively small coterie of military and security officers attached to the NIF, trying to mobilise all the resources of the country in pursuit of the goals of military victory and economic transformation and development.

Some elements of the NIF's Islamic state present an attractive face—at least it appears as a serious attempt to challenge the intellectual and political hegemony of the West and develop an alternative approach to Africa's problems. However, in practice the process of Islamisation is extremely violent. Not only is it forcibly imposed on Sudan's large non-Moslem minorities, but the majority of the country's Moslems are also bitterly opposed to a form of rule that brooks no dissent. Jihad has become the main element in the NIF programme.

Jihad is both the government's military effort against the SPLA and the non-violent struggle for an Islamic state (more widely, Jihad can be 'equality, freedom and struggle in the path of God'[14]). The NIF's war strategy is characteristically sophisticated, at both an ideological and a practical level. In the Sudanese media, and for the consumption of those who donate to Islamic relief agencies working under the aegis of the Comprehensive Call, they call for transforming jihad from the 'jihad through the gun' to another jihad in the field on investment through training and equipment of mujahadiin [holy warriors] for the reconstruction of the land.[15]

A form of Islamic humanitarianism is an important element in the Comprehensive Call. The NIF government has striven to break its dependence on international aid, including western relief agencies, by developing a distinctive Islamic model of relief activity.[16] In the war zones of Sudan, economic development and humanitarian relief are the counterpoints of counter-insurgency: when rebel-sympathising villages are razed to the ground, their inhabitants are relocated to 'peace camps' where they work as labourers for commercial farms.[17] Such 'peace camps' ring government garrison towns, and their food production ensures that the garrisons can withstand the SPLA sieges.[18] Humanitarian work provides security: the aim of 'civilising' the rural people of Sudan (especially those who happen not to be Moslems, at least not yet) converges happily with the aim of retaining their loyalty to the government, or at least their physical presence in government-held areas.

Despite its sophistication and the fervour with which it has been implemented, the NIF's political philosophy ran into insuperable problems. The NIF has never commanded majority support even in the majority Moslem north of Sudan. In the early 1990s the extremists had the good fortune of a weak and divided opposition. But by 1995 they had antagonised most of Sudan's neighbours, which allied to contain it and to support the Sudanese opposition, and by 1997 the project was in retreat. Although al Turabi and others saw their concessions as merely tactical manoevres, and the Ethio-Eritrean war removed the main military-political threat, it is unlikely that the NIF will ever be able to regain the paramount position it had earlier enjoyed.

THE 'NEW AFRICA' PROJECT: GUERRILLAS INTO STATESMEN

At the opposite end of the political spectrum, the neo-Maoist legacy of people's war has proved more enduring than many predicted. Governments in Eritrea, Ethiopia, Rwanda and Uganda all came to power after protracted 'people's war' in various forms. The success of these forms of war is because they are founded on principles that remain applicable: gaining the support of the local population and fighting with discipline and professionalism. 'People's war' is less about ideology and more about easily-applicable basic principles (such as Mao's rules). It also entails a return to better trained armies.

The military intellectuals who emerged from these struggles are also a remarkable group. Those in power (in Eritrea, Ethiopia, Rwanda and Uganda) have achieved their position after extended periods in the field. They have all experienced military onslaughts that appeared to put the very survival of their people in doubt, and have survived by linking their struggles, in concrete ways, to the aspirations of the people. The process of making this link is an important but little-studied area. In Ethiopia, the leaders of the TPLF[19] adopted much of their social programme from the demands of peasants, including methods of land reform, a pragmatic (free market) approach to trade, a relief society, self-governing village councils, and a self-appraisal mechanism known as *gagama* for regular examination of the performance of institutions.[20] Many military intellectuals who have emerged from this experience combine military prowess with progressive politics—a combination that has become virtually extinct elsewhere in the world.

In 1996-7, some journalists and commentators speculated about a conspiracy, planned by the leaders of Uganda, Rwanda and like-minded countries, or fomented by the United States, to impose a new order on Africa. This is not correct: rather it is that the experiences and outlook of a range of leaders led them to common positions on certain issues, while they differed, sometimes quite sharply on others—for example the role of ethnicity and multi-partyism in politics. Most importantly, common threats, especially from Sudanese Islamic extremism and the Zairean President Mobutu's readiness to house insurgents trying to overthrow neighbouring governments, drove them together. In an ad hoc manner, these governments developed a defensive interventionism: active involvement in the civil wars in Sudan and Zaire, primarily to protect their national interests, and secondarily in the hope of helping to install a like-minded government. Ethiopia sent peace-keeping forces to Rwanda; Eritrea was ready to assist in the pan-African alliance that overthrew Mobutu.

The 'new Africa' project did not last. It suffered fatal flaws. The most important is that all the leaders came to power by force, and continued to regard the use of force as a legitimate political response to internal and/or external problems they faced. Second, the leaders formed an informal 'club' and their mechanisms of internal government and regional cooperation were not properly institutionalised.

The links between the leaders as individuals were not however underwritten by strong democratic institutions that could have sustained these alliances through their inevitable difficulties. The leaderships were not constrained and continued to lean towards unilateral military action as a means of responding to problems. Links between the governmental bureaucracies in the various countries were not institutionalised, so that when disagreements occurred at the highest level, there were few if any mechanisms to take the strain. The project of regional economic integration made little progress. Perhaps most significantly, the project of building up subregional institutions, such as the north-east African Inter-Governmental Authority on Development (IGAD) also made little substantial progress. Ultimately, the success of the 'new African leaders' project (it appeared more as a common project from outside than from within) was founded on the Ethiopia-Eritrea axis, which had sufficient popular legitimacy, political stability, military capacity (and a willingness to use it), to influence the entire region. However, this political infrastructure did not prove strong enough to overcome tensions in the Eritrea-Ethiopia relationship, that erupted into conflict in May 1998, nor could it resolve the internal political problems of the Kabila government in the Democratic Republic of Congo.

Critiques of the leftist tradition have focussed on questioning the extent to which guerrilla armies really did establish reciprocal relations with local people. For example, Norma Kriger has questioned many of the claims made on behalf of liberation fronts during the Zimbabwean war.[21] There has also been some revisionism on the NRA, for example Mahmoud Mamdani argues that it failed to establish deep relations with the local populace.[22] We can expect revisionist accounts of the social strategies of the EPLF and TPLF as well, following on the unravelling of the prospects of the 'new African leadership' providing a model for the continent.

In little more than a year after taking power, Kabila's government had sunk into a state of authoritarianism, nepotism and corruption redolent of its predecessor—while the President lacked the Machiavellian skills of Mobutu. Unsurprisingly, it took more than a few months to reverse almost four decades of decay and fragmentation, but the readiness of the new leader to play ethnic politics was a depressing reflection of his inability to deliver tangible progress towards democratic rule or economic development. The territory of the renamed D.R. Congo was also hosting insurgents fighting against Uganda, Rwanda and Angola, a fact that provided the spark for a renewed conflict, as neighbouring states intervened to protect their interests, while a spectrum of the Congolese opposition took arms. Unexpectedly, Angola switched to support Kabila while Zimbabwe and Namibia both sent forces to fight against the rebellion, preventing what seemed the imminent overthrow of the Kabila government. The project of rebuilding a viable state in Congo is proving even more difficult than expected. However, contrary to the expectations of many, the country has not been partitioned or collapsed into anarchy.

The biggest setback to the emergent African leadership has been the Eritrea-Ethiopia conflict, which was sparked by a dispute over the border area of Badme in May 1998. Two countries that had until then been the closest of allies rapidly came to the point of armed conflict, exchanging air strikes and ground battles in June, followed by the large scale expulsion of the Eritreans resident in Ethiopia. In this conflict, two highly disciplined conventional armies face each other along their common border, while both governments mobilise their human and material resources. In February 1999 the Ethiopian government launched a massive conventional offensive that succeeded in pushing back Eritrean lines, at enormous human cost to both armies. The conflict is an immense setback to the prospects for the region. However, the war is anything but anarchic or 'new': it is redolent of 19th century European wars during the age of emergent nationalism. Mobilisation for conflict has increased the domestic legitimacy of both governments, as the populations rally to the nationalist call, and the governments seek to expand their bases of support.

The setback to the 'new African leadership' alignment should not obscure its genuine achievements. These include successfully challenging other hegemonic projects, and proving the viability of states in a region in which Afro-pessimist outsiders had predicted nothing but anarchy and famine. Indeed it is possible that the unanticipated consequences of the wars in the Horn and central Africa will be the consolidation of states in the region.

CONCLUSION

African countries have proved themselves highly susceptible to war. A full examination of the reasons for this would entail a comprehensive political economy of the continent, including an analysis of the politics of inclusion and exclusion. Both strong states (Rwanda, Ethiopia) and weak states (Liberia, Zaire) have been vulnerable to protracted or severe war. Authoritarian states (Uganda, Sudan under Nimeiri) and states at various points in transitions to democracy (Rwanda, Ethiopia in 1998, Sudan in 1986) alike have succumbed to war. Ethnically homogenous states (Somalia) have been vulnerable alongside states with sharp ethnic cleavages (most others). If there is one internal factor that stands out among vulnerable countries it is concentration of power at the centre. But peaceful states also share this feature: it appears to be factor that prolongs and sharpens conflict when it occurs, rather than being a factor in starting it.

In the 1990s, internal wars in Africa generally break out because there are military entrepreneurs who are ready to start them. They have most fertile ground in countries that have emerged from war, or where there is war in neighbouring countries. Once war has set in, the features of African states and the nature of most African warfare dictates that the conflict is likely to be bloody, prolonged and prone to escalation—geographically, ideologically and in terms of mass violence.

The implication of this analysis is in some respects rather conventional. Africa's wars must be tackled and settled on a case-by-case basis.

1. Wars must be geographically contained. Neighbours should not interfere in wars, and neither in peace agreements. Settlements must include a subregional element, to ensure stability.

2. Post-war transitions must be successfully managed, especially when it comes to disarmament, demobilisation and the reintegration of former combatants into civilian life.

3. The implementation of peace agreements should be carefully monitored, as failures in this regard are a major reason for wars re-igniting.

4. Extremist ideologies, including religious fundamentalism and ethnic exclusivism, are fostered during war and remain a threat to peace.

5. Political violence must be rendered wholly illegitimate. Recent OAU moves to outlaw the use of violence to gain state power are a very encouraging development.

6. Lastly, despite all the difficulties, state power remains in Africa: the state remains the framework within which solutions to wars will be found.

The absence of a superpower-dictated security order, and the failure of ideological hegemonic projects, mean that any future African system of peace and security will have to be based on a common consent among states. The outlines of such a system are gradually becoming evident, in the minds of political leaders, as the alternatives fail. The essential elements are good neighbourliness, a common culture of tolerance and pluralism, and respect for regional and subregional institutions. These challenges will be further elaborated in chapter 3.

NOTES

1. David Rieff, 'In defense of Afro-Pessimism', *World Policy Journal*, Winter 1998/9, 10-22.
2. Jean-Francois Bayart, Stephen Ellis and Beatrice Hibou, *The Criminalization of the State in Africa*, Oxford, James Currey, 1998.

3. Jean-Francois Bayart, *The State in Africa: The politics of the belly*, London, Longman, 1993.

4. Mark Duffield, 'Post-Modern Conflict: Warlords, Post-Adjustment States and Private Protection,' *Journal of Civil Wars*, April 1998.

5. Alex Vines, *RENAMO: Terrorism in Mozambique*, London, James Currey, 1991; William Minter, *Apartheid's Contras: An inquiry into the roots of war in Angola and Mozambique*, London, Zed Books, 1994.

6. Alex de Waal, 'Some comments on militias in contemporary Sudan,' in M. Daly and A. Alsikainga (eds.) *Civil War in the Sudan*, London, Taurus, 1994.

7. Paul Richards, *Fighting for the Rain Forest: War, Youth and Resources in Sierra Leone*, London, James Currey, 1996.

8. Fred Charles Ikle, *Every War must End*, New York, Columbia University Press, 1993.

9. African Rights, *Food and Power in Sudan: A critique of humanitarianism*, London, African Rights, May 1997.

10. African Rights, *Rwanda: Death, Despair and Defiance*, London, African Rights, September 1994.

11. Edward Mansfield and Jack Snyder, 'Democratization and War,' *Foreign Affairs*, May/June 1995, 79-97.

12. Alex de Waal, *Famine Crimes: Politics and the disaster relief industry in Africa*, London, James Currey, 1997.

13. Hassan al Turabi, 'The Islamic State,' in John L. Esposito (ed.), *Voices of Resurgent Islam*, New York, Oxford University Press, 1983, p. 243.

14. Gudrun Krämer, 'Islamist Notions of Democracy,' in J. Beinin and J. Stork (eds.) *Political Islam*, London, I. B. Tauris, 1997, p. 74.

15. Quoted in: *Al Sudan al Hadith*, 19 December 1992, p. 11.

16. African Rights, *Food and Power*, 1997, chapter 9.

17. African Rights, *Facing Genocide: The Nuba of Sudan*, July 1995.

18. African Rights, *Food and Power*, chapters 8 and 10.

19. Subsequently a wider coalition, the Ethiopian People's Revolutionary Democratic Front (EPRDF).

20. John Young, *Peasant Revolution in Ethiopia*, Cambridge University Press, 1998.

21. Norma J. Kriger, *Zimbabwe's Guerrilla War: Peasant Voices*, Cambridge University Press, 1992.

22. Mahmoud Mamdani, *And Fire Does Not Always Beget Ash: Critical Reflections on the NRM*, Kampala, Monitor Publications, 1995.

2

GENOCIDE AND ITS IMPLICATIONS

GENOCIDE IN THE 20ᵀᴴ CENTURY

The term 'genocide' was invented in the 1940s in response to the enormity of crimes against humanity being perpetrated by the Nazi regime. Since then, unfortunately there has been no reason to let it fall into disuse. The lay definition of genocide is the attempted extermination of an entire ethnic group, and under this definition there are three clear cut cases in the last hundred years—the Turkish massacre of Armenians, the Nazi Holocaust of European Jewry and the genocide of the Rwandese Tutsis in 1994. For central Africa today, as for Europe fifty years ago, the fact of genocide is a defining event for a continent.

The Genocide Convention was adopted on 9 December 1948, one day before the Universal Declaration of Human Rights. The convention definition of genocide is rather wider than the lay definition, and includes as genocide a range of measures intended to destroy, disperse or harm an ethnic, racial or religious group. Under this wider definition there are other historical instances that count as genocide, and even more borderline cases. Some definitions (for example in the Ethiopian penal code) are wider still and include the category 'political group', allowing the term genocide to be applied to cases such as Stalin's purges, Suharto's massacre of the Indonesian communists, the Khmer Rouge in Cambodia and the Ethiopian Red Terror.

ABSOLUTE GENOCIDE AND CONVENTION GENOCIDE

This chapter therefore distinguishes between 'absolute genocide' and 'convention genocide'. Furthermore, 'convention genocide' will be split into several categories. This may seem a distasteful exercise quantifying human suffering and measuring hatred is always a grim business but it is an essential one.

In absolute genocide, the state and its servants maintain that it is a duty to annihilate a particular group. The target group not only has no right to life, but there is a duty on other members of society to kill or cooperate in killing members of that group.

In convention genocide, there is mass killing, under an intent to kill or harm members of the target group, but this is mixed with other intentions which may be equally important or even more important to the perpetrator. Broadly, three sub-categories of convention genocide can be identified:

1. Ethnic cleansing. Under this, the target group has no right to be *here*, in this particular territory, and there is therefore a duty to remove them. As people do not usually submit to forced removal en masse, this usually involves killing and harming many, on various pretexts including the need for 'security.' Usually the group is ethnically defined, but in principle an economic or social class could also be targetted in this way.

2. Cultural, social or political cleansing. Under this, the target group and its members have forfeited its right to its culture, social institutions or political beliefs and institutions. The target culture and social and political institutions are therefore to be destroyed, along with individuals who resist. The forcible dismantling or assimilation of minority cultures are cases in point. Revolutionary or counter-revolutionary terror against particular political groups is another. I.e. people are not removed from the territory, but their identities are changed, and in the process large numbers are killed and harmed.

3. Borderline absolute genocide. This is a complex category, hence its unwieldy name. Under this, members of the target group have forfeited the right to life, but there is no positive obligation on others to kill them. They are simply left wholly without rights or

protection. Others may kill them, or they may choose not to. Commonly it occurs during vicious counter-insurgency wars in which the army is at liberty to kill or violate members of a civilian group suspected of being aligned with the insurgents.

The differences between the types are not clear cut. A single case of genocide can have elements of two or even all three categories. Moreover there is a slippery slope from ethnic or cultural/social/political cleansing to borderline absolute genocide and then to absolute genocide.[1]

It is important to stress, again, that all cases of convention genocide are genocide, for which there is a non-negotiable international duty of prevention and punishment. But they are also different, both qualitatively and quantitatively, from absolute genocide.

PROBLEMS OF DEFINITION

It will be clear that the ambiguities of the Genocide Convention and of scholarly study of genocide create serious definitional problems. Several points are important.

1. The 'Ethiopian definition' of genocide that includes political groups among the list of potential victims is an important improvement on the standard definition. This should be adopted generally throughout Africa.

2. The distinction between 'absolute' and 'convention' genocide has both positive and negative implications. Some of the advantages of the distinction have been described. The major disadvantage is that the distinction creates another criterion to argue over: it is already difficult enough to establish a consensus on what is genocide, without having a second controversy over what sort of genocide it may be. Moreover, the distinction might be used as an excuse for downgrading 'convention' genocide as a crime, and arguing that it is only necessary to use all necessary measures to prevent, stop and punish 'absolute' genocide. This would be very unfortunate.

3. Who is to decide what counts as genocide? The reluctance of the US and other major powers to recognise that genocide was being committed in Rwanda in 1994 is a warning that it is not easy even in apparently the most clear-cut case to decide whether the line between 'mere' massacres and war has been crossed into genocide. Leaving it to a government to decide whether an event counts as genocide is dangerous. Independent mechanisms for diagnosis are preferable. But multi-lateral mechanisms may have the drawback of being slow.

INSTANCES OF GENOCIDE

For Africa today, the classic case of genocide, and the sole case of absolute genocide, to which most attention will be devoted, is Rwanda. But we should also focus on some other cases which fit the convention definition, although they may be more controversial. Examination of these cases allows for greater depth and subtlety in trying to explain genocide and explore the measures needed to prevent and punish it. The following list is concerned solely with post-independence Africa. This is not to belittle the importance of the long list of cases of convention genocide (including borderline absolute genocide) of African peoples during the colonial conquest and 'pacification'. The mass killings and man-made famines that decimated, for example, the Herero of Namibia, were genocidal. The exactions of Belgian rule in the Congo and British punitive expeditions in Southern Sudan were arguably so. But because they were implemented by foreign powers, these cases are less relevant to the issue in hand. Some cases worthy of consideration are listed below. Many of these cases are not widely recognised as genocides, and it is highly contentious what would have been the right international response in such cases.

•Burundi, 1972: the systematic murderous elimination of a large section of the educated Hutu. The reciprocal massacres after the 1993 coup were also genocidal.
•Eritrea, Ethiopian military onslaughts at various points in its struggle for independence.
•Ethiopia under Colonel Mengistu, including (i) the Red Terror of 1977-8 in which tens of thousands of young people were murdered

on suspicion of being 'anti-revolutionary', and (ii) war and deportations in various regions including Tigray in the early 1980s.

•The mass killings perpetrated by the Obote II regime Luwero Triangle in Uganda in the mid 1980s.

•The destruction of Hargeisa and other Isaaq towns in north-west Somalia by the Siad Barre regime in 1988.

•Various experiences of marginalised peoples in Sudan including (i) the militia war against the Dinka of northern Bahr el Ghazal and (ii) the Jihad against the Nuba in 1992 which included mass forcible deportations and separation of men and women.

•The mass killings in eastern Zaire in 1996. The systematic killings of Zairean Tutsis in Kivu, especially Masisi, were an extension of the 1994 genocide in Rwanda. There were also mass killings of Hutu militiamen and civilians in the Rwandese/AFDL counter-offensive in 1997, the extent and nature of which have never been properly ascertained.

This list is not intended be comprehensive nor to minimise the gravity of human rights violations and mass ethnic violence or expulsion in other cases.

It is also important to mention some cases in which genocide was alleged but did not occur, notably Biafra in the closing stages and aftermath of the war in 1969-70. In Apartheid South Africa there were undoubtedly genocidal projects harboured and even planned by some extremists, such as projects to find diseases that selectively attacked black people, but this case was (a) never carried to fruition and (b) reflects a racist ideology that is, hopefully, of historical interest only.

Outside Africa, in addition to the Nazi Holocaust and the Armenian mass killing, the following cases are worthy of consideration:

•Stalin's deportations of entire nationalities that allegedly collaborated with the Nazis, including the Cossacks and Chechens. Stalin's pre-war purges of alleged counter-revolutionaries count as genocidal under the wider definition.

•Cambodia under the Khmer Rouge.

•The Indonesian massacre of the communists in 1965-6 and repression of East Timor after its annexation in 1974. The mass killings in East Timor after the independence vote in September 1999 may also count as genocide.

•Saddam Hussein's repression of the Iraqi Kurds and the Marsh Arabs.

•Ethnic cleansing in former Yugoslavia: cases include the expulsions of ethnic Croats and later Serbs in parts of Croatia, expulsions and mass killings of Bosnian Moslems, the mass expulsion and killing of Kosovar Albanians.

•A number of successful genocides against indigenous tribal peoples including native Americans and Australians (notably the Tasmanians).

THE EXCEPTIONALISM OF GENOCIDE

An exploratory framework for the issues surrounding genocide and international responsibilities pertaining to genocide can be derived from analysis of the Genocide Convention, the highest relevant international law.

The Genocide Convention of 1948 is perhaps the simplest of all international conventions, as well as one of the most widely ratified. It places an overriding moral obligation on its signatories to prevent and punish the crime of genocide. But the Convention is silent as to how these obligations are to be carried out. It does not specify any specific measures such as intervention with military forces, resort to sanctions, prosecution at an international criminal court, etc. This silence is important, and understanding the reasons for it is an essential precondition for appreciating the complexity of the relationship between genocide and the other principal instruments of international law (IL), international humanitarian law (IHL) and human rights law (HRL).

Why is the Genocide Convention silent on the means for discharging the responsibilities enshrined therein? We can identify three main reasons.

1. Genocide is almost always a state crime. Thus the same state that is obliged to protect its citizens from genocide is the one carrying out the crime. This makes the provisions of HRL vacuous.

2. Any effective response to genocide is likely to involve military intervention in a way that would be contrary to other fundamenta

principles of IL. Such intervention would contravene the IL principles of territorial integrity and non-interference in the internal affairs of sovereign states. I.e. it is an act of aggression. A military intervention to prevent genocide is perhaps the clearest case of a 'just war'. It therefore runs contrary to the presumption of IHL that belligerent parties are equal, and the principle of separating the right to wage war and rights in war.

3. One cannot legislate for how to respond to events as extreme and sui generis as genocide. The crime of genocide is so extreme and so rare, thankfully, and each instance is so particular, that it is extremely difficult to build a body of cases on which sound generalisations could be built. Thus, rather than trying to specify the exceptional cases in which IL and IHL should not apply, it is preferable to leave the matter unspecified. At the same time, absolute genocide is so easy to recognise when it actually occurs and so intrinsically horrible that there is little difficulty in identifying an instance as such.

In short, genocide is an event beyond the reach of normal mechanisms of IL, IHL and HRL. Preventing genocide requires ad hoc responses above the law, informed by the overriding principles of humanity and morality. The essence of an effective response to genocide is its disregard for lesser conventional laws. Humanity and ethics dictate arbitrary and summary action. Any such response will be determined by practicality—the justification for an intervention to prevent genocide will be found in its success.

We may call this argument the 'exceptionalism of genocide.' This case is implicit in the Genocide Convention. In the absence of an effective international response to genocide or the threat of genocide, other principles of IL and IHL are in serious jeopardy. No international order is meaningful while there is a real threat of genocide. Under the shadow of genocide, for those under threat, the only rule is survival by whatever means necessary. This is seen, more than a generation on, in the psychology and statecraft of Israel, which is based on exceptionalism and the constant reiteration that there is a threat to the existence of the state and the survival of the Jews as people. In other cases also, victims of genocide or borderline genocide who have later gained state power have been defensive to the point of paranoia about how they exercise that power. The post-1994 government of Rwanda has been profoundly influenced by the real fear that the genocidaires still intend to complete their project of mass murder, and these fears have prompted repeated military intervention in Zaire/D.R. Congo. In the 1970s and '80s, both the Eritrean and Tigrayan peoples justifiably felt that their existence was under threat (though at that time not from each other), and each has built strong defensive states since gaining state power. In any peace agreement in Sudan, Southerners and Nuba will be seeking extremely strong guarantees that they will never again be subjected to the kind of violence that has jeopardised their existence in recent years.

Those who seek to perpetrate genocide have no respect for IL or IHL. But they may invoke human rights or international law. Mostly this is a purely cynical exercise, such as the claims of the Rwandese genocidaires and their sympathisers that there was a 'double genocide' and therefore there should be a policy of forgiving and forgetting-and of course majority rule. But the perpetrators of genocide also commonly invoke a mentality of victimhood to justify what they are doing. Their targets are seen as being so threatening that every individual must be killed. The alleged threat may be cast in terms of human rights or law: the opponents are against human rights or democracy (i.e. majority rule); they are agents of a foreign power, etc. Many people in the society concerned may sincerely believe these arguments and support the genocidaires. Such arguments may also gain credence among observers who are not in full possession of the facts.

It is clearly both correct and self-interested for those threatened by genocide to respect IL and IHL to the extent possible. But where one party to a conflict is faced with absolute annihilation it is meaningless to speak about the state morality and warrior's honour that underpin IL and IHL respectively.

Similar considerations apply to various human rights requirements: they become vacuous. A restriction on freedom of expression to limit hate speech, racism and other extremes of intolerance is widely recognised as valid. In most societies these restrictions only affect the extremist fringe, but where there is a genocidal constituency, such restrictions will strike much more deeply into the liberties of that constituency. In cases of potential genocide against a minority it is also appropriate to consider the problems of majoritarian democracy. Electoral arithmetic can both return a genocidal government and validate the method of electoral engineering by selective murder.

The defence against threats of genocide (including the continuation of an uncompleted genocide) imparts a similar logic. If the international community and IL have failed to prevent genocide, the survivors have a colourable legal case to seek to implement the Genocide Convention even if this is in violation of other precepts of IL and IHL. I.e. the survivors can wage war, engage in acts of aggression, etc., as acts of legitimate self-defence.

But clearly this does not imply carte blanche to do anything. There must be a point at which the justification of exceptionalism ceases to be valid

1. At some point the threat of genocide may no longer be immediate (even though the intent may still remain). But it may be difficult for the survivors of a genocide to believe that the threat has been contained.

2. Arbitrary and summary actions, carried out systematically, may themselves approach the genocidal.

3. Reprisal abuses develop a self-defeating logic of their own, in which former genocidal killers, and the communities they represent or claim to represent, become victims with (some) legitimate grievances. (The practical logic of fighting genocide demands a respect for humanity.) The classic case of this is Israel, which has oppressed the Palestinians in a self-defeating spiral of reprisal.

The justification for exceptional measures also depends upon whether the case in question is absolute genocide or convention genocide. There is no clear-cut point at which one can say that the exceptional logic of resisting genocide ends and the conventional ethics of IL, IHL and HRL come into play. But, in short, we must seek to balance the imperative of preventing genocide with other very important demands of IL, IHL and HRL.

THE ORIGINS OF GENOCIDE

Investigating the origins of genocide in each specific case is an important exercise in historical scholarship. It is an academic exercise, but with important political implications, because an incisive analysis can help one see the potential roots of future genocides elsewhere. This chapter will not go into substantive detail on these issues, but give only a brief outline.

It is the prerogative of academic historians to seek to understand all, and therefore to forgive all. However, in the case of genocide, understanding and forgiveness must have their limits. Explanations are reductions, and reducing the crime of genocide to a particular model or set of causes is a simplification that runs the risk of denying moral responsibility. Individual people planned and implemented the crime of genocide, and while for some there may be mitigating factors, overall there can be absolutely no justification for this, the most outrageous crime.

Understanding is called for because it gives meaning to condemnation. Also, it is possible to see some of the same factors that contributed to genocide, alive elsewhere in the world. An obligation to prevent genocide entails being tough on the causes of genocide. The following discussion will take Rwanda as its central case but also bring in relevant examples from elsewhere.

ETHNICITY

Genocide is commonly defined by reference to ethnicity. This is a very complex subject. Certain points will be helpful at the outset.

It is important to distinguish between the moral ethnicity whereby membership of a particular ethnic group imparts a set of community, common values and accountability for the leadership, and political tribalism, in which ethnic ties are manipulated for chauvinistic political gain.

Customary ethnicity in Africa was and is complex and multi-valent. Contrary to the simplistic vision of a patchwork of autonomous tribes, ethnicity has always been multi-valent, with individuals utilising multiple identities. The idea of a simple unifocal ethnicity, and even more so the idea of an ethnically homogenous state, is a modern one.

These points should be enough to dispel any idea that genocide is merely 'traditional' inter-tribal conflict writ large, or conducted with modern weapons.

Ethnicity is necessary for the perpetrators to identify the target group, and also to identify themselves. Genocide is assisted by existing sharp ethnic, racial, religious or class divides. But, for absolute genocide, this is not enough. An ethnic ideology is necessary to turn an ethnic antagonism into a programme of extermination. This ideology needs to simplify ethnicity, removing ambiguity, deepen the divide between the perpetrator and victim group and change the status of the victims before people will be ready to isolate the victims and kill them.

Closeness and familiarity between the perpetrators and the victims do not prevent genocide. The clearest cases of modern genocide are the elimination of non-territorially based groups that were often very closely mixed in with the wider populace. The Armenians, Jews and Tutsis did not inhabit specific areas but were integrated, geographically and often socially. In the case of the Holocaust, many Germans were not aware of the Jewish identity of their neighbours, and the Jews themselves scarcely considered themselves as such, until their ancestry was researched by bureaucrats and the labels attached. The fact that the target group is mixed in and integrated may be a pretext for the architects of genocide to claim to fear them more, as alleged infilitrators and spies. Also of course if makes it more difficult for the victims to resist.

Territorial distinctiveness, or social, economic or cultural separation, are also no barriers to genocide. Attacks on territorially-based groups are either for colonisation (Tasmania) or counter-insurgency (Eritrea, Tigray, Luwero Triangle) or a mixture of the two (former Yugoslavia, Nuba Mountains of Sudan). However, where the target groups have a distinct territory, resistance is easier, and the success of genocide less likely.

In Rwanda, the ideology of ethnicity played a particularly important role. The politics of ethnicity in Rwanda is a vast and complex subject, in some respects unique, and in other respects comparable to the experience of other parts of Africa.

Hutu Power developed an ideology of politicised ethnicity initially in reaction to a colonial-inspired ideology that placed the Tutsi in a higher racial category than the Hutu. It was an attempt to compensate for an earlier relationship in which the Hutu were subjugated, exploited and victimised. The correlation between historic class and ethnicity, the alleged racial dimension, and the sharp ethnic bipolarity all helped set Rwanda apart from most other cases of political ethnicity in Africa.

Cases of convention genocide in Uganda's Luwero Triangle under Obote II, and northwest Somalia in 1988, lack a comparable ideological element. In these cases, the violence was driven by extremely hard-line counter-insurgency. The governments of Uganda and Somalia respectively were taking to extreme the dictum that to catch the insurgent fish one should drain the sea, and the latter entailed mass killing and displacement. The enemy may have been identified in primarily ethnic terms, but there was no ethnic or racial ideology as such behind the massacre. However, the reality of genocidal violence has its own implications for the dynamics of political ethnicity.

A comparable case is the extreme violence, including man-made famine, inflicted on Eritrea and Tigray in the 1980s. The Mengistu government had its ideological project: it was trying to implement a project that included 'Ethiopian unity' and the communist transformation of the country. Though not couched in ethnic terms, this gained an ethnic dimension through the labelling of Eritreans and Tigrayans as 'secessionists' (in the first instance accurately, in the second, not).

The cases of genocidal violence in Sudan are complex. The primary motive for the extremely bloodthirsty militia raids on the Dinka of Bahr el Ghazal from 1985 to the present is counter-insurgency and loot: the raiders sought to destabilise and impoverish an area of SPLA support. Similarly for the attacks on the Nuba of South Kordofan that reached a climax in 1992 with simultaneous major assaults and mass forced relocation of the population. But in these cases there is also a racial-religious ideology at work. The Sudan Government sought to mobilise forces under the banner of Jihad—'Holy War'. This legitimised a range of practises including mass killing, enslavement, population transfer, the separation of the sexes, and compulsory Islamisation of children, that amount to genocidal acts. Apologists for this brutal war argue that the Sudan Government is merely engaged in legitimate counter-insurgency against SPLA insurrection; government opponents focus on the ideological components of the war and cry genocide and slavery. The reality is that both elements coexist. The SPLA has primarily mobilised black non-Arabs in these areas, so that the racial distinctiveness of the two opposing armies is marked. Meanwhile, according to the government's 1992 Fatwa that supposedly legitimised the Jihad, those who took up arms against the state were ipso facto *kufaar* (unbelievers) who did not deserve the privilege of life. It is a case of borderline absolute genocide (no right to life, but no duty to kill) arising from a complex set of factors including war, racism and cultural cleansing. The ideology is a corruption of religion, while the framework within which it is implemented is racial-ethnic.

Therefore the ethnic component of genocide is important in that (i) it is the basic means of categorising and identifying the victim, (ii) it can be the foundation of an extremist ideology and (iii) it can be the means of identifying and mobilising a constituency in support of the killing. While counter-insurgent violence against an ethnic group, without other ideological overtones, can kill huge numbers of people, the clearest cases of genocide tend to include a powerful ideological element as well. Committing genocide is hard work, and it needs a powerful ideology to instruct the perpetrators that members of a certain group no longer have the right to exist.

CITIZENSHIP

The concept of citizenship, with its corollary converse concepts of expulsion of 'aliens', statelessness, etc, demands close attention in contemporary Africa. The principle of equality of citizenship has been honoured mostly in the breach.

Two strands to the concept of citizenship, as (mis)applied, warrant attention.

1. The idea of an ethnically homogenous state. This has a variant in the form of a religiously homogenous state. In the case of multiethnic states—i.e. almost every state in Africa—the main concern here is not with which is the 'core' or dominant ethnicity, but which marginal ethnicity is denied the right to citizenship, and in extremis, the right to life.

2. The idea that citizenship is a privilege not a right, and its corollary that state sovereignty encompasses the state's right to award or withdraw citizenship.

The 1990 war in Rwanda had its roots in the expulsion and exile of much of the Tutsi minority in the years after 1959. An early manifestation of the genocidal ideology of the 1990s can be seen at work in these killings and expulsions. The ideology of Hutu Power was initially that Tutsis—who, according to their fanciful reconstruction of history, were 'really' Ethiopians—had no right to citizenship in Rwanda and should therefore leave. (When it was clear that the Tutsis had no intention of leaving, the ideology claimed they should be murdered.) The denial of Rwandese citizenship was compounded by the later persecution and statelessness of the Tutsis in Uganda and by discriminatory nationality laws in Zaire. (Tanzania by contrast was ready to let a certain number of Tutsis become citizens.) Meanwhile, the 1972 genocide in Burundi, followed by the failed transition to democracy in 1993 and the reciprocal mass killings that followed the Tutsi extremist putsch, also helped fuel the fears of Hutus.

An exclusivist ethnic definition of citizenship is both alarming in its own right and also a warning light for potential genocide. Most African countries have citizenship laws that contain a latent ethnic component, usually in the form of requiring a certain number of ancestors resident in the territory. But overtly ethnic definitions are rare. Their imposition commonly requires either the retroactive revision of nationality laws, the arbitrary and selective enforcement of such laws, or overriding the law altogether. Unfortunately this is not uncommon in many parts of Africa. Ethnic violence, scapegoating, discrimination, expulsion and withdrawal of nationality are a standing challenge to concepts of citizenship.

Rulers some of them supposedly democratic in countries such as Zambia and Ivory Coast have tried to prohibit rival presidential candidates from running for office on the grounds that they are not citizens. This is a blatant use of xenophobia for personal political gain.

The clarification of citizenship laws is particularly important when a country divides, with one part claiming the right to self-determination or independence. This issue must be resolved in a peaceful, lawful and consensual manner. Ideally it should be resolved before any exercise of self-determination. The failure to resolve these issues in advance of the Croat and Bosnian declarations of independence from Yugoslavia was a crucial factor in the genocidal violence that erupted there. Similar failures plagued the USSR's successor states in the Trans-Caucasus region, and, earlier, the separation of India and Pakistan. The failure of Ethiopia and Eritrea to resolve the citizenship status of Ethiopian citizens of Eritrean descent resident in Ethiopia after 1991 contributed to the mass expulsion of Eritreans from Ethiopia in 1998-9. If another major African country were to break apart into two or more recognised successor states, the potential for mass inter-communal violence and mutual expulsion would be very great.

In Africa, citizenship is specially to be prized. The ethnic complexity of many African states, and the way in which international borders cut through the territories of ethnic groups, renders the continent especially vulnerable to the selective exclusion of certain people from citizenship rights. There is a pressing need for a jurisprudence of citizenship in Africa.

WAR

Genocide may be implemented as the most extreme form of counter-insurgency. The state responds to the threat of insurgency by physically eliminating all potential or suspected supporters of the insurgents. The largest number of cases of convention genocide fall into this category. Mass killings and forced flight in Eritrea and Tigray, north-west Somalia, Southern Sudan and the Nuba Mountains, the Luwero Triangle of Uganda, the war in Zaire in 1997, and other cases, are all approximations to this. War can also be a pretext for genocide launched for other reasons, and the exceptional measures adopted by wartime governments (censorship, conscription, martial law) can assist in perpetrating genocide (a case is the expulsions of the Kosovars in 1999).

In the case of Rwanda, the war against the RPF provided the pretext for the genocide. The non-combatant Tutsis were uniformly portrayed as 'accomplices' of the RPF who therefore needed to be eliminated. The killing of Tutsi children was justified as a form of pre-emptive counter-insurgency: otherwise they would grow up to become enemies. Apologists for the genocidaire have argued that the RPF 'provoked' the genocide by its 'aggression' of 1990.

In the Rwandese case, it is clear that state policy was the annihilation of the Tutsis, and military and police units and citizens were commanded to carry it out to the last person. To describe the genocide as 'normal' massacres in war or a 'response to a threat of aggression' is wholly incorrect, and in fact is a form of genocide denial (see below).

In recent African cases other than Rwanda, motivation and command for genocide are less clear cut. For example, it is often argued that the Sudan Government has a genocidal policy in Southern Sudan. Certainly the level of violence and destruction wreaked by its servants are potentially genocidal—and, as has been argued in this chapter, several instances undoubtedly count as convention genocide. But much of the violence is inflicted by militias that, while set up and supported by the government and military command, are not directly controlled by the central authorities. The activities of raiding, burning, killing and enslaving are given tacit approval and ideological legitimation—Southern Sudan has become an 'ethics free zone' for Sudanese military officers, in which soldiers can kill with impunity. However, government policy could also be legitimately construed by army or militia commanders to entail a much lower level of violence and violation, compatible with maintaining security (in fact a more enlightened approach is likely to prove more effective at discouraging insurgency). Thus one garrison commander could preside over the massacre of hundreds and the flight of thousands, while his successor could maintain a reasonable level of restraint. Hence the level of cruelty exercised by front line troops is critical in whether a ruthless war turns into an act of genocide.

Similarly, considering the famine policies of the Mengistu government in Ethiopia which were arguably genocidal, the government was probably not aware of quite how devastating its use of food as a weapon would be. In Somalia, the zealotry of individual army officers acting with the authority of the state behind them was instrumental in the near-genocidal level of bloodshed in the north in 1988. An aggregation of war crimes targetted at a particular group can amount to a genocide.

The 'Ethiopian definition' of genocide includes the massacre of members of political groups and allows us to include cases of mass killing on the basis of political orientation alone. These are akin to counter-insurgency genocide merged with class war taken to extreme. The Ethiopian Red Terror was a particularly bloody and indiscriminate form of urban counter-insurgency, implemented partly with the aim (as its name suggests) of terrorising citizens into compliance. In Cambodia's Year Zero under the Khmer Rouge, ideological extremism was taken to its logical end point. In the Indonesian case, counter-revolutionary fervour motivated the massacre. European early modern history also furnishes cases of similar mass killing on a purely religious basis, that had little or no ethnic components.

As Clausewitz noted, war tends towards the absolute. This is true in ideological and political terms as well as in weaponry and military strategy. During war, the two sides usually become more entrenched. War is the ideal environment for the growth of extremism. As noted in chapter 1, it is common to see political, religious and ethnic extremism hardening during war. The enemy is demonised: enemies (and their accomplices) have no right to exist. This makes genocide more probable.

Human rights law and humanitarian law makes it absolutely clear that an abuse by one party is no justification for an abuse by the other. Humanitarian law is very precise about the conditions under which reprisals are permitted, and prohibits reprisals against civilians. The excuse of 'provocation' and the issue of who started the war are irrelevant to the consideration of legal responsibility for violations of IHL and genocide.

Nevertheless, insurgents must be aware of the potential unanticipated consequences of their actions. War is inherently unpredictable and tends towards the absolute.

There are some exceptions to the rule that genocides are perpetrated during war. Stalin's deportations were implemented with enough cruelty to make them cases of convention genocide. They took place in the aftermath of war, targetting alleged accomplices of the Nazis. The tribal genocides of America and Australia are the exception to this: in these cases, the killers simply believed their victims to be subhuman, and that it was legitimate to exterminate them as vermin.

CONCENTRATION OF POWER

One of the familiar arguments made by proponents of one-party or military governments is that pluralism encourages tribalism and inter-communal violence. For some Kenyans, for example, the genocide in Rwanda is an argument against multi-party politics.

The issues here are not simple. During President Habyarimana's period of single-party rule (1973-90), the Rwandese Tutsis suffered various forms of discrimination and were wholly excluded from political power, but were not subject to violent attack. The period of mounting violence coincided not only with the civil war but also with the advent of multi-party politics and the freeing of the press. However, the genocide was planned and implemented by a small clique that had virtually absolute power over the state's security and military apparatus.

In the case of Rwanda, the genocide arose from an unfortunate conjunction of absolute power and an ill-planned multiple transition to peace, democracy and a market economy. Before 1990, the Habyarimana government enjoyed an extreme concentration of the power in the executive presidency. In a region marked by centralised government authority, Rwanda was an extreme case. There was no effective separation of powers between executive, legislature and judiciary. Nor was there clear separation between state and 'civil society', notably between state and church, and state and academia, nor was there a clear dividing line between politics and business. Contrary to many descriptions, the crisis in Rwanda did not arise from 'anarchy' or a failing state, but from an excess of state power.

When the prospect of power sharing arose in the aftermath of the RPF invasion and the donor demands for a multi-party system, this concentration of power created a highly dangerous situation. Rwanda between 1990 and 1994 is a model of the mismanagement of a transition to democracy and peace. The country was expected to simultaneously undergo an economic austerity plan, merge two hostile armed forces into a national army, and abandon a one party system and hold multi-party elections. The clique that had held power were losing simultaneously on several fronts, and unsurprisingly, were not willing to abandon their privileged position.

The extreme political stresses generated by the transition to democracy, especially in the context of war, were seriously underestimated by the international community. The formal apparatus of democratisation and an apparently thriving human rights movement were taken, misleadingly, as encouraging signs, allowing the disturbing developments mentioned above to be ignored or minimised. The high level of international engagement, including the far-reaching requirements of the August 1993 Arusha agreement, the wide role of UNAMIR, and the activism of a number of donors, may have given a misleading impression of the depth of international commitment to democratisation and human rights in Rwanda. But the UNAMIR force commander was instructed to interpret his mandate in a very conservative manner, so that he could not use force to raid arms caches. When the genocide was actually launched, the UN force was cut back, and left in a depleted condition with virtually no logistical support or even food, as a spectator to the carnage. The fact that the small number of troops were able to save approximately 30,000 Tutsis and moderate Hutus from otherwise certain death is a testament to the individual officers and men who were stationed in Rwanda; the fact that they were impotent in the face of a genocide they could have minimised and perhaps even prevented is an indictment of their political masters.

What was the role of corruption? The Habyarimana government, in common with its neighbours in Burundi and (particularly) Zaire, was a classic instance of the 'criminalisation' of the state, including the control of power by a shadowy mafia-type network behind the formal executive, close links with foreign governments and commercial companies acting in ways with questionable legality, the privatisation of the means of violence in clan, party and commercial military forces, etc. This was certainly an element in the concentration of power, and a potentially serious problem if Rwandese society had been opened up. The criminal networks helped in obtaining illicit weapons supplies, and providing the appropriate skills and mindset for assassination squads. Corruption and criminality were therefore background components in the creation of the Rwandese genocide, but not, it seems, the central elements.

Genocide was a means whereby the leaders of Hutu Power consolidated and increased their power. They mobilised people around a manifesto of hatred. The mass killing was an event in which very many people participated, creating collective involvement and guilt. For people who had not killed before it was a sort of initiation ritual into a special club, namely a new Hutu-ism. There were also rewards to be distributed, namely the land, assets and surving women of the Tutsis.

All cases of absolute genocide and most cases of convention genocide are also marked by extreme concentration of power. In Africa, this applies to the 1972 government in Burundi, Siad Barre in Somalia, Mengistu in Ethiopia, and the NIF in Sudan. Outside Africa, there is of course Nazi Germany, and also Stalin's USSR, the Khmer Rouge in Cambodia, and Suharto's coup in Indonesia. Slobodan Milosevic is an interesting case in that, while he enjoyed considerable authoritarian power from 1991, this was never as absolute as many of the other cases considered. One of the uses of ethnic cleansing was to help build a Serb nationalist constituency, and therefore increase his power.

But there is an interesting exception, which shows that an insecure elected government or a contested transition to democracy can also witness extreme violence. The case in point is Sudan in the late 1980s, when there were genocidal militia attacks on northern Bahr el Ghazal, which took place when Sudan had an elected government and free press. These attacks also witnessed the creation of an unusually severe famine and a resurgence of slavery. How did this come about? Most important, there was war. The first militia raids were initiated before the 1986 elections, during a transition with democrats in an uneasy compromise with military hardliners. The enemy was a powerful and uncompromising insurgent army, the SPLA. The government cultivated an already-entrenched racist nationalism in northern Sudan. This amounted to de facto withdrawal of citizenship from Southerners, exemplified in the extraordinary Arabist jingoism that followed the SPLA capture of the small town of Kurmuk, just inside northern Sudan, in 1987. While there was no formal declaration of jihad at this stage, the South was already becoming an 'ethics-free zone'. Lastly, the northern public knew very little about what was going on. Access to the war areas was restricted, and was difficult and dangerous in any case. Moreover, the concerns of northern democrats rarely extended to the war areas, as shown by the desultry press coverage of the war, famine and issues such as slavery, even when evidence did belatedly emerge.

This case indicates that democracy can be an antidote to genocide, but that certain conditions must be met. Notably, a democracy cannot remain healthy in the context of a civil war, and institutionalised racism.

SOCIAL CONSENSUS

Absolute genocide requires a state apparatus including development and propagation of ideology, use of the media, mobilisation of state resources, complicity or at least acquiesence of a wide swathe of civil society. It demands extreme internal conformism. It does not occur when it can be debated internally in a democratic atmosphere.

In the case of Rwanda, this conformity is extremely striking. In the run-up to the genocide, there was an extraordinary degree of consensus among the country's major institutions in support of Hutu extremism, and once the killing had started, in support of the genocide itself. All the government institutions, including the army, police, all levels of administration, all ministries and departments, Radio Rwanda and other news outlets, were in total conformity. More strikingly, academics and journalists, businessmen, and senior members of all major churches, also supported the government. Large numbers of teachers, health workers, members of religious orders, relief and development workers, and even some erstwhile human rights activists, joined the killing or supported it publicly. Those who resisted were few. This widespread conformism owes much to the hierarchical nature of Rwandese society, and the unquestioning obedience expected by those in authority. It also reflects the thoroughness with which the genocide was prepared. Finally it reflects the way in which the genocidal government was able, for the few months of the genocide, to completely rewrite morality. Genocide was ordered by those in authority, genocide was being perpetrated by loyal citizens, it was normal, therefore it was the correct thing to do. Only those with powerful and independent consciences were able to resist.

Many Hutus and indeed the entire Hutu collectivity became victims of the genocide too. A large number of Hutus were bystanders or reluctant accomplices in the genocide. Although they survived, their moral standing has been seriously undermined. Meanwhile it is easy to blame 'the Hutu' for the genocide, thereby criminalising an entire people. This of course was one of the aims of the architects of the genocide. In the world's popular consciousness, the Hutu collectivity is irredeemably stained by the genocide. This is very negative.

The case of the massacres in Southern Sudan during the 1980s parliamentary government illustrates a more passive conformism. The killings were far away and invisible, their scale probably not known to more than a few army officers and militia commanders. The consensus in this case was not to look, to avert the official gaze, and the northern public acquiesced. Similar public ignorance about the true level of violence also facilitated the extreme violence of counter-insurgency operations in northern Somalia (1988), northern Ethiopia and Eritrea (1980s), and other cases. It is easier to not ask too many questions, and remain in the dark.

SECRECY

A genocidal government may be able to construct an internal consensus in favour of genocide. This is much more difficult internationally—or in a large and complex country. Hence the need for secrecy.

Genocide thrives in the dark: it rarely persists when it is exposed internationally. The debate over what the Allies (and also the Swiss Government, the ICRC, the Vatican not to mention German citizens themselves) knew about the Holocaust remains bitter, because it is widely believed that not even the Nazi regime would have been able to continue with its exterminations had these received the public condemnation of the Allies and neutrals. In all cases, the perpetrators of genocide have sought to deceive the outside world, while also trying to mobilise an internal constituency in support of their heinous acts. War is the best pretext for secrecy, and all modern genocides have been carried out in times of war.

There are cases of international organisations being complicit in keeping genocide secret. Some of the untruths endorsed by the UN Emergency Operation in Ethiopia in 1984-5 are belatedly coming to light. International NGOs also tried to maintain 'access' in

Uganda's Luwero Triangle at the cost of remaining silent over Obote's genocide. These silences were matters of policy that have become more difficult to maintain in the 1990s, with freer information. But the silence of UN organisations and NGOs operating in Khartoum over the case of the Nuba, after full evidence became available in 1995, is somewhat disturbing. The inaction and complacency of senior UN staff in the run-up to the 1994 genocide in Rwanda has belatedly become a scandal. The readiness of many UN and NGO staff to identify with the Rwandese 'refugees' in eastern Zaire and defend their collective innocence, in 1994-6 is also disturbing. The latter case is perhaps a variant of the 'Stockholm syndrome' in which hostages come to identify with their captors and support their cause.

It is remarkable how, even after the exposure of the reality of a genocide, many people, both domestically and internationally, refuse to recognise the reality. This is not because the material evidence for genocide is lacking: it is because they refuse to acknowledge the evidence. There are many possible reasons for this that will be explored below. But it is unfortunate that many genocides remain denied even after their completion.

ECONOMIC CRISIS

It is commonplace to recognise the economic factors that contribute to conflict. They are also a factor in genocide. In the case of Rwanda, the strains of structural adjustment, including austerity measures within the government establishment, coinciding with external economic shocks such as the collapse in the coffee price, large-scale internal displacement due to fighting and drought, coincided with political liberalisation and war. The economic packages were negotiated by Rwanda's western donors without any apparent recognition of possible political ramifications of a sudden increase in unemployment and fall in farm incomes. The responsibilities of foreign donors and international financial institutions are of concern here: the strains unleashed by simultaneous political and economic restructuring may be too great for a country to bear.

Participation in the genocide entailed economic incentives. Many of those who participated were relatively poor and marginalised themselves, and the possibility of looting property, livestock and land was undoubtedly attractive. But, before attributing the killing to the individual greed of frustrated youth and peasants, it should be noted that the great majority of the looting benefitted senior officials and politicians: their eyes were on businesses and land. Only the defeat of the genocidal government prevented them from completing their acquisition. Meanwhile, the ideology of obliteration meant that the houses of Tutsis were burned, their cattle slaughtered and eaten, and their crops left to rot in the fields. The genocide did not make economic sense, at any level.

(The genocide also did not make military sense. The diversion of men and material from the front line fighting the RPF to massacreing civilians hastened the defeat of the Hutu extremist government. In that respect, the ideology proved self-defeating. One is reminded of Hitler's diversion of war material from the Eastern Front to help complete the extermination of the Jews before the arrival of the Russian and Allied troops.)

Those who seek a mechanistic explanation for genocide in population pressure and a supposed life-and-death struggle over meagre resources should try to explain how these grand factors translate into the mechanisms for selective mass murder. Even cursory examination reveals that no such links exist. There are no Malthusian or similar reductionist explanations for genocide.

PREVIOUS GENOCIDE

Perhaps the most common precursor of genocide is genocide, or extreme violence or dispossession that has genocidal elements. Many of the cases discussed in this chapter had precursors, e.g. the expulsions and killings of Rwandese Tutsis between 1959-66, and the genocidal killings in Burundi in 1972 were a precursor of the genocidal violence that began again in 1990, and the killings and expulsions of Southern Sudanese were a precursor of the militia war of 1985-8.

One of the most important cases is the 1996 genocide in eastern Zaire. This began in late 1995 as the exiled genocidaires from Rwanda turned on the local Zairean Tutsis, especially the Banyamulenge and the Masisi Tutsis, and systematically massacred them. The prime reason was simply that they were Tutsis. This was no more than a continuation of the 1994 absolute genocide in Rwanda a project which its perpetrators had not abandoned. It was associated with resurgent genocidal killings of Tutsis inside Rwanda and a plan to reinvade the country. The RPA response was similar to that of 1994, except that this time it was swifter and more decisive. There were no negotiations, but instead a military campaign waged in former Zaire in alliance with both Zairean forces and some international allies. This prevented further genocide of Tutsis and meted out summary punishment to the genocidaires, driving them far away from the Rwandese border even as far as Angola and Congo-Brazzaville.

This campaign was also bloody, and many militiamen and civilians lost their lives.[2] Some human rights and humanitarian agencies have preferred to describe these latter killings as 'genocide.' It is possible that, if sufficiently numerous and systematic, they may qualify as an instance of counter-insurgency genocide. This however remains unproven not least because no independent examination of the evidence has been permitted.

More widely, genocide has become a common, even normal, part of the political programme of armed groups in central Africa. The elimination of ethnic groups or their forced removal has become a standard instrument of power. Genocide is becoming normalised. This is of course disastrous.

IGNORED WARNINGS

Predicting genocide is not easy, and there are real dilemmas for those concerned with predicting and preventing genocide.

Each case of modern genocide has appeared to the world as a surprise. But in retrospect, in each case, clear warning signs and statements of intent were there beforehand for all to see. Step by step, abuses mount up until the they arrive at the threshhold of genocide. In the normal course of life, genocide is literally unthinkable. Militarists and extremists are unfortunately common, in and out of government, and such people often make statements about their aims of 'crushing' their enemies and suchlike. At the same time members of the same government will be reassuring, insisting that such extreme things can never happen here. And often of course they are right. The Nigerian forces did not commit genocide after the defeat of the Biafrans, neither did the EPRDF after defeating Mengistu, nor the RPF after the defeat of the former government of Rwanda despite many observers' predictions. Hence it is all-too-easy to dismiss warnings of genocide as exaggerated fears.

Moreover, most genocides are slow. They take several years to unfold, during which time the international community has time—in theory—to assess the evidence and respond. It could be argued that the speed of the Rwandese genocide was exceptional, and that no international organisation could realistically be expected to respond in time. But this argument has several major flaws:

1. The genocidal killings began in 1990-1, and by early 1993 they had positively been identified as genocidal by an international commission of inquiry. The scale of the 1994 genocide should not permit one to overlook these earlier massacres. These, which were the first stage of the genocide, provided a warning as incontrovertible as one could ask for.

2. There were authoritative public and confidential warnings of the impending genocide in late 1993 and early 1994. The UNAMIR force commander was aware of these and requested permission to take the necessary preemptive action. Permission was not forthcoming.

3. The French and Belgian governments sent troops to Rwanda within days of the outbreak of the absolute genocide to evacuate foreign nationals, with US Marines standing by in neighbouring countries. These forces abandoned Rwanda to its fate. And when the French government decided to intervene with Operation Turquoise, the necessary troops arrived in days, and the UN approved the Chapter VII mandate in record time. (Meanwhile the UNAMIR force in Kigali was still without equipment, ammunition or supplies, even basic foodstuffs, and was still operating under a Chapter VI mandate.)

All the other genocides in recent African history also had ample warning and good information. The massacres in the Luwero Triangle in Uganda became known to the outside world, which chose not to act. The killings in Southern Sudan and the Nuba Mountains were known about, albeit within limited circles. The same was true of the crimes of the Mengistu regime and Siad Barre regime (although the speed of the eruption of the 1988 war in northern Somalia caught all by surprise). The international community was fully aware of the war and killing brewing in eastern Zaire in 1996, having made its contribution to the process and agonised ineffectually over its role, but failed to react in time (and when it did finally react, did so in a counter-productive manner).

GENOCIDE REVISIONISM

It is impossible to be dispassionate about genocide. It is a matter for strong emotions. Among the survivors and their relatives, there are many deep and complex emotions, some of which will be touched on in the following section.

Among the perpetrators, it is also deeply emotional and stressful. Mass murder takes its toll on even the hardest of hearts. For genocidaires, the best refuge is collective denial: they seek the social support of their fellow killers and construct a collective myth that all are innocent, reproducing the conformism that facilitated their evil enterprise earlier on. They seek to deal with their anger and anguish by projecting it onto others, especially of course the victims. It is well known from psychological experiments that someone who harms another for no reason quickly seeks to invent reasons for their action—the commonest stratagems are to deny free will ('I was ordered and had no option'), to deny that the victim felt pain ('such people aren't sensitive like us'), or to claim that the person deserved it ('he must have been a criminal', 'she asked for it'). Later on, they many deny that the event even happened at all.[3] Such responses are common among those who planned, perpetrated or acquiesced in genocide.

Among third parties, the responses to genocide are more complex. For some, it is an issue of utter clarity on which they can focus their energies, assisting victims and hunting down murderers. Given the size of the international human rights community, such individuals are remarkably rare.

Our concern here is more with those third parties who prefer not to recognise genocide for what it is. Their motives are varied. Some were allies of the genocidaires, who have their own guilty secrets to reveal. Others were personal friends of killers, who did not abet the genocide, but who find it hard to believe that their

kind friends are murderers. Still others are guilty about their failure to act, or their failure to believe. The UN as an institution, for
example, seems to be fatally compromised by its inaction in the
key months of early 1994. Until it recognises and comes to terms
with its failing, it seems improbable that it will be able to play a
constructive role in central Africa.

This section attempts a preliminary categorisation of the various kinds of genocide revisionism. The focus is chiefly on Rwanda,
but there are parallels with other genocides that will be apparent.

1. Genocide denial. This is simply ignoring the genocide, either
claiming it did not exist, or starting one's history of central Africa
in July 1994. For some international humanitarians, for example,
the pivotal event in the region is the war in Zaire in 1996-7—a
view that overlooks how this war was merely another round of
what had earlier happened in Rwanda. For others the main event
was the flight into Zaire in July 1994 and the subsequent cholera
outbreak.

2. Minimisation of genocide. A variant of the above, this is to play
down the numbers involved. The true numbers of people murdered
in Rwanda in April-July 1994 is not known, but a figure of 800,000
has become generally accepted and is a symbolic minimum. Occasionally, much lower figures are quoted, with the implicit intent of
saying 'it wasn't that bad.'

3. Justification of genocide. For some, blame for upsetting the tran-
quility of Rwanda lies with the RPF, who must therefore carry
responsibility for the genocide: 'They provoked it.' (Few who claim
to be remotely objective would dare say, 'they deserved it'.) There
are some bizarre variants of this, such as the argument that the
RPF were spearheading an Anglo-Saxon imperialist plot in central
Africa.

4. 'Banalisation' of genocide. This is one of the most insidious of
arguments, particularly favoured by those who have seen only the
post-genocide conflicts in Rwanda and eastern Zaire/D.R. Congo.
This view is summarised by the words, 'It is just massacres during

war,' and 'It is just tribal fighting.' International human rights organisations have also developed their own variant of the 'banalisation' approach by treating the post-genocide period as 'business as usual', and giving the same space (if not more) to post-genocide revenge killings as to the genocide itself. (Between April and September 1994, Amnesty International produced one eleven-page report on the genocide and one eleven-page report on alleged revenge killings, many of which, incidentally, were not substantiated.)

5. A variant of the above is the thesis of the 'double genocide': the idea that both sides committed genocide, so that the score is even. Attempts to brand the RPF as the 'khmer noir' were a clumsy attempt at this. A slightly bizarre version of the 'double genocide' thesis is the invention of the term 'genocide by starvation', which was used to describe the situation in the camps in eastern Zaire in early November 1996 by no less a figure than the UN Secretary General. Not only was this a remarkable legal innovation, but as events over the following few days demonstrated, there was in fact no starvation in the camps at that time.

All the above can be invoked by those who support the genocidaires. They can also be invoked in the name of reconciliation. While reconciliation is a noble and worthy aim, it can also be pursued carelessly without regard to its necessary preconditions.

Parallels of the above will be evident to those who have followed the other genocides mentioned in this chapter.

RESPONSES TO GENOCIDE
There is no adequate response to genocide once it has taken place. All cases of genocide leave a legacy of conflict and bitterness that takes generations to subside.

SURVIVOR'S SYNDROME
Holocaust survivors have been intensively studied by psychologists, and much is known that is relevant to survivors of the Rwandese genocide and other genocides. The cluster of responses is known as 'survivor's syndrome.'

One of its main components is pathological grief, arising from the survivor's inability to mourn the dead adequately. There are simply too many dead, they have not been buried or had any memorials erected to them, and proper mourning procedures have not been followed. In African traditions, proper public mourning is particularly important, and if they are not followed, the relatives of the deceased often feel tormented. (The belief that the dead are not at peace, and their spirits are still abroad, may also torment the killers.) Given the scale of killing in genocide, and the fact that whole families and lineages have been wiped out so that there many be no-one left to mourn many of the dead, any process of commemoration will be inadequate. Nonetheless it is essential.

Another component of survivor's syndrome is isolation. Survivors are lonely because they have lost many of their family and friends. But they are also lonely because they cannot properly communicate their experience to others, except other survivors. They often feel that others simply fail to understand their point of view, and sometimes give up even trying to explain.

Survivors can be deeply distrustful. They are searching for security but rarely if ever finding it. Bitterness and vengefulness are also understandable aspects of survivor's syndrome, directed not only at those responsible for killing, but those who were not involved (and did not intervene) and those who fail to understand their situation. Acts of vengeance are normal and to be expected.

KILLER'S SYNDROME

Genocide, in its various forms, also has a profound effect on the killers and the wider society that produced the killers. Those who plan genocide usually do not anticipate these effects.

Killers also suffer guilt, grief and anguish. They may be tormented by the thought of all those they have killed or seen killed; they may fear the revenge of the spirits of the dead; they may fear the final reckoning with their creator. At the same time, their readiness to continue killing may be high. Having already been engaged in mass murder, it is easy for them to resume killing.

In some cases, soldiers and leaders involved in genocide may be accepted back into their communities, and even hailed as heroes. In other cases, they are rejected and shunned.

JUSTICE, REMEMBRANCE AND FORGETTING

In the aftermath of genocide, justice is always inadequate but it is also essential. Various methods have been used to bring genocidal criminals to justice and to expose the truth. They include:

· Truth commissions and commissions of inquiry.
· Prosecutions, using the regular courts.
· Special prosecutors.
· International criminal courts.
· Local, traditional courts and mechanisms for truth-telling and accountability.

These responses are usually couched in terms of achieving absolute 'justice' and 'truth'. They can also be seen as means of constructing an account of the past which makes it possible to live with the future. For example, trials can be used to single out the main architects of genocide, while simultaneously allowing the majority of (lesser) accomplices to escape, on the understanding that they collaborate in condemning the genocide and cooperate in building a post-genocide order.

Faced with the magnitude of genocide, only major perpetrators are ever successfully brought to trial. The majority of criminals escape. However they continue to live in the knowledge that there is no statute of limitation on crimes of genocide, so that if evidence is brought against them years or decades later, they can always be exposed and prosecuted.

Lesser measures such as public exposure and denial of civil rights (e.g. the right to hold public office) can also be invoked.

In Africa, the most systematic judicial process against the perpetrators has been in Ethiopia. While the principle of the Special Prosecutor's Office has been applauded by all (except uncompromising opponents of the death penalty), its operation has been subject to many criticisms on accounts of long delays. While justice may not (yet) have been done, the process has at least the consequence of allowing the wider population to argue that those responsible have been identified and isolated and are subject to due process which will in time lead to punishment. The issue of killers being still 'out there' is thus resolved in principle and, largely in fact.

In the case of Rwanda, the situation is much more difficult, because (i) the number of perpetrators is extremely large and it is simply not feasible to bring them all to trial and (ii) the genocidal ideology and many genocidal leaders remain active and at large. The process of prosecution has been scarcely faster than in Ethiopia despite the setting up of an international criminal tribunal in Arusha.

The basic element in post-genocide justice is remembrance. The genocide should not be forgotten. Physical memorials are important. (They can also assist with the grieving process of survivors.) Remembrance days are important. Keeping open the possibility of prosecuting criminals years afterwards is also important, as it keeps the memory active.

In Uganda, the post-genocide Human Rights Commission was not successful in prosecuting individual criminals, but did succeed in the wider objective of educating the public about human rights abuses under previous regimes and the need to respect human rights in the future.

Cases of successful genocide (e.g. the elimination of the Tasmanian Aboriginals) are forgotten by the perpetrators, while there are no survivors to remember. Near-successful cases, which leave the perpetrators in power, are also forgotten or considered unimportant by those who carried them out or their descendants—but the survivors and their descendants do not forget. The descendants of immigrants to Australia and North America are very belatedly being forced to contemplate the sins of their grandparents. Reconciliation usually waits for the next generation, at the earliest.

Slavery is a lesser crime than genocide, but the legacy of slavery in the US demonstrates the difficulties of reconciliation and coexistence several generations on. Britain which benefitted as much as America from the Atlantic slave trade has never been forced to confront its historical responsibility because the problem was kept safely out of sight there were scarcely any slaves or ex-slaves actually on British soil.

REPARATIONS, RESTITUTIONS, RESPONSIBILITIES
In most cases of genocide, the issue of restitution and reparation has not been raised. The main exception is the Nazi Holocaust. In this case, the Europeans escaped from territorial reparation or res-

titution by making the Palestinians pay by giving up their land. Belatedly, financial reparation for the Holocaust has become an issue, with companies and banks that profited from the genocide and associated war crimes being forced to pay compensation to survivors and their families. This process has not been driven by a general sense of international responsibility, but by survivors taking legal action in the courts.

Similar action through the courts has yet to be taken in Africa. But in principle there is no reason why not. There is no international mechanism for examining accountability to the Genocide Convention. In the aftermath of the Rwanda genocide, several countries (Belgium, France) and donor consortia (the Danish funded joint evaluation) have held inquiries into their roles, but these have been largely internal and have not satisfied the Rwandese demand for accountability. The OAU Panel of Eminent Personalities holds the potential of creating a new and more thorough mechanism for accountability.

POLITICAL RESPONSES: THE QUEST FOR SECURITY

The basic political response to genocide is the search for security. There are four principal kinds of response, and most instances involve two or three of them.

1. The territorial response: the victimised group seeks its own defensible and preferable sovereign territory.
2. The power response: the victimised group seeks to control sufficient political and military power to prevent future genocide, while denying any such power to the perpetrator group.
3. The ideological response: the elimination of the genocidal ideology. In the case of extreme communist and anti-communist ideologies, these have now passed out of political fashion. Ethnic extremism has not.
4. Reconciliation: the former perpetrator group lives together with the survivors in harmony, or at least peaceful coexistence. This is invariably called for but rarely achieved. If it does occur, it is usually in the context of a successful response of type 1-3 above.

An element that is sometimes found across these different responses is the legitimation given to the group that has ended the genocide, especially when that group is also associated with the victims of genocide. In the case of Israel for example, the legitimacy of the state is founded on the memory of the Holocaust, which also gives the Israeli government a moral argument for acting with impunity against its real or perceived adversaries. Genocide survivors, and those who claim to be acting on their behalf, can enjoy moral impunity. This impunity can have a number of negative effects:

1. Judicial measures taken against those guilty of genocide are not matched by measures against those responsible for reprisals. Double standards can creep in. These can be institutionalised: the post-genocide government can claim that it is justifiable for it to act outside the law.

2. Critics of a post-genocide government can be disarmed or discredited, with the argument that they are supporting the genocidal forces, or they have no moral authority to criticise as they did nothing to stop the genocide.

3. The guilty conscience of the international community can lead to uncritical support for the post-genocide government.

Genocide has commonly given a strong impulse to separation—the territorial solution. The survivors of genocide have sought to set up their own state, as the best means to secure themselves. The Jewish state in Palestine was a result of the Holocaust, and Israel has subsequently been highly militarised and often shown disregard for international law. The Armenians have also established their state, albeit in very different circumstances. Some of the victims of Stalin's deportations have sought separation, for example the Chechens. The Kosovars' response to Serbian ethnic cleansing will undoubtedly be to seek independence. The East Timorese may have done likewise. In Africa, the same phenomenon is clear. Eritrean nationalism was greatly boosted by the extreme violence employed by the Mengistu regime and Eritrea duly achieved its independence. The genocidal attacks on the Isaaq by Siad Barre fuelled Somaliland separatism, and the territory unilaterally declared independence in 1991. (Within Somaliland, however, there has been an extensive process of reconciliation, in the context of Isaaq dominance.) In these cases, co-existence is possible in the context of separate statehood, the two peoples separated by a sovereign barrier. This separation allows each party to ignore the other if they so wish, and reconcile if they both wish.

In Sudan, Southern secessionism has been boosted by genocidal violence and enslavement, and the Nuba response to the government's genocidal jihad has been to raise claims for self-determination. The Southern Sudanese search for security may yet lead to the division of Sudan, unless the Khartoum government is able to provide strong enough constitutional guarantees on their rights.

In all these cases, note the common threat of international lawlessness that arises from genocidal violence. Existing state structures are not strong enough to contain the pressures that arise in the wake of genocide.

The case of Tigray in Ethiopia is a case in which the power solution comes first and the territorial second. Ethiopia's ethnic federalism, which gives the right of self-determination to territorially-defined nationalities within the Federal Republic, is aimed at securing collective rights. This approach confronts the 'nationalities question' head on, in a radically different manner to the Ugandan response. However, this approach also has many problems, including difficulties in defining nationalities and establishing borders, and the implicit legitimation of ethnic discrimination (though the Ethiopian government will hotly dispute this). The Ethiopian model has been workable in the context of the complete defeat of the previous regime, the dismemberment of its armed forces and security apparatus, the imprisonment and prosecution of its leading members, and their replacement by a new regime under the domination of the Tigrayan element. The Tigrayans' security is guaranteed first by their dominance of the national army and security forces, and second by the devolution of power to Tigray and the constitutional right to self-determination.

Note that in all cases where a territorial solution is sought, one implication is the politicisation of ethnicity. Therefore, although the specific ideology that led to the genocide is eradicated (e.g. Naziism in Germany), the general possibility of ethnic ideologies is not removed, and in fact may be reinforced. The fact that many states created in the aftermath of genocide have continued to engage in conflict with an ethnic component bears this out. The classic case is of course Israel. The territorial solution comes at a high price for both the survivor group and its neighbours.

In the Ugandan case, the power response came first and the ideological second, with the territorial response barely visible. The NRM government took power, giving strong representation to the victim groups, and embarked upon a concerted attempt to eliminate tribalist ideologies and depoliticise ethnicity. The survivors' security is assured by the NRM's control over the state, their powerful representation in the state and NRM, the prosperity that underpins this, and the geographical separation between them and the perpetrators—who are meanwhile weak and divided. But a return of political leaders associated with the days of genocide would raise the ghosts of the past and could prove very divisive. The success of this strategy can only be proven over time.

The price of the ideological solution is that political pluralism must be limited, in order to suppress politicised ethnicity. Many countries in Africa adopted single-party systems in the name of counteracting tribalism, but often this amounted to no more than a disguised tribalism, and ethnic conflict was actually sharpened. The case of Somalia is instructive: the 1988 genocide was perpetrated at a time when only one party was permitted and it was actually illegal to use clan names, but the regime was undermining this official policy with its cynical manipulation of clan politics.

In cases of political/ideological genocide, there is no territorial solution. Survivors and perpetrators must continue to coexist within one state. Such is the case in Cambodia. Fortunately, while there are individual criminals who can threaten individual survivors, the Khmer Rouge's genocidal ideology no longer remains a force. The same is true for the survivors of the Red Terror survivors in Ethiopia: their security is provided by the demise of the genocidal ideology. In Indonesia, there is as yet no solution, while government and the principal opposition parties refuse to take seriously the question of accountability for the killings of 1965-6 and those in East Timor. A repeat of those mass killings may be unlikely, but the prospect of other large-scale violence remains very real.

Reconciliation is not a common response to genocide. If reconciliation occurs, it is when the victim group has successfully ensured its security using the above strategies. The case of South

Africa is instructive. While genocide was not perpetrated, the model of the response to decades of Apartheid—a Truth and Reconciliation Commission—has been widely admired and has been proposed for elsewhere. For example, Archbishop Desmond Tutu, one of the inspirations for the TRC, has urged Rwandese to forgive and reconcile. But this appeal was not well received in Rwanda. Reconciliation requires an admission of guilt by those responsible, which was not forthcoming. It requires an abandonment of the genocidal ideology, which was not forthcoming. It requires acts of restitution, which were not forthcoming. Constitutional guarantees for security and power sharing are not enough, when those responsible for genocide are not ready to take up the opportunities offered.

The case of Uganda is perhaps the closest to real reconciliation, based on the relative security of the former victim group and the anti-tribalist approach of the government. The bitterness between the Luwero residents and the northerners, who supported the Obote government, appears to have abated—though political antagonisms remain. Reconciliation has occured in the context of the political marginalisation of the groups associated with genocide, and the enjoyment of power and prosperity by the groups that suffered. However, serious problems remain in the north. Blame for this must be divided between the NRM government, the northern political leaders, and those implicated in the mass killing. One of the problems is the failure of the northern communities themselves to reconcile with their members who were part of Obote's genocidal army. The victims of the northern insurrection have been the northerners themselves.

There is no territorial solution in Rwanda or Burundi. The option of mass relocation of the targetted group to a safe distance does not exist. Even if the victims obtain a separate state, by dividing the current territory (as some naive observers have proposed) they are still neighbours to those they fear. An ideological response is a theoretical possibility, as in Uganda, in which ethnicity is suppressed. To some extent this has been pursued by governments in both countries, which have tried to stress common citizenship rather than ethnicity. But in both countries, the power response has been paramount.

Following the 1972 genocidal killings in Burundi, there was a growth of militant Hutu extremism, especially in exile. This matched the existing Tutsi supremacist ideology in the government and army (although it was disguised by an attempt to deny ethnicity). This polarisation and hatred contributed to civil war and reciprocal mass killing in 1993 and subsequently. This is the most serious instance of vengefulness—the growth of a reciprocal genocidal ideology. However, the well-demonstrated capacity for mutual destruction by both parties, and the incapacity of either one to rule alone, may yet bring about the conditions in which reconciliation, or at least peaceful coexistence, is possible.

In Rwanda also, the genocide was ethnic, but no territorial solution is on offer, making it an extremely difficult case. There can be no sovereign barrier between victims and perpetrators, which would give time and space for co-existence and possible long-term reconciliation. This makes security for the survivors extremely difficult, and therefore co-existence difficult. Currently, the survivors' security is provided solely by the RPF control of state power and national security—there is no fall-back option of territorial defence or self-determination open to them. An ideological solution along the Ugandan model would theoretically be possible including the prosecution of the ringleaders, a truth commission, and a consistent and widely-supported attempt to minimise ethnicity. But this has not been effectively pursued and probably cannot be while the genocidaires remain at large and active. The continued presence of the genocidaires in neighbouring countries (particularly Zaire/D.R. Congo) and the continued acceptance of the genocidal ideology by some Rwandese leaders and their foreign allies, was and is an extremely serious threat to the survivors and the Rwandese Tutsis in general. In the medium term, the implications of the genocide in Rwanda have included the destabilisation of Zaire, the fall of Mobutu and the current civil war in D.R. Congo, a war with nearly continent-wide ramifications.

In the long term the solution for Rwanda can only be the demise of the genocidal ideology, which can be the basis for reconciliation. But unlike extreme communism and anti-communism, ethnicity does not go out of fashion.

CONCLUSION

Genocide is the ultimate crime. The above analysis has shown how genocide challenges the basic order of international law and makes human rights law and international humanitarian law irrelevant. Preventing and punishing the crime of genocide is therefore of paramount international importance, not merely for reasons of humanity, but because no international order can remain stable in the aftermath of genocide.

It is unfortunate that, in addition to the absolute genocide in Rwanda in 1994, Africa has also seen a number of cases of 'convention genocide'. Moreover, the threats of genocide are still very real in central Africa, Sudan and elsewhere. Fighting genocide demands many measures, some of which have been alluded to. Perhaps the most important is reiterating the commitment to fighting genocide. States that have not signed the Genocide Convention should do so, and others should reaffirm their commitment and incorporate the Genocide Convention into domestic law.

The most important components in preventing genocide are depoliticising ethnicity and the related measure of minimising the ethnic element in citizenship. There are no satisfactory solutions once genocide has occurred.

Given that most genocides are ethnic, the ideological response to genocide is to depoliticise ethnicity. This is rarely followed after a genocide. The only successful case (so far) is Uganda. The price is limited pluralism. Instead, most victim groups seek a combination of a power solution (controlling the state and armed forces) and a territorial solution (self-determination and preferably independent statehood). The price is continued political ethnicity and potential for conflict. In such cases, African governments and intergovernmental organisations should recognise the legitimacy of the demand for self-determination, and subsequently invest effort in ensuring that the potential for future conflict is minimised.

The case of Rwanda is exceptionally difficult. No acceptable territorial solution has been offered, nor is likely. The ideological solution is very distant indeed. The only option is a power solution—Rwandese Tutsis have effective control over the state apparatus and security services. This is intrinsically unstable, because it denies full civil and political rights to the majority Hutu populace, and implicitly places their interests below those of the minority who still feel under the threat of genocide. It is the task of the international community, including African nations and interstate organisations, to make this solution as humane, just and democratic as possible.

Notes

1. Note that the defense of the 'double effect' does not work in cases of genocide. Even if the principal intent was to suppress insurgency (or whatever), as long as this involved deliberate acts involving killing or harming members of an ethnic group, indentified as sucyh, then it is genocide.
2. UNHCR and some humanitarian agencies claimed that 200,000 'refugees' had 'disappeared' in the RPA's 'final solution.' Those who were sceptical of such figures, given the total lack of reliable statistics about teh number of residents in UNHCR's camps in eastern Zaire, were reassured when suddenly 170,000 Hutu refugees appeared in the forests of Kivu in April 1999.
3. Among behavioural psychologists, this is known as cognitive dissonance, and among psychoanalysts essentially the same phenomenon is known as defensive projection.

3

STRUCTURES FOR REGIONAL
PEACE AND SECURITY

WHAT IS REGIONAL PEACE AND SECURITY?

The last quarter of the 20th century has witnessed the development of numerous regional and subregional structures to promote peace and security around the world. In retrospect, this may emerge as one of the most significant developments of these decades. Responsibility for the principle of collective security, enshrined in the United Nations charter and organisation, is increasingly being shared with a range of organisations concerned with specific regions. In line with UN Secretary General Boutros Boutros Ghali's 'Agenda for Peace,' on a case-by-case basis, the UN Security Council has requested regional and subregional organisations to take the primary responsibility for resolving particular peace and security crises. These organisations are extremely diverse in their compositions, mandates and mechanisms of operation, reflecting the different political histories of different parts of the world.

Regionally-based security systems are a reality in most parts of the world. Africa is only catching up. Where a dominant regional power exists, the UN has either had no role or a more limited role under very close supervision by that power. Thus in the conflicts in the former USSR (Trans-Dniestr, Chechnya, South Ossetia, Abkhazia, Georgia, Nagorno-Karabakh, Tajikistan), the UN has played virtually no role, and Russia has played the policeman in its 'near abroad.' The US has done the same in the Caribbean and Central America, keeping a tight rein on the one UN programme in the region (El Salvador). The EU tried to play the lead role in Former Yugoslavia but in the end NATO took the lead. Only in Africa has the UN been left to play a major role in initiating conflict resolution.

There is no single model for a successful peace and security structure. Even those models that appear to be successful may fall apart as circumstances change. A decade ago, for example, the European conflict prevention and resolution structures were considered a model, but after the wars in former Yugoslavia they can scarcely be considered to have succeeded.

WHAT MAKES FOR ROBUST REGIONAL PEACE AND SECURITY?

1. Formal inter-state structures, created by treaty. While each has some resemblance to the United Nations model, they are also extremely varied. These take time to develop and gain the credibility and legitimacy that earns them respect.

2. Complementary networks and mechanisms, for example inter-parliamentary unions, environmental, economic and other organisations, human rights commissions, religious associations and networks, citizens' groups, etc.

3. Other inter-state ties, notably economic cooperation and integration. Stable inter-state power relations. The power relations extant in the region or subregion, specifically whether there is a hegemonic power structure (one major power with uncontested dominance), stable balance of power among states, or a contested power structure. A variant of this is a coherent structure, aim and ideology in the face of a common external threat (e.g. NATO against the Warsaw Pact). Unfortunately Africa did not benefit from the partial stability of the Cold War era.

4. Enforcement capacities, including sanctions and interventions. (Details of this issue are dealt with in chapter 4). Note that an enforcement capacity depends upon prior credibility and legitimacy-no interstate organisation can gain legitimacy solely by the use of

force.

5. Consensus on shared basic values of democracy and human rights and a commitment to peaceful resolution of disputes among member states and their citizens. This may be facilitated by the presence of a common external enemy. There are important roles for civil society organisations in this respect.

The following sections examine each of these requirements with respect to Africa. Africa is in the unenviable position of needing good peace and security structures more than any other region, but lacking them more completely. It is evident that Africa will need to develop its own peace and security institutions, even while its conflicts continue to sap its energies and undermine its confidence.

AFRICAN CONFLICT RESOLUTION STRUCTURES AND MECHANISMS

African structures and mechanisms for conflict prevention and resolution are young. Most are only a decade or less old. They have hitherto been marked by a stress on formal inter-governmental structures with formal commitments. The OAU is broadly modelled on the United Nations, with the subregional organisations—ECOWAS, IGAD, SADC, AMU etc—broadly similar. For some conflicts, such formal structures are ideally suited, while for others they are singularly inappropriate. The Ethio-Eritrean conflict demands first-rate professional diplomacy resulting in a peace treaty. The Somali conflict requires a more patient and unconventional approach. Over time, these organisations are certain to develop and change, becoming better suited to the varied challenges they face. In the meantime, however, they are relatively weak, and face enormous challenges which are wholly disproportionate to the resources they command and the political consensus they can summon.

In the 1990s, the OAU has assumed greater responsibility for conflict resolution. The OAU Central Organ, and the OAU Mechanism for Preventing, Managing and Resolving Conflicts were established at the 1993 OAU Summit in Cairo. While restating the OAU norm of non-interference in the internal affairs of states, the mechanism also assumed a mandate for dealing with internal conflicts.

Some of the motivation for the OAU conflict resolution mechanism was prefigured in the May 1991 Kampala Conference on

Security, Stability, Development and Cooperation in Africa. At the time this was somewhat ambitiously dubbed 'the African Helsinki' and it was an auspicious start to the development of a regional peace and security order. However the notable absence of human rights from the Kampala 'calabashes' suggested that enduring jealousies over the privileges of national sovereignty still held strong sway. And the Kampala document was not subsequently adopted at the OAU, including OAU Central Organ and mechanism for conflict prevention and resolution.

In 1997, the OAU took a major step in resolving that it would henceforth refuse to recognise governments imposed by the use of force. There should be no more short cuts to power. Since then there has been lively debate concerning the status of governments that have recently taken power by unconstitutional means, whether they should be given 'red cards' or 'yellow cards.' Ensuring that this principle is properly recognised and enforced will be one of the biggest challenges for the OAU and subregional organisations in the 21st century.

There are many challenges that must be met to enable the OAU conflict resolution mechanisms to work more effectively. These include:

• Greater financial capacity and more human resources at the OAU. Training in methods of conflict resolution has already been provided to OAU staff but there is scope for more.

• Improved coordination between the OAU and subregional organisations, so that initiatives can be shared and mutually supported.

• The creation of OAU-NGO fora so that there are more lines of communication between the OAU and African civil society. This will enable the OAU to have a more effective early warning and prevention system.

• Increase the options open to OAU conflict resolution initiatives. One worthwhile option is to have 'missions of long duration' for conflict-prone countries.

• Special attention to the particular challenges posed by refugee flows, humanitarian crises, and disputes over minority rights. The OAU's capacity with regard to humanitarian and refugee affairs warrants strengthening, including gaining expertise and increasing its liaison with existing specialist institutions. The OAU could also consider appointing a special unit, or a special commissioner, for national minorities. (The model is taken from the OSCE).

One proposal that is frequently made is that there should be a 'conflict early warning system'. This is an inherently difficult proposal, which is discussed in chapter 6. It is likely that a formalised specialist early warning system for conflict would simply become an information gathering exercise. It is probable that the best form of early warning is improving the skills and capacities of existing conflict prevention and resolution mechanisms.

It is notable that the OAU and Kampala Conference both reflect a very formal, summit-based and treaty-based approach to peace and security. This is one model for inter-state cooperation, and it has been followed for example in the successful Arias plan for Central America. However, there are other models also worthy of consideration. The ASEAN model of cooperation is based less on formal commitments and more on discreet closed door negotiation between leaders who share a common determination to present a united face to the world, resolving their differences in private. Possibly, once the formal systems have matured and become well-established, the opportunities for developing other, more flexible systems will increase.

SUBREGIONAL SYSTEMS: ECOWAS

ECOWAS is much more advanced than other subregional systems in Africa, with active military and political engagement in Liberia and Sierra Leone. The case of ECOMOG is the most significant African experience in peacekeeping.

ECOMOG draws its mandate from ECOWAS and in turn from the OAU and the UN. The ECOWAS states embarked upon a subregional peace and security order two decades ago, beginning with the 1978 protocol on non-aggression and the 1981 protocol on mutual assistance in defence. The latter was an ambitious document that called for an Allied Armed Forces of the Community, a common defence budget for ECOWAS, and a Deputy Executive Secretary General for Defence. Common action was specified in the case of external threats, and not internal conflicts. Although the 1981 Protocol entered into force five years later, its key provisions were not implemented. Instead, the ECOMOG force was created a decade later in a more ad hoc manner, heavily reliant on the Nigerian contribution.

ECOMOG intervened in Liberia when no others were willing to do so. The intervention was criticised as having a political agenda-specifically, the Nigerians sought to deny military victory to Charles Taylor. In that respect, the ECOMOG intervention resembled all other humanitarian military interventions including the UN operations in Cambodia and Somalia. The intervention has also been criticised for excessive use of force, for corruption and human rights abuses, and for placing political and military interests above humanitarian concerns. This is not the place for an examination of these allegations, or a judgement of the overall ECOMOG record. However, the controversy over the ECOMOG performance points to the importance of having independent assessments and mechanisms for recourse in such cases. The lessons must be learned for future interventions.

The ECOMOG intervention in Sierra Leone is even more controversial. There was in fact no decision by either the UN or by an ECOWAS summit to authorise the Nigerian military action against the 1997 coup leaders-the resolutions called for the restoration of the elected government but did not specifically authorise the use of force. The Nigerian military presence in the country was based on a bilateral defence agreement with the former Sierra Leonean government, not on an ECOMOG mandate-making it arguable that the force should not be referred to as an 'ECOMOG' force at all. It has also been argued that the ECOMOG blockade on Sierra Leone, which was extended to all commercial goods and humanitarian aid, was unlawful and exceeded the sanctions imposed by the UN Security Council. There was also much comment on the irony that the former military government of Nigeria was prohibiting democracy at home, while trying to impose it by force abroad.

However, the Nigerians also won praise for their robust action in a situation in which the international community was unwilling to do anything other than provide modest humanitarian aid. In situations such as the May 1997 coup, swift and decisive military action may be the most effective response, although in this instance it was not successful.

Economic capability is an essential basis for any form of intervention. The ECOMOG intervention in Liberia and Sierra Leone may have cost as much as US$4 billion, a bill that only Nigeria could afford. The OAU by contrast has a budget in the tens of millions of dollars and many states are deeply in arrears in paying their dues. This is an indication of how Africa's economic crisis is closely interlinked with its failure to find political solutions to its conflicts.

OTHER SUBREGIONAL SYSTEMS

In the late 1990s, SADC has rapidly developed an active peace and security mechanism. SADC intervened (with South African troops) in Lesotho, and SADC member states sent troops to the Democratic Republic of Congo to support the government there. SADC interventions raise similar questions of legality, effectiveness, respect for human rights and accountability as the ECOMOG operations, underlining the need for independent mechanisms for evaluation. Operation Blue Crane in April 1999 indicates that SADC member states may be ready to go further than ECOWAS in putting their forces under a unitary command.

In north-east Africa, IGAD has a peace and security role, and has played a part in seeking peace in Sudan and Somalia. However, IGAD is considerably weaker, both financially and politically, than either ECOWAS or SADC. IGAD member states have preferred to reserve their armed forces for use in pursuit of the national interest alone and IGAD has yet to put together any enforcement capacity. This will become a particular challenge in the case of Sudan, where IGAD has taken the lead in the peace process, which may lead to a self-determination referendum for Southern Sudan-which will require some form of supervision and monitoring.

COMPLEMENTARY STRUCTURES, NETWORKS AND PROCESSES

It is also important to look at parallel and complementary structures of various kinds. These fall into various categories.

Economic structures

Most African subregional organisations began with an agenda for cooperation over economic policies, infrastructural development, etc. These are less contentious areas in which interstate cooperation can more easily be obtained. These fora are important.

They enable bilateral economic disputes to be identified at an early stage and resolved within a multilateral framework, thus helping to minimise one potential source of conflict.

By assisting the negotiation of economic cooperation, integration and convergence, they create a web of ties within and between countries that help mitigate the potential for conflict.

They are a meeting point for leaders, providing opportunities for formal and informal discussion of problems.

However, economic organisations in themselves are not sufficient to prevent conflict. Economic development and integration may reduce the potential for conflict but they cannot eliminate it entirely, and economic fora are rarely the right place for the resolution of non-economic disputes.

Environmental organisations

There are a number of specialist multi-lateral organisations that can play a role in promoting security.

• Riperain associations, such as the signatories to the Nile Waters Agreement. There is a school of thought that maintains that the conflicts of the coming century will be 'water wars', with states (especially in the Middle East and north-east Africa) going to war over contested water resources including the Nile, Indus, Tigris, Euphrates and Jordan. This may be an exaggerated fear, but the potential for friction and dispute over water resources is always present. Fortunately, most states are already acutely aware of these problems and institutions and mechanisms exist, which continue to function even when there are other disputes between the relevant governments. (For example the disputes between Sudan and Uganda have not jeopardised the Nile Waters Agreement.) In cases such as Somalia, however, which has no functioning government, problems could potentially be stored up if Ethiopia should decide to divert a substantial part of the waters of the Jubba and Shebelle rivers.

• Livestock and pest control agencies, such as the desert locust control organisation. The smooth functioning of these organisations can prevent minor but significant disputes between countries. Internally, the independent functioning of water supply and veterinary agencies can help mitigate conflicts involving pastoralist populations.

Informal 'clubs' of leaders
Many of the independence generation of African leaders shared a common set of aspirations and values, and were ready to make considerable sacrifices to support one another. They shared a common heritage of the struggle against colonial rule, and many were close personal friends. In the 1970s and '80s, there were comparable 'clubs' of military rulers, especially in west Africa, who shared common values of militarism and contempt for democracy and human rights. More recently, a 'club' of 'new leaders' briefly emerged in central and north-east Africa, with a shared history of internal armed struggle against oppressive regimes and a common commitment to a solution to the region's interlinked problems. While such clubs of leaders can achieve a great deal—and often they can succeed in areas where more formal arrangements between governments cannot make progress—they also have their shortcomings. These include:

• Insufficient institutionalisation. Cooperation may not extend beyond the leadership level, so that membership of the club is wholly dependent upon the head of state and his immediate entourage. If the head of state dies or is overthrown, or if two leaders quarrel, then there may be no mechanisms lower down the governmental structure to help contain the dispute.

• Insufficient transparency and democracy. Clubs are inevitably secretive and exclusive, and develop a mystique. These are not conducive to democracy. The sense of shared membership in a common multinational project may not extend from the leaders to the citizens.

• Neglecting formal channels. Agreements between members of a club are commonly based on informal agreements, and may not be written down. If something goes wrong, this creates many possibilities for dispute and misunderstanding. Formal diplomacy, while cumbersome, minimises these dangers.

• Neglecting rules. A successful club generates its own internal rules, which may be highly informal. But international action based on informal understanding between leaders has a long-term danger of undermining formal structures for mediation and dispute resolution.

• Exclusivity. Such clubs of leaders are commonly created partly by a common enemy (e.g. Apartheid). But they tend to exclude others too, who by virtue of personality or history have a somewhat different outlook. Clubs can generate counter-clubs in opposition to them.

These considerations imply that we should be very careful about promoting or supporting informal clubs.

'Seminar diplomacy'
The speed of change and development in the international arena is such that it is difficult for even the best-informed—and this includes senior political leaders—to keep themselves up to date. Keeping abreast of current thinking in economics, politics, the environment, etc, may be even more difficult than staying well-informed about current events.

The rapidity of change of economic, political and security paradigms creates its own dangers. The worst scenario is misunderstanding between political leaders about what is politically acceptable or legitimate. More widely, there are missed opportunities for developing a common understanding of priorities and strategies.

Structures and mechanisms for 'seminar diplomacy' may prove

to be an effective long-term instrument of peace and security. They provide an opportunity for leaders to discuss in discreet and informal ways, and develop greater understanding of common problems and challenges. 'Seminar diplomacy' also should not take place in isolation from investment in research, publishing and teaching at African universities and research institutes on these subjects. Educating the coming generation of African graduates in contemporary affairs—with a distinctively African perspective—will be a major investment for the future.

Africa lacks a continental centre for security studies, which could be a centre of excellence and a hub for academic and policy-related networking on the issues. In Europe, academic and policy-related think-tanks have helped to bring together specialists on crisis-prone countries, and have played the important role of providing a platform for academics and journalists from the affected countries, whose voices might otherwise not have been heard.

Interparliamentary structures
There is scope for inter-parliamentary associations and unions. At present these are likely to be chiefly an educational and cultural exchange exercise but are valuable nonetheless. The greater the political and economic cooperation between countries, the more significant such associations become.

Legal structures
Slowly, Africa is developing continental legal and human rights organisations. These, including the African Commission on Human and People's Rights and the African Court of Human and People's Rights, have an important potential for creating multilateral mechanisms for investigation and adjudication of certain sorts of complaints. The mechanisms for presenting cases to the African Commission however need to be simplified and the Commission needs to be more accessible to the citizens of African countries.

Citizens' assemblies
Informal parliaments and assemblies can play an important role in certain situations. In Europe, the Helsinki Citizens' Assemblies

were active in Bosnia, trying to help maintain relations between the different communities there during the war. There is certainly a potential for comparable initiatives in Africa, for example under the banner of the Pan African Movement. However there are serious obstacles to the organisation of such assemblies in Africa. One problem is communication and logistics. A second is that the requisite freedoms of association and expression only exist in certain countries. A third is that most citizens of African countries are understandably preoccupied with their national problems and are therefore less able and willing to mobilise support for initiatives concerning other countries. A final difficulty is that such international initiatives have a tendency of being hijacked by certain interest groups, such as communists or churches.

Religious structures

Religious leaders often speak of peace and reconciliation, and occasionally play a constructive role in that direction. Religious institutions are not immune from their own politics including potentially divisive internal political differences. The All-Africa Conference of Churches could potentially play a role in conflict resolution, but that is likely to be some time in the future. The Roman Catholic Church is enormously influential in many African countries, and some bishops have been prominent in promoting democratic transitions, but the Vatican has yet to take on a wider role regarding peace and security, and is not likely to try to do so.

The role of the World Council of Churches in the negotiations that ended Sudan's first civil war in 1972 was the biggest success for church mediation, but credit must be placed primarily with the personal qualities of the facilitator, the backing of the Emperor Haile Selassie, and the readiness of the parties to reach an agreement. The Community of Sant Edigio in Rome played an important role in the Mozambique peace process, a good example of a low-profile and low-expectation mediation role by a private religious institution.

Islamic structures and leaders have played a role in several efforts at conflict resolution, for example in Somaliland. Religious extremism, both Christian and Moslem, has been a negative influence throughout the continent.

Extra-continental structures

• United Nations. The UN retains a more important role in Africa than elsewhere in the world, and Africa is important to the continued relevance of the UN, especially its specialist organisations.

• The UN Security Council is the premier peace and security organisation in the world, and much of its time is spent on African issues.

• Arab League. Ten African states are members of the Arab League. However, the League has played no significant role in the conflicts that have afflicted any of these countries.

•Organisation of Islamic Conference. The OIC has yet to play a constructive role with regard to the promotion of peace and security in Africa.

•Non-Aligned Movement. This has unfortunately become something of a historical curiosity. It is however an opportunity for heads of state and foreign ministers to meet.

•Commonwealth. The (British) Commonwealth is an interesting example of an international organisation that could never be created from scratch, but, given that it exists, has come to play a significant role. Created as an association of former British colonies, it has succeeded in shaking off the image of an imperial relic. It has a membership of 54 states, and is growing. For example, Mozambique—never a British colony—has joined because all its neighbours were members and were enjoying the benefits that followed. The Commonwealth has no enforcement capacity. Its only force is moral—which can be rebuffed, as in the case of its suspension of Nigeria. Its chief roles lie in promoting trade, human rights, and democracy, through assistance, agreement and persuasion. The 1991 Harare Declaration adopted principles of human rights and democracy as an integral part of the Commonwealth principles, which is credited with helping nine African countries make the transition from authoritarian or military rule to democracy.

•Francophonie. The association of former French colonies is a rather different creature. Unlike the Commonwealth, it has a preponderance of African members, but is dominated by France. After decolonisation, the economic and security links between France and its former colonies remained extremely close, so that the Francophone club became a much tighter organisation—but by the same token less flexible and open to change.

ECONOMIC TIES
After World War II, France, Italy and the Benelux countries decided to tie Germany into an ever-closer economic union in Europe, with the aim—among others—of making it impossible for Germany to go to war with its neighbours again. This succeeded. It has given rise to the vision of economic integration bringing an end to conflict on a world-wide scale. In Africa, however, that vision is a long way from being realisable. Economic factors can be both a force for peace and a contributor to conflict. Economic development in the context of neoliberal globalisation creates economic interdependence that should militate against conflict. However, the trade disputes within the European Union and between the EU and the United States, among others, indicate that neoliberal doctrine does not abolish economic national interest. The same is true for Africa, especially as most African economies are very unevenly integrated into the global economy, and the level of state intervention in economic affairs is rather high. No fewer than fifteen African countries are landlocked and rely on their neighbours for access to the sea, creating many potential sources of friction over transit of goods. Many find themselves competing for supplying agricultural commodities to the same, rather limited world markets.

Economic integration should help limit inter-state conflict, because there are strong countervailing interests against a break in relations between economically-integrated neighbours. Similarly it should militate against internal conflict, as there are economic interests vested in maintaining a well-functioning internal market. However, this does not always prove so simple in practice. Until the conflict of May 1998, the economies of Eritrea and Ethiopia were among the most closely integrated on the continent—but that very closeness created friction. The 1999 Trade, Development and Cooperation Agreement between South Africa and the EU will bring benefits to South Africa, but some losses to its neighbours. In particular Botswana, Lesotho, Namibia and Swaziland will lose a substantial proportion of their customs revenues. In a number of internal conflicts in Africa, there are strong economic forces that have benefited from war. For example, some traders have made windfall profits from the high prices of goods in besieged garrison towns, or from the resale of looted goods, or from the acquisition of farmland forcibly emptied of its former inhabitants.

At independence, many African states were financially and economically integrated. This was particularly so for the Franc Zone in west Africa, the East African Community and the Central African Federation. However these associations rapidly fell apart, or, in the case of the Franc Zone, failed to develop. Following the adoption of the 1980 Lagos Plan of Action that announced a pan-African programme of economic cooperation and integration, a new start seemed to have been made. But a number of factors militate against effective economic integration:

1. Most African countries are exporters of raw materials, and compete with one another for markets.

2. Integration between neighbouring African states is usually the integration of unequal partners, and the benefits of the arrangement are usually polarised towards one partner. For example South Africa is the major beneficiary of the Southern Africa Customs Union, and has therefore allowed compensatory mechanisms to be built in that benefit the other smaller members. Although integration is a sum-sum exercise, the disproportionate allocation of benefits may create frictions.

3. A very low level of international trade is between African countries. In the Southern Africa subregion (excepting South Africa), for example, no more than 5% of international trade is between member states, and most of this is accounted for by Zimbabwe. This level did not change despite the efforts of SADCC in the 1980s.

Moreover, few if any developing countries have experienced rapid economic growth on the basis of intra-regional trade, as opposed to exporting to world markets.

4. Most trade between neighbouring states is informal or illegal. Lowering tariff barriers does not address the constraints on this trade. It also does not address the main transaction costs of formal trade, which consist of informal duties and tolls exacted by underpaid officials and soldiers.

5. There is a low level of implementation of treaty obligations. This is due to (a) unwillingness to sacrifice sovereignty, leading to (b) unwillingness to incorporate international treaties into domestic law and give powers to supranational bodies and (c) a low level of institutional development, so that the hard bureaucratic work of implementing obligations is rarely actually carried out.

6. Some of the requirements of preferential trade areas are contradicted by the demands of structural adjustment programmes required by donors and creditors, whose priorities are more usually to promote competitive exports to the global market.

As a result, the outcomes of attempts at creating common markets and developing subregional economic integration have been disappointing. More modest functional cooperation on specific projects and in particular sectors has had a better record. Infrastructural projects (building or rehabilitating road and rail links) have often been more successful. These have often been donor-funded.

Economic cooperation and integration entails a complex agenda that is beyond the scope of this chapter. They are desirable ends in their own right, will contribute to more sustainable and equitable development, and should also provide means of mitigating the potential for conflict. But the prospects of using a process of economic cooperation and integration as a robust conflict-prevention mechanism are not bright.

STABLE INTER-STATE POWER RELATIONS

Probably the most significant factor in creating a regional environment conducive to peace and security is the existence of a stable inter-state order. This order does not have to be just or democratic—just stable. Under Soviet hegemony, eastern Europe at least had the virtue of not suffering internecine warfare, while the balance of power across Cold War Europe froze conflicts for more than a generation, enabling the creation of two mutually-antagonistic interstate treaty organisations.

During the Cold War, large parts of Africa (the whole of southern Africa and the Horn) were the site of violent contest for power between geo-strategic interests. The Cold War was never cold in Africa—there was always organised violence and destabilisation across the continent. The end of the Cold War created an opportunity for American hegemony, but the US was not ready to actively pursue that option. France sought to maintain its power in substantial parts of Africa, but discovered that this was costly, unpopular and unproductive. As a result there has been a vacuum of strategic interest. This has created conditions in which a new power scenario may emerge, perhaps with subregionally dominant powers or subregional balances of power. But in the meantime, states have to test the limits of their power and discover their roles. The particular politics of different subregions may make for chronic instability for some time to come.

WESTERN POWER

The main feature of the western engagement in Africa, especially since the collapse of the Somali intervention in 1993, has been its lack of seriousness. Western powers, and notably the United States, are simply unwilling to risk military resources and above all the lives of their troops in Africa. Policy has been marked by only a 'soft' engagement; verbal and symbolic commitments not backed up by resources or hard political and diplomatic work.

United States policy has not been assertive. There have been opinions and emotions, but little more. The Administration has consistently supported Egypt for reasons unconnected with Africa, and has admired Nelson Mandela, but little more. Aid policy has been confused, with multiple conditionalities that often contradict one another. After much internal struggle within the State Department and National Security Council, a policy was beginning to emerge in 1996-7 which consisted of supporting the 'new leadership' and opposing Sudan. But loud noises translated into virtually nothing on the ground: the Sudanese opposition received no military support worth speaking of, and promises of humanitarian aid to be channelled to the opposition-held areas in northern Sudan failed to materialise. This policy collapsed in 1998 with the Ethio-Eritrean conflict. In retrospect, the only workable part of that policy was to stand back as some African countries (notably Rwanda and Eritrea) intervened militarily in their neighbours' affairs.

The main outcome has been a crisis of credibility for international mediation or peacekeeping. Neither the US nor any European country has been ready to invest the time and resources to sustain a credible peacemaking effort, even where political interests are at stake, such as Congo, Sudan or Ethiopia-Eritrea.

American military doctrine with regard to Africa is symbolised by the August 1998 cruise missile attack on the al Shifa factory in Khartoum. This was a projection of US military power: overwhelming force with no possibility of American casualties. It has similarities with 19th century colonial punitive expeditions, intended to show that America can wreak its vengeance where and how it likes. The strike almost certainly hit an innocent target, illustrating poor intelligence. It was in blatant disregard for international law. It contrasted with the protracted failure—despite symbolic acts to the contrary—of the US to provide any serious assistance to the Sudanese opposition forces. It was counter-productive, in that it wrong-footed the Sudanese opposition and delivered a propaganda coup to the government. Its sole virtue was that it was limited: it caused few casualties and did not lead to an escalation to all-out war.

In short, the US missile strike had rather more in common with the 'cowardly' acts of long-distance terrorism it avenged than its authors might like to admit. Ultimately it was an irrelevance, a firework display that showed US impotence in Africa. This impotence has not come about because Africa is beyond hope or is in the grip of political process that cannot be influenced by outsiders. It has arisen because of the self-imposed paralysis of US policy.

Should the US administration, or any European government, wish to become constructively engaged in seeking political solutions to Africa's crises, the opportunities are there—but this will demand sustained and perhaps expensive commitments, which at present are not in prospect.

The French government has shown more realism and determination in its dealings with Africa. It has also been highly cynical, particularly in Rwanda in 1991-4 and in Zaire in 1994-7. But the limits of French power have also been shown up by the readiness of countries such as Rwanda to confront the French army when necessary.

In summary, Western powers have not generally had a coherent strategy for Africa. On the occasions where they have had clear tactical or strategic goals, they have rarely followed them with commitment. And on the occasions when the commitment has been there (e.g. the US in Somalia, the French in Rwanda and Zaire), the results have not been positive.

HEGEMONIC PROJECTS

The last decade has seen several attempts at continental or subregional hegemonic projects. These have been discussed in chapter 1, and include:

• The humanitarian interventionism of western governments at the behest of some special interests.

• Extremist Islamic internationalism.

• The coalition of the 'new leaders', briefly allied in pursuit of a progressive new order.

• The plan for a post-genocidal Hutu Power order in Rwanda and the neighbouring areas of central Africa.

None of these projects has succeeded, for very different reasons. Although it would be unwise to rule out resurgent hegemonic projects including extremism in various forms, the current failure of these hegemonic ambitions leaves the international political arena to more conventional state interests.

The largest countries in Africa's subregions could potentially play a decisive role in regional peacekeeping and peace enforcement, but there are major political and technical obstacles to them doing so.

NORTH-EAST AFRICA

The north-east African region has no natural dominant power. Briefly, the Ethiopia-Eritrea axis looked as though it might begin to establish subregional hegemony, but this possibility vanished in 1998. Egypt is the obvious country to dominate the region, being the wealthiest by far, and it has always sought to have a controlling influence in the Nile Valley and by extension the Horn. However, Egyptian diplomacy and projection of power have never been skilful enough to enable it to play such a role. Moreover in north-east Africa, many of Egypt's southern neighbours look upon it as a quasi-colonial power, eager to keep its African neighbours in a state of under-development so as not to lose any Nile waters to their irrigation schemes or hydroelectric projects. Whatever the truth in such a perception, it colours attitudes towards Egypt. This places a major challenge before the Egyptian government: how can it overcome these suspicions and play a constructive role in peacemaking in the region?

Establishing a stable inter-state order in north-east Africa will be peculiarly difficult. There are sharp and long-standing cultural and political divides in the region, which will be overcome only with great difficulty. There is a legacy of war and militarism in the region that makes each country vulnerable to the outbreak of conflict. The relations between northern and southern Somalia, and between Somalia and its neighbours, cannot stabilise in the absence of a government there. The relationship between the constituent parts of Sudan, and between Sudan and its neighbours, are also marked by deep distrust. Eritrea and Ethiopia each suspect that the other has designs on its territory or power. Overall, the subregion is cursed by zero-sum politics: each state looks at its neighbours and calculates that the other's gain is its own loss, and vice versa. This is not a sound basis on which to develop practices of mutual trust and cooperation, which require sum-sum thinking.

One fortunate aspect of the north-east African subregion is that, while the major conflicts have all influenced each other over the years, they can be treated on a case by case basis. The governments of Djibouti, Ethiopia and Kenya have learned to contain the instability in Somalia so that it does not critically destabilise them (though it continues to be a headache and intermittently a danger). Ethiopia and Eritrea have managed to insulate the Sudanese conflicts from their bilateral war. In a curious way, despite its chronic conflicts, the Horn of Africa has achieved a level of inter-state stability. However, whether this will endure is a difficult question, as there are short-term potentially destabilising factors (e.g. the demand among many Southern Sudanese for an independent state) and 'sleeper' issues such as disputed borders that always have the potential for reigniting conflict.

Without a dominant subregional power to take the lead, and with all states aware of the potential for serious armed resistance by a militant minority, there is unlikely to be military intervention in north-east Africa in the near future. It is possible that a settlement to the war in Southern Sudan will include provisions for international guarantors, but few countries—including the near neighbours—are likely to want to place significant peacekeeping forces in the territory. Peace and security mechanisms in the subregion are therefore likely to be based very substantially on formal multi-lateral negotiations, resulting in detailed treaties, signed at high level summits. A considerable period of positive experience of such agreements may be required before more flexible arrangements become viable.

This approach may be ill-suited to the special demands of Somalia. The reconstruction of Somalia probably demands the abandonment of conventional forms of diplomacy and state building and their replacement by other more flexible doctrines. But the states of the subregion are not well-placed to engage in such innovative practices, and Somalia's unfortunate citizens will probably continue to suffer.

WEST AFRICA

In west Africa, Nigeria is the obvious dominant power. Its population and economy are greater than those of all the other west African states combined. In the 1990s, Nigeria began to play an assertive role in the subregion, using its controlling stake in ECOWAS to despatch military forces to Liberia in the wake of the civil war there. After a long and difficult entanglement in the Liberian war, political scene and economy, ECOMOG did succeed in stabilising the situation in the country. But the limits of that are illustrated by the ultimate success of Charles Taylor in the Liberian elections: one of ECOMOG's principal aims at the outset had been to prevent Taylor from taking power. Similarly, ECOMOG intervened in Sierra Leone in the wake of the civil war there and the 1997 military coup that overthrew the elected government. In 1998, Nigerian ECOMOG troops restored the elected president, Ahmed Tijan Kabbah, to power. However, subsequent events in Sierra Leone have demonstrated both Kabbah's political failures and the hazards of relying on an external peacekeeping force to keep a government in office: by January 1999, the former army and rebels, in alliance, had re-entered the capital Freetown. One reason for the rebels' success appears to have been the concern among some smaller west African states that Nigeria was becoming too dominant in the subregion:

They unwilling to extend themselves in support of a Nigerian initiative. Whether Nigeria has the military capacity and the political will to fight a protracted war in Sierra Leone remains to be seen-especially now it is under democratic government.

The second power in the subregion is Ivory Coast, which is the leading Francophone country. However, the divergent interests and relatively small size of the Francophone west African nations makes it difficult for them to form a cohesive bloc, despite the advantages of a common currency and the related economic cooperation.

Nigeria may have learned the limits of its power, but it remains the dominant force in West Africa. A stable and prosperous Nigeria will undoubtedly become a force for stability in the subregion. It will have no option but to play that role. It is therefore important that Nigeria, within the context of ECOWAS, begins to develop appropriate doctrines of collective security, intervention and peacekeeping for the subregion. With the right leadership, west Africa could be poised for innovative developments in this regard.

SOUTHERN AFRICA

In southern Africa, the Republic of South Africa enjoys a dominant economic position, and there are widespread expectations that this will translate into a hegemonic military-political role. In terms of arms sales, this is certainly the case, but as the arms exporters are ready to sell to both sides of any conflict, this role tends to be politically self-negating. The same holds true for South Africa as a supplier of private security services, including mercenaries.

In terms of peace and security, South Africa's role has yet to be established. South Africa has been actively engaged in the Zaire-Congo crises of 1997-9, but not always successfully. When renewed war broke out in the Democratic Republic of Congo in 1998, several members of the Southern Africa Development Council (SADC) took the opposite stand to South Africa and intervened militarily on the side of the Kabila government. Zimbabwe exhibited a degree of jealousy at the leading role that South Africa was assuming, and sought to counterbalance it with a contrary initiative. Angola has a considerable military capacity which it is ready to use, if necessary projecting it over a substantial distance, but solely in pursuit of its own self-interest. Another setback to South Africa taking on the role as subregional policeman was its intervention in Lesotho to reverse a military takeover. The operation suceeded, but at the cost of much destruction and bloodshed, calling into question the effectiveness of the South African National Defence Force as a regional peacekeeper.

Post-Apartheid South Africa has been quick to learn the limits of power. But, like Nigeria, it will have no choice but to play the dominant political-military role in the subregion, especially with respect to its immediate neighbours. Thus, we can expect to see a relatively interventionist peace and security practice in southern Africa, necessitating an effective doctrine of intervention and peace-keeping. As with west Africa, there is room for innovative approaches to collective security.

CENTRAL AFRICA

Central Africa is cursed with a potential dominant subregional power—the Democratic Republic of Congo—that has been turned into a force for destabilisation and insecurity. Unfortunately, DRC's smaller neighbours cannot play a constructive role in stabilising the subregion because several of them are engaged in zero-sum political struggles with subregional ramifications.

The zero sum game of ethnic politics in Rwanda has an immense knock-on effect throughout the region, creating the preconditions for continued instability. While the Hutu extremists continue to want to destroy the Tutsi minority, and the Tutsi minority continue to seek security in military and political power, there is an insoluble conflict that can only end with the destruction or surrender of one side or the other. While this conflict continues, the politics of Rwanda will destabilise the entire subregion. Unfortunately, in the wake of the 1994 genocide, the Rwandan zero-sum game is real, and cannot be negotiated away. This will take a long time to resolve.

Similarly Angola, because of its wealth and the intractable nature of its conflict, also continues to destabilise the subregion. DRC will be unable to achieve peace while the Angolan war continues. Angola's readiness to project force beyond its borders in defence of its interests was also demonstrated in its 1997 intervention in the Republic of Congo (Brazzaville)—an action that flouted the principle that governments should not be changed by force of arms.

The nature of the subregion is such that each conflict influences the other, and neighbours cannot stay out of one another's conflicts.

Peace and security in central Africa therefore demands an approach different to each of the other African subregions. No single country or coalition can impose a new order. The conflicts cannot be treated in isolation on a country-by-country basis, with detailed formal treaties. The war in central Africa demands the engagement of the entire African continent and all its intergovernmental organisations, so that the different inter-related conflicts are settled together.

A CONSENSUS ON VALUES

Peace and security is more than a question of realpolitik and statecraft. More elusive qualities such as common principles and cultures are also important. This final section will examine some of the challenges to the achievement of a consensus on common values across Africa, or at least its subregions. Let us begin with the positive aspects.

There are no states in Africa that deny the right of others to exist, in a way that Arab states have denied the right of Israel to exist. There is however the case of Western Sahara, and potentially divisive cases such as Somaliland may emerge.

Africa is a weapons of mass destruction free zone: South Africa no longer possesses nuclear weapons, and it should be straightforward to investigate allegations of chemical weapons in Sudan following a peace agreement in that country.

Africa has a convention forbidding the use of mercenaries. Many African countries have a common history of collectively resisting colonialism and Apartheid, and therefore there is a fertile ground for promoting pan-African solidarity (though there is a regrettable tendency to downplay this, demeaning the previous generation of African struggles—when the current problems are surmounted perhaps the founding fathers of African independence can properly be celebrated once again). There is a strong consensus on the imperative of democratic rule. Military governments are no longer considered legitimate or acceptable. The hegemonic projects of the 1990s, which by their nature were exclusivist, have not succeeded. With electronic and satellite communication, governments cannot isolate their citizens from the currents of world affairs.

There is an emergent doctrine that governments cannot be changed by force. Though there are exceptions, when coups and invasions have not been condemned, the trend is definitely towards an unequivocal condemnation of such actions.

All conflicts are now the legitimate subject of international concern. Every internal or inter-state war is now immediately taken up by international bodies, and states are no longer able to argue that these are purely domestic affairs. But there are also very substantial challenges to the emergence of a truly effective continental consensus on peace and security. The negative aspects must also be listed:

Democratic institutions are still weak in many countries, and too many elected governments do not represent all sections of the electorate. There are too few democratic institutions that cross national borders, that allow citizens of different countries to collaborate. In many countries, force is still seen as a legitimate political instrument. Frustrated army officers and even civilians are ready to take up armed rebellion, and governments are ready to threaten and use force in settlement of disputes, both internally and with their neighbours.

Political, ethnic and religious extremism discolours several nations, creating inter-communal tensions and violence. Such extremism often has an international dimension so that neighbouring countries can be affected too.

There are major cultural divides within and between nations that have yet to be fully bridged. For example, may countries still suffer an enduring political and cultural problem between farmers and administrators on one hand and pastoralists on the other.

These challenges will take time and effort to surmount. They will require education and the development of institutions, the maturation of democracy, and the free exchange of ideas. Broadly speaking, the challenges are greatest in north-east and central Africa, where there is least consensus on values and a strong history of war and violence.

IMPLICATIONS

The paradox facing the world is that where peace and security institutions and mechanisms are most needed, they are least effective. Africa is more riven by war than any other continent, but it has neither a hegemonic power ready to enforce a new order (as NATO is doing in the Balkans), nor effective regional mechanisms for mediation and conflict resolutions. Africa has to invent the peace and security mechanisms that it needs, in the middle of debilitating conflicts that undermine the capacity and credibility of the governments and intergovernmental institutions that need to act effectively and credibly to create peace and security. The challenge is therefore rather substantial. But it can be met.

The challenge of peace and security must be met at many levels. Formal inter-governmental structures are needed, which entails strengthening the OAU Central Organ, developing appropriate doctrines and practices for ECOWAS and SADC, treating the conflicts in north-east Africa on a case-by-case basis by negotiation and treaty, and summoning a collective effort to address the many interlinked conflicts in central Africa. Wider institutions such as the UN, and the Commonwealth can also be involved where appropriate.

Complementary and parallel mechanisms are needed. These may include parliamentary unions, citizens' assemblies, economic organisations, religious organisations, etc. A consensus on common values of peace, tolerance, human rights, democracy, good neighbourliness, and the necessity of peaceful political processes, should be developed. Specific measures such as 'seminar diplomacy' and the development of university courses in peace and security will prove a good investment.

Ultimately, peace and security across Africa depends on political stability within and between nations. Unfortunately, history shows that the legacy of wars lasts for years if not decades, so no quick fixes can be anticipated. But the outlines of a stable and democratic order are at least becoming evident.

Africa needs progress on all fronts in order to build a robust peace and security order. This includes investing in formal interstate structures, building complementary and parallel structures (especially non-governmental ones), and trying to strengthen the consensus on peace, democracy, human rights, good neighbourliness and the necessity of political change through peaceful processes. The killing must end; organised violence must cease to be a legitimate tool of politics.

4

Interventions and Sanctions

Intervention . . . is a high and summary procedure which
may sometimes snatch a remedy beyond the reach of law.
Nevertheless it must be admitted that in the case of intervention, as that of revolution, its essence is illegality, and
its justification is its success.

—Sir W. V. Harcourt, 1843

Responsibility for response to threats to peace and security, including the security dimensions of humanitarian crises, is increasingly falling upon African intergovernmental organisations. As a
result, Africa needs to develop appropriate doctrines for enforcement measures, notably military interventions and sanctions. Circumstances are difficult: the array of conflicts in Africa is daunt-
ing. Fortunately, the recent experience of coercive measures allows us to learn from the mistakes that have been made.

In the last ten years, the international regime of military intervention and sanctions has undergone a series of dramatic changes.
First, there was an ambitious if badly-thought out attempt to create
a 'new world order' using UN-based multilateralism at its centre.
In Africa, this came apart between Mogadishu in 1993 and Zaire
in 1996. Instead, a more confusing and more overtly interest-driven
order has emerged. The US and its NATO allies have reverted to a
policy of indifference where their perceived national interests are
not at stake (e.g. most of Africa), punctuated by occasional unilat-

eral warfighting redolent of colonial punitive expeditions (e.g. the US missile attack on the al Shifa factory in Khartoum). In between, there may be a role for traditional UN blue helmets. Meanwhile, in line with Boutros Ghali's 'Agenda for Peace', and various UN Security Council resolutions, African countries and subregional organisations are taking on the primary responsibility for interventions.

This chapter will first consider intervention. It will review the 'old system' of military intervention and peacekeeping. This system has important virtues that should not be carelessly abandoned. It will discuss the 'post-cold war' order, based on the 'post-modern' conflict paradigm. with its corresponding model of humanitarian intervention called for and dominated by international agencies. Thirdly it it will make some specific suggestions for practical improvements in the conduct of military forces in humanitarian crises.

The logic of sanctions is in many ways the converse of the logic of humanitarian intervention. Sanctions compel civilians to make humanitarian sacrifices for what is seen as a greater political good, while intervention is premised on the argument that longer-term political objectives should be considered secondary to immediate human need. But sanctions are also enmeshed in a wider system of conditionalities on aid and trade, and a related philosophy of how aid donors should use their power to enact political change among aid recipients. The chapter examines some of the problems that emerge when an aid donor uses the essentially arbitrary and opaque process of sanctioning in order to promote 'democracy' or 'good governance.' When considering both sanctions and interventions, it proves impossible to separate means and ends: democracy and human rights can only be promoted by mechanisms that are themselves subject to democratic accountability.

'OLD SYSTEM' INTERVENTION
The 'old system' of military intervention during the Cold War period was characterised by a formal respect for state sovereignty combined with an active interventionist policy by the two superpowers and their principal allies. While formal military doctrines were based on the idea of a Clausewitzean inter-state war, actual war practice more often consisted of 'dirty wars' in which states

used very brutal methods of counter-insurgency and destabilisation. Interventions in these circumstances consisted of:

• Covert, indirect and occasionally direct involvement by major powers in other wars, based on bilateral agreements with governments or rebel movements. This was the norm: examples of US, Soviet, French, British, Portuguese, Israeli and Cuban involvement in other wars are too numerous to list. These are not often called 'interventions'-but that is what they were.

• Multilateral intervention in Korea in the exceptional circumstances of the Soviet boycott of the UN Security Council. 'Traditional peacekeeping' in which UN blue helmets oversaw a negotiated peace, operating with light weapons with the consent of both sides. This began in the 1956 Suez crisis but has been widely applied.

• More ambitious UN intervention in Congo in the 1960s. The failure of this mission led to a reluctance to attempt any more such missions for 25 years. Exceptionally, unilateral intervention in the face of extreme humanitarian problems (also usually justified as the response to aggression. E.g. Tanzania-Uganda and Vietnam-Cambodia).

Many of the actual wars were protracted guerrilla struggles, sectarian conflicts or involved collusion between covert engagements and criminal syndicates. 'Traditional peacekeeping' was utilised by the main powers when they had an interest in containing the conflict, and the two sides were also committed to freezing the conflict. It was not designed for other sorts of war which were resistant to mediation, either because of the intractability of the internal dynamics, or because the powers were themselves engaged in the conflict. Many of these 'old wars' were hidden, and outside involvement was often clandestine. Many have subsequently been forgotten. When looking at contemporary wars it is important to have a historical memory.

The UN Charter makes no mention of the possibility of humanitarian intervention, and no international law developments in the Cold War period mention it either. Critics of the concept of humanitarian intervention maintain that this is no accident. They argue that the concept (which had existed in customary international law before World War 2) had become so discredited by misuse that it was worthless. Such critics would point to cases such as the 19th century imperial ventures, especially in the Middle East, that were justified by the alleged need to protect Christian minorities, and Hitler's invasion of the Czech Sudetenland to 'protect' the German minority there. This historical experience indicated that no consensus was possible on the issue of humanitarian intervention, and in particular that it was easily misused and was always subject to political judgement. Humanitarian intervention was also subject to the law of unintended consequences: intrusion into another country could always have unexpected results.

Arguably, the concept of 'humanitarian intervention' remained valid in customary international law, and the drafters of the UN Charter knew it. The 1948 Genocide Convention implicitly allows for it. But by refusing to incorporate a specific doctrine of humanitarian intervention into the law, they were recognising that it is such an exceptional measure that it cannot be legislated for. To be 'humanitarian', intervention does not have to be multilateral or UN authorised, it just has to be an effective response to an exceptional circumstance. The slow process of obtaining legality may conflict with the imperative of speedy action for example there may not be enough time to achieve a multilateral consensus. As Sir William Harcourt put it, its essence is its illegality and its justification is its success.

Two important virtues remain in the 'old system'. These are the value of 'old fashioned' peacekeeping by consent, and scepticism about the right of humanitarian intervention.

'POST-COLD WAR' SYSTEM
The immediate post-cold war era was characterised by a concerted challenge to the concept of state sovereignty and a parallel development of a theory of 'post-modern' wars. This doctrine of intervention that followed was less a coherent ideological or political programme and more an ad hoc reaction to circumstances prevailing but it borrowed from concepts current at the time, and developed its own rationale and ideology.

THE CHALLENGE TO SOVEREIGNTY

The challenge to state sovereignty in Africa was rooted in the historical fact that many African rulers in the 1970s and 1980s refused to entertain criticism of their human rights record, still less to allow outside assistance or monitoring, on the grounds that this was a violation of their state sovereignty and territorial integrity. The crimes of the Mengistu government in Ethiopia and the Amin and Obote governments in Uganda were but two of the most egregious examples in Africa. The Khmer Rouge in Cambodia and Saddam Hussein's campaign against the Kurds were two other appalling examples.

Humanitarian agencies learned from this the simple and obvious lesson that sovereignty does not legitimise gross abuses of human rights nor prohibiting humanitarian assistance. This lesson was applied in Sudan, when Operation Lifeline Sudan was set up in 1989. Under this agreement, the Sudan government agreed to allow humanitarian assistance to go to civilians in areas under SPLA control. A similar agreement was reached in Angola but was not fully implemented.

Problems began to arise with the question of who was authorised to act on behalf of a people whose sovereign interests are not represented by their government, or who have no government at all, or who are a minority facing extreme repression by a government claiming to represent the will of the majority. The United Nations is the obvious repository for such unexercised or abused sovereignty. But in practice it was not well-prepared to assume this mantle. Those in favour of an assertive multilateral interventionism were well-organised and influential. They included much of the international NGO community, many in the UN, and influential figures in western governmental and military establishments. From the south, some governments argued in favour of a conservative position on maintaining state sovereignty. Asian governments were particularly vigorous on this. In Africa, the voices in favour of the status quo were often discredited by their appalling human rights records—the Mengistu government in Ethiopia is a case in point. Other African voices favoured 'international rescue' in one form or another. A coherent critique of assertive humanitarian interventionism was only to emerge later.

However, in the early 1990s the problem was urgent: Liberia and Somalia were at the point of collapse, and the disastrous impasse in Cambodia needed to be broken. African governments acquiesced in the US-UN intervention in Somalia in 1992. A few years later they would have put up a spirited critique of the idea, as for example many African governments did in response to the French proposal to send a force to Zaire in 1996.

Meanwhile, African states were developing their own ad hoc responses to selected crises, including the wars and Liberia and Sierra Leone, and the threat posed by the fugitive genocidaires in eastern Zaire. These have begun to crystallise into a doctrine, that forcible seizure of power will not be tolerated. This new doctrine has been reaffirmed at OAU summits, and enforced in Sierra Leone (with sanctions imposed upon Burundi).

FAILING STATES AND 'ANARCHIC' WARFARE
Theories of failing states and 'anarchic' warfare were part of the ideological justification for humanitarian agencies and the UN Security Council assuming a 'super-sovereignty' in Africa in the early 1990s. One important approach is the 'neo-barbarism' of some followers of the journalist Robert Kaplan, whose 1994 article 'The Coming Anarchy' proved influential in encouraging western policymakers to regard Africa as a lost cause. A second approach is the 'criminalisation of the state' hypothesis, arguing that many elites in Africa have been using state power in a criminal manner to acquire wealth and power. A variant of this is the 'neo-medievalism' approach. While disagreeing with Kaplan—specifically by saying that Africa is witnessing 'post-modern conflict'—this argument comes to almost exactly the same conclusion, namely that African politics is and will be characterised by warlordism and 'post-adjustment rulers' who in effect rule over collapsed states. The latter argument, in several variants, has been widely adopted within the humanitarian international.

Such arguments converge on various beliefs, including:
• African states can no longer exert a monopoly of violence;
• African security is becoming privatised, dominated by militias and mercenaries;
• Economic globalisation renders African state structures largely irrelevant;

• Predatory and criminal economic structures are the most sustain
able in poor countries;
• In Africa, social and political programmes have given way en
tirely to ethnic and patrimonial politics.

Some of the phenomena on which these analyses were built are
real. Some states have largely collapsed. It is unfortunate that there
has been too little considered response to these deeply pessimistic
theories of African politics and statehood.

AGENDAS BEHIND UN 'HUMANITARIAN' INTERVENTION

The agendas behind 'humanitarian' intervention in the early 1990s
were complex. The sense of confusion among western humanitarians, academics and policymakers should not be underestimated.
Many believed that the then-current wars were 'new' and that it
was necessary to 'do something' about them. Others were identifying new threats: Islamic extremism, 'the coming anarchy', resource wars. At the same time many thought that, at last, humanitarians and international bureaucrats could run the world, and it
would be a better place as a result. This was linked to the feeling of
post-Cold War disorientation in the west: including alternate eu-
phoria and dismay.

In particular, the new doctrine of humanitarian intervention was
influenced by the following: Armies and their suppliers were searching for new roles. The US and European defence industries have
undergone an important but little-noticed consolidation, and have
retained their grip on economic and security policy making. They
discovered they did not need a new 'threat' to justify their existence: they just needed to wield enough influence in their capital
cities. But in the 1990-94 period (approximately) their futures
seemed to be in doubt, so multi-national interventions were an
important potential role.

Humanitarian organisations, which were finding it difficult to
maintain their 'market share' in development and peacetime relief, were looking for a new niche in 'complex emergencies'.This
was only possible if physical security and some guarantees of long-
term programmes were provided. In Somalia, it was senior officials of CARE who proposed to 'move in and run' the country
(their words).

Some European governments and armies (e.g. France and Belgium) were seeking prominent international roles in Africa to avoid becoming marginalised in the new US-dominated world order. France has long linked its national status to the prestige of the Francophone bloc, while Belgium is too small to justify having a modern army for its national defence alone: hence if its army could become the international 'expert' at African peacekeeping, it would remain in business. There was an optimistic readiness to take special measures to address long-running problems (Cambodia). Many believed that once the 'orphans' of the Cold War were settled, there was a prospect of the 'end of history'.

Related to this was an idealistic readiness to make a 'real' UN (e.g. over Iraq's invasion of Kuwait) and to develop a new foreign policy tool of 'humanitarian intervention' (e.g. in Somalia). But simultaneously there was a pessimistic fear of new wars needing new instruments (notably in Bosnia). These pressures all led to an unprecedented readiness to send troops, usually under UN auspices, to different conflict-stricken countries around the world. Although the ideologies and circumstances were disorienting, the doctrine of humanitarian intervention served very real material interests.

Alongside this, professional soldiers in western armies (who have good reasons for being practical-minded), had a more realistic acknowledgement of the complexities of real wars and the hazards of getting engaged in them. It was not that the wars were very different from in the past, it was just that before the 1990s, western armies were very reluctant to become involved. The inactivity of the OAU and sub-regional organisations during this period (with the important exception of ECOWAS policy in Liberia) created a vacuum in which these non-African interests could play a dominant role.

Since ambitious western military interventions fell out of fashion, the institutional agendas among western humanitarian agencies have become complicated. Some—notably UNHCR—still stick to an interventionist agenda with disregard for sovereignty. Others—such as UNDP, which is supposedly the coordinating agency in humanitarian emergencies—have reverted to an old-fashioned deference to state sovereignty. As a result the situation is confused, and decisions often reflect internal power struggles within the UN system rather than any appraisal of the needs of the particular situation. These realities are not well-suited to the development of coherent doctrines and best practices.

MULTIPLE MANDATES

The implication of these new interventions was that the previous rather strict mandates for UN peacekeeping forces became extremely complex, ad hoc and often ambiguous. Some of the tasks they were called upon to do included the following:

- Creating enclaves (Iraqi Kurdistan, 'Operation Turquoise' in Rwanda).
- Protecting relief agencies (UNPROFOR in Bosnia, Somalia).
- Creating a temporary international trusteeship (Cambodia, Kosovo).
- Overseeing peace agreements and transitions to democracy (El Salvador, Angola, Mozambique, UNAMIR in Rwanda August 1993-April 1994).
- Overseeing referenda and decolonisation (Western Sahara, Namibia).
- Reversing coups (Haiti).
- Enforcing/overseeing disarmament or arms embargoes (Somalia, Mozambique, Angola, UNAMUR on the Rwanda-Uganda border).
- Border monitoring to prevent conflict spreading (FYR of Macedonia).
- Enforcing peace (IFOR in Bosnia).

Many of these operations had important political motives too. The French interventions in Rwanda and planned intervention in Zaire would have served certain perceived national interests.

From the point of view of the intervening forces, the most important change was that while traditional peacekeepers operated with the consent of the parties, under some of these conditions consent might be partial or might be withdrawn, or there might be no consent at all. This completed altered the context of 'peacekeeping' operations. Instead of white vehicles and blue helmets and no intelligence-gathering capacity, multi-national forces began to operate as war-fighting units.

The legal basis for these interventions were ad hoc improvisations on international law and IHL adopted at the UN Security Council. Many of these resolutions were hard-won compromises-often they had to be phrased in terms of humanitarian priorities in order to gain acceptance from countries such as China and Russia. Though each resolution might have been acceptable in its specific context, a series of precedents were set that have far-reaching implications for the legal basis of the international order: they gave almost complete authority to the UN Security Council to impose its 'super-sovereignty'.

LEGAL IMPLICATIONS

The experience of 'humanitarian intervention' in the 1990s has indicated that the 'old' doctrine from the Cold War era had its value. Some of the main legal problems in trying to develop a doctrine of humanitarian intervention included:

• The 'mandate dilemma'. Classic peacekeeping using restricted mandates is premised on the goodwill of the parties—i.e. they really want to make the agreement work. Intervention in circumstances where some elements may seek to derail the agreement is more hazardous and calls for a warfighting capacity. This is a slippery slope that has its dangers. But unless an intervention force commander can threaten to escalate his use of force, and if necessary carry out that threat, then the intervention can easily be rendered useless.

• Slow procedures for obtaining legality entailed obtaining consensus, which meant that decisions could not be made in time (e.g. in Rwanda in 1994). The more elaborate and cautious the mechanisms for approval, the higher the degree of legality—but the lower the chances of practical success. When decisions were made quickly, they were railroaded through, were based on extremely subjective political judgements, and therefore discredited the whole doctrine (e.g. the French Operation Turquoise in Rwanda in 1994, the planned intervention in Zaire in 1996).

•The readiness of the US to bypass the UN altogether when it wishes to intervene-notably in Kosovo. The doctrine of 'humanitarian impunity' made interventions ineffective and damaged their credibility. 'Humanitarian impunity' entails that the supposed humanitarian aims of the mission justify arbitrary or abusive behaviour by the forces and organisations involved. In 1999, the UN Security Council specified that UN forces should henceforth explicitly be bound by international humanitarian law.

• The apparent arbitrariness and double standards governing intervention. Africans have repeatedly noted that the UN appears much readier to act in Europe than it does in Africa. In 1999, the UN began developing objective criteria for intervention that could be used to tackle this problem of double standards. At the very minimum, such criteria could be used to discover whether double standards are actually used.

• Note that interventions on behalf of legitimate governments (i.e. governments enjoying a measure of democratic respectability) to defend them against insurgencies may be classed as merely the normal exercise of the sovereign rights of self-defence and making foreign alliances.

The principle that unilateral intervention (aggression) is outlawed, and only multilateral intervention is permissable, remains sound. But, unfortunately, the record of multilateral interventions and the abuse of multilateralism by the UN Security Council, have done untold damage to this principle. In this context it is difficult to condemn unilateral interventions (e.g. the RPF offensive in Rwanda in April-July 1994, the AFDL-Rwandese attack on the former Rwandese armed forces in November 1996). Arguably, the doctrine of humanitarian intervention is best left as an ad hoc, in extremis response to exceptional circumstances, while endeavouring to improve the legal framework and practical implementation of multilateral interventions.

PRACTICAL PROBLEMS
The main problems faced by the intervention forces on the ground were not legal but practical. They simply did not have the resources, expertise, integrity or equipment to do what they were supposed to

do. The two biggest failings were lack of resources, information and planning, and incoherence of command structures.

Intervention forces rely on major western governments for their resouces, and the decision to provide resources is inevitably a political decision. In 1999, there was an astonishing discrepancy between the resources provided for refugees from Kosovo compared to African refugees: sixty times more per head was spent on the Kosovars. Intervention forces in Africa rarely obtain the resources they need for effective operation. UNAMIR in Rwanda in August 1993-March 1994 never achieved the full strength called for in the Arusha agreement.

Intervention forces rarely acquire their resources rapidly enough. Delays in despatching forces can undermine their effectiveness, sometimes fatally. The delay in despatching UNAMIR I in late 1993 undermined its credibility, and the delay in sending reinforcements during the genocide was fatal. In Somalia in 1992, the very slow despatch of forces for UNOSOM I also undermined the mission. The UN simply does not have the cash flow to pre-finance such missions. There is a pressing need for a revolving emergency security and humanitarian intervention fund which can be utilised at short notice for such missions.

Lack of good information has meant that key decision-making, especially in the early days of interventions, can be badly flawed. The first ECOMOG troops to arrive in Monrovia, Liberia, found that they did not even have a reliable map of the city. The UN analysis in Somalia in 1992 was notoriously poor, and major decisions were made on the basis of unsubstantiated reports including newspaper articles, NGO reports etc. In Europe, institutions such as the SCSE and the International Crisis Group have been able to provide accurate and up-to-date information and analysis, drawing on the expertise of academics, journalists and other specialists from the affected countries, to enable far better-informed decision making.

Good strategic and comprehensive planning is nearly impossible in the absence of good information and analysis. This problem is compounded by the public relations imperative for international intervention forces to describe their mandate in humanitarian terms, so that that planners and commanders are tempted to neglect political aspects of their mission.

Lack of a coherent, single chain of command has bedevilled a number of intervention missions. The non-cooperation of different national contingents in UNOSOM, especially during the battles against General Aidid's militia, became notorious. In Rwanda, the Belgians took the unilateral decision to withdraw in April 1994, without coordinating with the UN command or other contingents. In Liberia, ECOMOG forces often responded to the orders of their national chiefs of staff, not the ECOMOG commander.

Meanwhile, intervention forces in Africa have a very mixed record in terms of their cultural sensitivity and behaviour towards the host population. The presumption of 'humanitarian impunity' allowed them, to get away with murder (sometimes literally), because of the 'humanitarian' nature of their mission. Basic failings in relations with local people undermined their credibility. These included:

- Serious human rights violations by the UN forces (notably in Somalia);
- Lack of procedures for citizens to complain about abuses and receive compensation;
- Low level rampant corruption (notably in Cambodia and Bosnia);
- High level corruption in Western Sahara;
- Prostitution rings in Mozambique and elsewhere;
- Racism and contempt for the citizens of the countries where they were operating, often compounded by lack of translators and complete absence of local knowledge and sensitivity;
- Lack of social and political intelligence, including reliance on international NGOs and diplomats for information;
- Inadequate backup including logistical support, regular rotation of troops, etc.;
- Lack of training in civilian policing methods, compounded by a tendency to send combat troops (especially elite paratroopers and marines) rather than engineering units etc;
- Lack of contingency planning for outbreaks of violence;
- Slow and cumbersome means for revising mandates as situations changed;
- Unwillingness to make a long-term commitment to a country;
- Unwillingness to take casualties.

These are lessons that must be learned if future military interventions are not to repeat the same mistakes. Overall, western led military interventions suffer from the problem that western governments want to portray their actions as overwhelmingly humanitarian, and they are not willing to take the necessary political and military actions to ensure that a durable solution is found-because this would involve long-term commitment and a risk of casualties. Unless the intervening force is ready to fight and take casualties, stay for the long term, and adopt a political strategy, an intervention cannot succeed.

Most analyses of the failings of military interventions focus on the legal shortcomings of mandates and the command and control systems within the intervening forces themselves. The personal behaviour of the troops on the ground and their relations with the ordinary citizens are absolutely vital. One of the major reasons for the collapse of the Somali intervention was that many of the contingents had deeply alienated wide sections of the Somali populace, who would otherwise have been sympathetic, by their routine everyday brutality and unwillingness to hear complaints. Those who did try to complain were intimidated, beaten up and even killed. As a result, senior commanders simply did not know, or did not care to know, just how hostile the population was becoming, and the strength of popular support for armed resistance against the UN forces took them completely by surprise. It has taken more than four years for the true extent of human rights abuses by many of the UN troops to be revealed: a major failing not only of ethical standards but of military intelligence.

Thuggish behaviour is not necessary, even in difficult circumstances such as Somalia. The excellent community relations and respectful behaviour of the Botswanan contingent resulted in very calm relations with the local people. This was despite the fact that the Botswanans had one of Somalia's toughest postings, and had only a third of the number of troops of the US forces whom they replaced, and no heavy weapons or helicopters. (Most other African contingents did not distinguish themselves and some were responsible for serious abuses of human rights.)

Any intervention that is destined to fail is by definition unethical. An essential component of any intervention is its success. In this regard, the rather poor record of interventions is discouraging.

IMPLICATIONS

It is very unfortunate that the principle of multilateralism, which seemed to be riding so high at the beginning of the 1990s, has sunk so low at the end of the decade. The failures of UN interventions have been unfairly blamed on the principle of multilateralism, whereas in fact the main culprit has been careless legal ad hoccery by the permanent members of the UN Security Council (particularly the US and France) and very poor implementation. The most important failure—in Somalia—was almost entirely an American responsibility.

One of the important agendas for the coming decade is for those who have most to benefit from multilateralism—that is, any countries other than the US—to build an effective coalition to rescue the basic principles of international law and collective action. Africa has perhaps more to gain from a robust doctrine of multilateralism than any other region, and should take the lead in this.

AFRICAN AGENDAS FOR INTERVENTION

The legal foundations for intervention exist at the OAU and in the charters of subregional organisations. But the actual process of authorising and implementing intervention has been much more ad hoc. A major factor has been the political readiness and financial capacity of leading states to despatch troops.

In contrast to western-led interventions under the UN flag, African interventions have not portrayed themselves as primarily humanitarian. They have sought to justify their actions with reference to political criteria, specifically the protection or restoration of democracy, or the preservation of regional security. African interventions have the following characteristics:

The intervention troops have been ready to fight and take casualties; The intervening governments have been ready to make a long-term commitment; The force has been ready to undertake long-term political engagement in the country concerned. For example, ECOMOG forces have been in the field for a decade, taking many casualties and adopting an agenda with explicitly political aims. No American or European intervening force could have done this. These should be seen as positive aspects of African intervention.

They make it possible to achieve long-term success. Unfortunately, interventions have been criticised on precisely these grounds. NGOs have criticised ECOMOG for not giving priority to humanitarian concerns and for not being politically neutral. These criticisms have undermined support for these interventions both in Africa and in the west.

While there are many justifiable criticisms of ECOMOG and other African interventions, such criticism should allows us to conclude that these interventions are inadequate because they do not measure up to the western-UN model. As we have seen, the western-UN model has major flaws, and some African interventions do not share these flaws. The remainder of this section addresses some of the challenges of developing a coherent doctrine and practice of African intervention.

A DOCTRINE FOR AFRICAN INTERVENTION

The basis for African intervention in Africa needs to be elaborated. A first and fundamental step is to reaffirm multilateralism: interventions should be carried out on the explicit authority of a mandated multilateral organisation such as the OAU in coordination with subregional organisations. However, in order to avoid the paralysis, slowness to respond and arbitrariness of response that has undermined the credibility of UN interventions, mechanisms for assessment and decision-making will need to be expedited. If African peacekeeping or Chapter VII-style operations are to work, the OAU Central Organ will need to become a very credible, decisive and respected institution.

Humanitarian crises in Africa are a worldwide responsibility. Coordination between the OAU and other multilateral organisations (primarily the UN, but also the EU, Arab League, etc) is an important task. The political basis for African interventions has been made clear. However, the humanitarian aspect needs greater attention. This is a matter of doctrine (clear elaboration of principles), partly a matter of public relations (stressing the humanitarian dimensions of interventions) and partly a matter of practices (building institutions that can react to the humanitarian dimensions, and ensuring that the political and military strategies are pursued in a way that does not contradict humanitarian requirements).

Africa's doctrine of intervention is primarily political. This is positive because it allows for a strategic engagement with the country subject to the intervention, and the prospect of a long-term political solution.

But Africa also needs a humanitarian dimension to its doctrines of intervention. This can take two forms:

1. The development of humanitarian institutions and practices that can meet the humanitarian needs of peoples during an intervention. Related to this there needs to be a code of conduct for intervening forces to ensure that restraint is used and human rights abuses avoided.

2. The acknowledgement of a humanitarian dimension to the rationale for an intervention in the first place. Humanitarian intervention has become discredited in many circles, but the basic philosophy, that extreme human suffering demands action, remains sound. Severe humanitarian crisis should be one component in the justification of an intervention—but it should never cause the intervening forces to forget the need for a political strategy.

There is a danger that, without these humanitarian dimensions, African interventions will not gain credibility and legitimacy outside the continent. This may encourage special interest groups in Europe and the US to try to undermine or oppose them, and may create a vacuum in certain humanitarian crises in which western powers are tempted to call for western-led UN interventions once again.

Improved public relations is one aspect. African interventions do have a humanitarian dimension—but it is often not presented well, or even presented at all. A greater consensus is needed on the criteria for intervention. Currently, there are too many opportunities for criticisms on the grounds that the interventions are arbitrary. Given the confusion within the UN specialised agencies, it is likely that there will be instances in which UN agencies refuse to cooperate with African interventions. There is an outside possibility that they could be challenged, legally, politically, or even militarily by another power. However it must be stressed that the exceptional, 'illegal' nature of humanitarian intervention should remain. The 'mandate dilemma' cannot be resolved by any legal doctrine: it has to be treated on a case by case basis.

IMPROVEMENTS IN DECISION-MAKING

Rapid, informed and effective decision-making is essential if African interventions are to be improved in their quality.

1. Improved information and analysis is essential. Africa needs better policy-oriented academic and think-tank institutions that can utilise the expertise of host-country academics, journalists and other specialists, in a way that can be relevant to those who plan and implement responses to crisis.

2. Expedited mechanisms for responding to crises are necessary. The OAU cannot simply wait for the next meeting to decide how to respond to a crisis such as the unconstitutional removal of a government. As with the UN Security Council, measures for emergency reaction and decision-making are needed.

3. Related to the above, there is a need for the development and utilisation of a formal nexus between the OAU and subregional organisations, so that OAU and subregional responses can be properly coordinated.

4. Strategic, comprehensive planning is essential for effective interventions. This must not rule out the ability to respond rapidly and effectively to an unfolding situation. Each intervention—whether under the auspices of the OAU or a subregional organisation—will require an operations room on 24-hour watch, backed up by advisers and a group of ambassadors and senior officials at the OAU and subregional organisations, to ensure that the intervention remains on track.

PRACTICAL IMPROVEMENTS IN MILITARY INTERVENTION

Military intervention is ultimately a practical measure. It works not if the lawyers say it is legal, but if the humanitarian agencies and the troops on the ground can do the difficult job. In the 1990s there has been some discussion about the creation of a special African crisis response force. To date, the prospects of a multilateral pan-African army are remote. The prospects for improved military cooperation among OAU member states, including coordinating training and doctrine, are rather better (especially in the SADC subregion). There is much work to be done to enable African intervention forces, drawn from different countries, to be able to work together on the ground in a way comparable to the convergent practices of European and American forces under NATO.

Concerning the actions of the intervening troops, some practical improvements are in order:

- Unity of command is essential for an effective intervention.
- Many interventionary tasks are more akin to policing than combat. It follows that training in police methods should be provide vided or even civilian police forces sent on interventions.
- Intervention troops should have some education in international humanitarian law.
- Intervention troops should have public relations officers and humanitarian sections.
- Intervening forces should have institutionalised mechanisms for complaints, so that citizens can seek justice and compensation for wrongs committed by the intervening forces.
- Cooperation with the ICRC should be institutionalised.
- The OAU should provide independent observers to monitor interventions. Military intervention also calls for effective hu manitarian action. This will involve clarifying the relationships between intervention forces and international humanitarian agencies (which will be easier for some than for others), and if possible developing African humanitarian institutions as well.

SANCTIONS AND PUNITIVE CONDITIONALITIES

Economic sanctions, arms embargoes and aid conditionalities are a major instrument of foreign policy, for both African countries in relation to their neighbours, and more commonly for western donors in relation to African recipients. All of these have a legitimate purpose, and in some cases they have been well-chosen and well-used. But in many cases they are an arbitrary and undemocratic instrument ostensibly used to promote human rights and democracy, and the contradictions in this approach have become evident.

This and the following sections are concerned with the use of embargoes and sanctions to promote human rights and democracy (or more commonly, to punish alleged violations of human rights and military coups). They will not look at economic conditionality in donor finance, such as imposed by the IMF, though there are obvious similarities in:

- the imposition of particular external models and a coercive approach to effecting change;
- the way that those imposing the conditions tend to conflate their own material interest with moral concern;
- lack of transparency and no due process or court of appeal in the imposition, terms and lifting of the sanctions.

The logic of conditionalities and sanctions, as practised at present, is the opposite of the logic of the 'humanitarian principles' advocated by many international NGOs. The purity of humanitarian aid is commonly defended on the slogan that 'a starving child knows no politics' and that it is indefensible to allow the innocent to go hungry or ill in order to punish the guilty. For conditionalities and sanctions the logic is that our aid (or trade or whatever) should not go to an unpleasant regime, and that it is acceptable to allow a civilian population to suffer in pursuit of a political goal. But sometimes the same organisations advocate both (Oxfam supported sanctions against South Africa but opposed conditionalities on assistance to the Interahamwe-dominated camps in eastern Zaire.)

This chapter argues that there is little or no evidence that either economic sanctions or aid conditionalities, as actually practised, work. That is, they do not deliver their main aims and they may in fact inflict damage. This is chiefly because they are an extremely blunt instrument for dealing with very complicated situations, partly because they have numerous side effects, and partly because they are so inconsistently applied. But they are a simple and widely accepted way of expressing international disapproval of a regime that stops short of intervention.

Arms embargoes are potentially an effective weapon in a continent highly dependent on arms imports. However, they are commonly adopted as symbolic acts, and there is a need for them to be fine-tuned, and properly enforced. The following sections will first examine arms embargoes, then economic sanctions, and finally make some modest proposals for an African agenda on these subjects.

ARMS EMBARGOES

Africa imports the great majority of its arms. Many of the most war-affected countries, such as Angola, Congo, Sierra Leone, Somalia and Sudan, are highly or wholly dependent on arms transfers. In theory, arms embargoes could therefore be effective mechanisms for limiting war and pressuring belligerents. However, arms embargoes as they are currently utilised suffer from several problems:

They are commonly imposed too late, when belligerents have already stockpiled large quantities of arms and ammunition. There is, as yet, no pre-emptive mechanism for preventing arms build-ups that may lead to war. There are often imposed without the creation of mechanisms for monitoring, enforcement, and sanctioning of violators (both suppliers and recipients). As a result, arms embargoes (on Somalia, on Rwanda) have been widely violated with complete impunity by arms manufacturers and neighbouring states.

They may fail to make any distinction between belligerents when such a distinction is important. For example, the military forces in control after the coup d'etat in Sierra Leone deserved being the target of an arms embargo, but it was absurd to extend that embargo to the forces of the former elected government, trying to regain power in accordance with international wishes. Similarly, the post-genocide government in Rwanda inherited the arms embargo imposed on its genocidal predecessor.

Arms embargoes are sometimes no more than symbolic, an instance of gesture politics. They are the minimum that the UN Security Council is able to agree to, when its powerful members are reluctant to act. They can however be strong gestures with moral effect. The main problem with arms embargoes is enforcement. This is difficult enough to achieve in Europe, and more so in Africa because of the difficulty of monitoring long borders and Africa's vast airspace. Without a worldwide system of monitoring arms transactions (legal and illegal), the possibilities of sanctions-busting will always be there.

ECONOMIC SANCTIONS

Sanctions are often adopted symbolically. It is as though the sanctioning country or its public do not want to be sullied by contact with the rogue regime (Apartheid South Africa, Nigeria after the execution of Ken Saro Wiwa or whatever). It is more to do with the sanctioning countries' own demand for moral purity than a coherent political plan for achieving the desired political change. Many sanctions sceptics may then follow the plan for sanctions because they want to express solidarity or do not want to be seen to be failing in their moral duty.

SUCCESSES FOR SANCTIONS

Sanctions can be successful in two respects:

1. One is if the sanctioned country is already very economically and politically weak, and the sanctions are combined with other decisive political action. Thus for example the sanctions against Sierra Leone after the May 1997 coup prevented the new military government from establishing a firm base and helped pave the way for the ECOMOG military action to return the elected government of Ahmed Tijan Kabbah to power.

2. As sanctions are primarily a symbolic expression of outrage and isolation, symbolic sanctions—focussed on sporting and cultural links—may be most effective. There are some suggestions that the boycott of South African sportspeople was the most politically effective element among the Apartheid sanctions, and certainly the exclusion of the Nigerian national football team from the 1998 World Cup would have put pressure on General Abacha in the months before he died.

THE PROBLEM OF BLUNTNESS

Sanctions are an extremely blunt instrument. They may be highly targetted but mild, for example trying to prevent government officials from travelling abroad. These are easily evaded. Or they may be far-ranging but chiefly hit the wrong target, that is affect ordinary people in the country concerned. Rulers—particularly authoritarian ones—are likely to be the last to suffer from economic sanctions, while ordinary people may undergo massive hardship. Sanctions against Iraq are estimated to have cost the lives of hundreds of thousands of Iraqi children. ECOMOG sanctions against Sierra Leone undoubtedly caused suffering for the civilian population. (The case has also been argued that ECOMOG forces exceeded their legal mandate in blocking commercial goods and humanitarian supplies bound for Sierra Leone.)

If a country is economically strong, then sanctions are even less likely to have an effect on the rulers. A case in point is Nigeria: no country seriously considered taking the one step that might genuinely damage the Nigerian economy, namely an embargo on oil exports. Special interests in the sanctioning countries may also undermine their effectiveness. For example the soft drinks industry in the US uses gum arabic in its manufacturing processes, and successfully lobbied for gum arabic to be excluded from US trade sanctions on Sudan.

If a country is economically weak, however, sanctions can have effects far beyond pressuring the government. This is a particular problem for African countries.

THE PROBLEM OF COMPOUNDING ECONOMIC PROBLEMS

Africa's economic problems are deep rooted and have been present for years. They will outlast current rulers. Sanctions inevitably make such problems worse. While they may make life difficult for those in power at present (who may not care if the people suffer), they will make it even more difficult for those who follow them, particularly if they have an agenda of meeting the basic aspirations of the people.

Take the case of Sudan. Some human rights activists and opposition politicians have been calling for oil sanctions against Sudan or its expulsion from the IMF. These measures would create massive hardship for the Sudanese people but would probably not decisively affect the outcome of the political and military struggle in the country. But a democratic government coming to power in Sudan and inheriting a bankrupt and oil-starved economy, and a debt of $18 billion with the country unable to begin formal negotiations for debt forgiveness, would face literally unsurmountable obstacles. If Sudan were facing legislative sanctions imposed by the US Congress, it might take several years to lift these sanctions-during which time the new government would suffer. In April 1999, the US government belatedly admitted that food sanctions against Sudan, Cuba and North Korea had been ineffective and counter-productive, and lifted them. (Sanctions on Iraq stayed.)

A further problem is that African countries can ill-afford to impose sanctions on their neighbours. It is much easier for western countries that are much wealthier and have only a minute fraction of their trade with Africa to take the moral high ground. But for Chad to impose sanctions on Sudan, or Tanzania on Burundi, entails facing serious economic hardship. This hardship may be politically destabilising, and compound the existing problems.

Africa's economic problems are so profound that economic warfare between African states can only damage the entire continent. Excepting very specific circumstances, economic sanctions will only have a negative impact.

THE PROBLEM OF MONITORING EFFECTIVENESS

If sanctions are ostensibly imposed for human rights grounds there should be some independent system for monitoring their effectiveness. None exists. Human rights organisations may be ready to call for sanctions but they seem unwilling to examine the consequences, let alone take responsibility for them.

The first task is for those who legislate for sanctions to specify their goals and deadlines. If they have particular objectives in mind they should be able to specify them, which will facilitate assessing whether the aims have been achieved or not, and therefore whether it is worthwhile maintaining the sanctions (or intensifying them, or lightening or changing them).

There is therefore a need for an independent monitoring organisation at an inter-governmental level. If the UN is unwilling to set up such a body—and there are strong interests among the permanent members of the Security Council that would be averse to such an organisation—then the OAU or subregional organisations could consider doing the same task. There are some western governments and multilateral institutions (e.g. the World Bank) that may be ready to collaborate with such an initiative. Economists, nutritionists and others could be asked to report regularly on the impact of sanctions on the affected country. Alternatively, when an interstate organisation authorises sanctions, it should form an ad hoc sanctions monitoring committee specific to the country in question, which should report back on a regular basis.

IMPLICATIONS

The emerging world order in which African regional and subregional organisations take prime responsibility for peace and security in Africa has laid down major challenges. The OAU has taken a bold position on the unacceptability of the use of force to change governments. Developing this principle into a workable doctrine is a challenge.

Beginning this process at the turn of the century allows Africa to learn the lessons from multilateral exercises in coercive action by the UN over recent decades. It is an opportunity to analyse and recognise why many military interventions and sanctions have failed to achieve their goals. In terms of intervention, Africa has made an auspicious start by avoiding some of the disabling problems of western-led interventions, namely the unwillingness to fight and take casualties, and the unwillingness to engage politically over the long term. African interventions however have failed to prioritise humanitarian aspects of intervention, with possible costs in terms of public support, credibility and effectiveness.

Africa is not well-placed to impose sanctions on any African country—the negative effects on the country and its neighbours may well outweigh any positive outcomes, however laudable the intentions. However, sanctions cannot be readily abandoned as a tool of coercive diplomacy. They should at least be carefully monitored and assessed.

5

DEMOCRATIC POLITICAL PROCESS AND THE FIGHT AGAINST FAMINE

INTRODUCTION

This chapter examines the linkages between certain sorts of political processes and institutions and the prevention of famine. It begins with an examination of the 'democracy prevents famine' hypothesis, which is found to be in need of elaboration. Democratic political institutions and processes can play a lead role in the struggle against famine, but this depends upon the development of political coalitions in the countries concerned, and the strategies they use. In Africa, the challenge of democratic anti-famine politics is complicated by the nature of famines, the political history of anti-famine measures, the prevalence of war, and the level of international aid. The chapter introduces the concept of a 'political contract' against famine.

Amartya Sen has famously remarked that famines do not occur in countries with democratic political institutions.

> The diverse political freedoms that are available in a democratic state, including regular elections, free newspapers and freedom of speech, must be seen as the real force behind the elimination of famines. Here again, it seems that one set of freedoms—to criticize, publish and vote—are usually linked with other types of freedoms, such as the freedom to escape starvation and famine mortality.[1]

This observation is commonly simplified and presented as 'there is no famine in democracies'. Sometimes it is rather smugly presented as an endorsement of liberal electoral systems plus a free press as both necessary and sufficient for the conquest of poverty-and as a rejoinder to those who argue that socialism in China or Eastern Europe made great strides in combating hunger. The reality is not so simple. While there is no shortage of historical and contemporary material to analyse, it is not easy to test the 'democracy prevents famine' hypothesis. There are important counter-examples, which require us to make some major clarifications and revisions to the hypothesis. The major difficulty is that democracy has often failed to play a role in preventing chronic hunger-indeed, as Sen himself as repeatedly pointed out, democratic India has conspicuously failed to overcome widespread undernutrition. What is the dividing line between this extensive chronic poverty and hunger, and the phenomenon of famine? In addition, demonstrating an empirical association between liberal democratic institutions and the absence of famine is not enough to prove the causal link. We need to investigate further and detail some of the exact processes and mechanisms that have enabled democratic institutions to play a pivotal role in famine prevention. The 'democracy prevents famine' argument seems to assume that just because liberal institutions can be used to protect famine vulnerable people, it automatically follows that they will. It implies that, in a free press, journalists and editors will automatically be concerned with the threat of famine and will use this concern to push for effective governmental action, and that electors will reward representatives who protect them against famine, but vote out those who fail to do so. These assumptions do not always hold true. In short, we need to problematise both 'famine' and 'democracy' before a sensible analysis can be made of the 'democracy prevents famines' hypothesis.

This chapter will attempt to identify what is meant by famine, disaggregating the components of famine and identifying some of the main variants. It will also try to identify some of the elements in political democracy that make it possible to prevent famine. This does not amount to a theorisation of democracy—such a task is beyond the scope of a modest chapter—but rather it is a preliminary identification of some of the broadly democratic processes, mechanisms and institutions that can serve in the struggle against famine.

War is now the commonest cause of famine, and no theorisation of famine or the struggle against it can ignore warfare. This chapter covers the by-now familiar ground of the various ways in which war creates or contributes to famine.

This chapter is primarily concerned with Africa, as the continent most susceptible to famine, but some cases are drawn from Asia and some conclusions may be relevant to protection against famine in countries such as Bangladesh and North Korea.

THEORIZING FAMINE

Sen has pointed out that most definitions of famine are in fact pithy descriptions of what happens during famine, usually based on a few selected extreme cases.[2] They are not much help in diagnosing when a borderline case actually counts as famine, and they are little better when it comes to identifying the component parts of famine.

Famine is in fact extraordinarily difficult to define. Most definitions break down when one tries to use them-chiefly because many cases diagnosed as 'famine' do not meet textbook definitions, or because the definitions are too subjective and give no guide for how they are to be used. The definitions of other comparable terms does not help. 'Poverty' can be defined by income or assets. 'Drought' can be defined meterologically. An epidemic can be defined by an epidemiologist. In all these cases, there is a certain mismatch between arbitrary scientific cut-off points and popular perceptions. But for 'famine', there is no discipline that can lay claim to the right of definition. Demographers, or agricultural or nutritional statisticians may aspire to take precedence, but no definition based on excess mortality, food supply, food consumption, or nutritional status alone is workable. Everyone can diagnose a famine when they encounter one, but identifying its crucial elements is rather more difficult. One of the main reasons for this is that statistics (on death rates, on food supplies) tend to confound lay impressions—for example the disastrous Sahel famine of the early 1970s passed without measurable excess mortality, while several major famines are famous for having occurred without a decline in food availability. A comparison between the measured mortality rates in different districts of Bengal in the 1940s and the recorded impressions of government administrators confirms that observers' estimates for the gravity and nature of famine can be highly unreliable.

One of the important reasons for needing a workable definition of famine is that the distinction between chronic poverty and acute famine is essential for any attempt to examine the 'democracy prevents famine' hypothesis. This is because no-one argues that democracy prevents poverty (at least not in anything but the very long run). While it is easy to identify the extreme cases, especially in South Asia where major famines are dramatic, visible and rapid onset events, there are many instances of famine, especially in Africa, that are borderline. A number of African societies have lived for years in a sort of economic twilight, suffering extreme dislocation and poverty, and occasionally attracting international media and relief attention that points to starvation and famine. Some communities, for example in Southern Sudan, will argue that they have suffered famine continuously for several years. (But in their languages, the words 'hunger' and 'famine' are usually cognates.)

Anthropological research has found that local definitions and diagnoses of famine are commonly more subtle and complex than those of outsiders, such as nutritionists and economists. This is not surprising. But the concepts used by one community (e.g. in Bangladesh) may not transfer to another (e.g. in west Africa) with very different social structures and economic history. It is notable however that all distinguish in some way between chronic poverty and hunger and more exceptional outbreaks of famine.

In short, famines are not a natural kind, and nor are they a convenience of disciplinary nomenclature. But while there can be no precise definition of famine workable across the world, and no diagnosis that is not subject to some contestation, it is possible to identify what famines have in common, and thereby begin to develop a general account of how they may be caused or prevented.

COMPONENTS OF FAMINE

The most profitable approach to the definition of famine is to disaggregate the components of famine, and argue that what we identify as famines tend to combine many, sometimes all, of these elements in varying degrees. This allows us to combine the insights of different famine-affected peoples across the world and the analyses of the various relevant disciplines.

The four main components are:

1. Hunger. This includes subjective feelings of severe and prolonged hunger, the socially-defined going without acceptable food, and the measurable fact of undernutrition.

2. Impoverishment. This includes loss of livelihood, income and assets, and other components of increased poverty. For most rural people threatened with famine, the most concrete fears arising from famine are those associated with the threat of destitution.

3. Social breakdown. Famine commonly has social symptoms such as distress migration, splitting up of families, etc. For many famine-affected communities, these are not 'symptoms' of famine, but are intrinsic elements of the unpleasant experience itself.

4. Mortality. Many famines are accompanied by increased levels of mortality, usually concentrated among vulnerable groups such as children, the aged, and migrants. (Interestingly, in all famines for which demographic information is available, death rates are higher among men than women.) The highest death rates are invariably found in camps and other concentrations of destitute people. When social disruption is such that there is mass migration to camps, death rates tend to shoot up.

A fifth component of famine must also be mentioned, namely, the resistance of individuals, families and groups to each of the above. The study of social and economic 'coping strategies' has become an important subdiscipline since the 1980s drought-famines in Africa, during which many rural people showed a resilience in the face of extreme food shortages that astounded many observers and aid providers. For example, in western Sudan in 1984-5, journalists and aid workers predicted deaths in the millions. In fact, excess mortality was probably about 200,000—unacceptably high, but well short of the figures confidently forecast. (The exaggeration of imminent famine mortality is in fact a commonplace: predictions of mass deaths reaching a million or more are a staple of relief agency funding appeals, but are invariably erroneous.) The nature of a famine, and its impact, is therefore shaped by the social and economic responses to the threats by the affected population. Most research indicates that coping strategies are primarily geared to the protection of livelihoods and assets. This is usually because the processes of impoverishment are predictable and thus to some extent preventable, while mortality in famines is chiefly a function of epidemic disease and health crises, which are inherently less predictable and less controllable by those affected by famines.

SEVERITY OF FAMINE
A second dimension of analysis of famine relates to the degree of severity. This is not a simple linear deterioration from mild to severe. Rather, as famines unfold, they can cross thresholds into qualitatively different kinds of disaster. Some analysts have compared the onset of 'outright' famine to the difference between 'ice and freezing water.'[3] This has been noted in South Asia and Ethiopia, at the point in which an affected society reaches a critical point and suddenly (to use a different metaphor) 'crashes'.

In a simplified manner, we can identify three different degrees of famine severity:

1. Famines involving primarily hunger and impoverishment.
2. Famines in which there are elevated rates of mortality.
3. Famines in which there are spectacularly high death rates alongside severe social dislocation and collapse.

Standard English language definitions of famine refer to types 2 and 3, whereas most local definitions include type 1 (sometimes explicitly making the distinction between the different kinds). But diagnoses of famine usually agree in including all the types.

It is important to note that the difference between these various kinds of famine does not lie solely in the extent of loss of entitlement to food, but also in the factors creating the famine and the socio-economic response to those factors. If a famine shifts from a less severe, type one famine, to a more severe type two, it may be because the affected population's coping strategy involves widespread migration which changes disease patterns and thus increases the incidence of disease, thereby heightening death rates. A shift to a type three famine may occur because large groups are concentrated in relief shelters, perhaps because their home areas have been devastated by war or because they have been forced into the camps by armed groups. The 'crashing' of some agrarian societies (such as parts of highland Ethiopia in 1973 and again in 1984) suddenly brings large number of very poor peasant families on to the road in search of food and money, creating a dramatic crisis of displacement, congregation around relief shelters, and rapid spread of infectious disease.

Responses to famine change over time, and affected people learn. The sad experience of relief shelters in western Sudan in 1984-5 led many rural people to avoid migration to towns in the drought and famine of 1990-1. This probably helped keep death rates down, although (in common with most contemporary African famines) there are no reliable figures for mortality on which to base any meaningful conclusions.

TYPES OF FAMINE
The final dimension to the theorisation of famine concerns the type of famine. A simplified typology of famines can be attempted, based on the kind of society affected and the main causal elements.

1. Pastoral. These are famines that affect herders. Usually their short-term cause is drought and resulting lack of pasture and water for animals. The longer-term cause is alienation of pastures for farms and plantations, and restrictions on nomadic movements. These are slow-onset famines. Because of the mobility of pastoralists, these famines tend to cover wide areas, but often they are invisible outside the pastoral areas. They may be extremely protracted. Coping strategies are relatively more important than relief interventions. As well as relief distributions, effective responses can include buying up livestock at guaranteed prices and providing credit.

2. Agrarian/smallholder. These are the paradigmatic African famines, affecting scattered farming populations. Commonly, drought-related production failures are the proximate cause, with deeper causes including exclusion from land, exploitative economic relationships, etc. These are also usually slow-onset famines. They can often be highly localised, and the more severe famines are often akin to a series of interconnected localised famines in which each locality is unable to assist its neighbour. Often there is an 'epicentre', from which waves of grain price rises and distress migrations move out. Only severe agrarian famines become visible outside the affected area. Coping strategies are usually much more important than relief programmes. A wide range of programmes and policies, ranging from land preservation to prepositioning food stocks, can help prevent such famines, and a range of responses including food relief and labour-based relief projects can help ameliorate the effects.

3. Class-based/occupational. In this category, wage labourers are often the worst hit occupation. These are the paradigmatic Asian famines, in which whole classes of people (farm labourers, artisans, fishermen) are suddenly rendered destitute by a collapse in the demand for their labour or a rise in the price of staple food. Some recent African famines have become closer to this type. These famines tend to be rapid onset and cover a wide area, selectively affecting certain groups. They can be highly visible, with affected people flooding towns, and townspeople themselves suffering. In these famines, coping strategies are less effective, and state intervention is far more necessary. Grain price controls and employment guarantee schemes are the most effective relief measures.

4. Wartime. Wartime famines are usually associated with a catastrophic collapse of the livelihood base, either by physical destruction or confiscation, or by severe restrictions on movement and economic activity. The nature of the famine depends very much on the nature of the war and the determination with which the belligerent parties pursue their famine-creating strategies. These famines can be very rapid, or can take years to develop (perhaps affecting societies that are not normally famine-prone); they can be

highly localised, or can cover a huge area. Occasionally, coping strategies can be forcibly prevented by belligerents, leaving affected people wholly reliant on relief. Sometimes these famines are almost completely invisible—deliberately kept that way by the belligerents. A more detailed theorisation of war famines will be attempted later in this chapter.

Note that many famines are compounds of the above. Agrarian famines are commonly, though not always, associated with pastoral famines. Grain price rises caused by an agrarian or wartime famine can cause a secondary class-based famine in adjoining areas, for example nearby towns. In Ethiopia in 1984/5, some of the highest mortality was recorded in areas which did not themselves suffer a major production failure, but which were suddenly (and to their residents, inexplicably) struck by high food prices and immigration of destitute labourers.

At a high level of generality, we can note that the characteristic 'Asian' famines that have given rise to the most sophisticated famine theorising have been class-based, rapid-onset, and high visibility. With coping strategies relatively ineffective, state action is important-and such famines sometimes have a dramatic political impact. Most African famines have been more locality based, slow-onset, low visibility, and with greater roles for coping strategies and less for public action. This contributes to their lesser political impact. This contrast is important when it comes to explaining the role of political processes in famine creation and prevention.

DEMOCRACY AS AN INOCULATION AGAINST FAMINE

Liberal democracy is no antidote to homelessness or widespread chronic undernutrition or the selective murder of girl babies. The examples of the US and India demonstrate this amply. Why should it be an inoculation against famine? The answer is that it isn't—at least not simply.

First, there are important examples and counter-examples from the history of famines that indicate that the relationship is not a simple one. Second, the means whereby democracy does (often) act as an antidote to famine demonstrate the complexities of the relationship.

FAMINE AND DEMOCRACY: CASES FROM HISTORY

The famous, paradigmatic cases of democratic institutions preventing famine are India and Botswana. Each of these demands a careful historical discussion in its own right. In summary, however, it is important to notice that the mechanisms whereby democratic mobilisation and democratic institutions prevented famine were historically constituted. In the case of India, the critical events occurred over nearly a century in the later colonial period. First, in the 1880s, the colonial government realised it needed to intervene to prevent mass deaths from famine, and began to develop the famine codes. The motivation was political—to maintain security—rather than benevolent. Second, at about the turn of the century, the failures of the famine codes to prevent disastrous famines became an embarrassment in Britain and a danger in India (where famine became the rallying cry of the Congress), leading to a thorough overhaul of anti-famine policy. Third, in 1943, the British failed to prevent a needless famine in Bengal, causing at least one million deaths and decisively undermining the Raj's aspirations to legitimacy. As a result, one of the main imperatives of the independent Indian government was to prevent famine. In the case of Botswana, a comparable sequence of events between the 1970s and 1990s created the political (and electoral) imperative for an efficient drought relief policy.

Some of the counter-examples, in which democratic or liberal institutions have failed to prevent famine include the following:

1. Bihar, India, 1966-7. Although mass deaths were prevented, a famine in the sense of widespread hunger, destitution and social breakdown occurred. This reflects the wider phenomenon that the Indian government has failed to tackle the extent of chronic immiseration in the subcontinent, and the economic processes that create endemic hunger.

2. Bangladesh, 1974. The liberal institutions failed to prevent this famine. They were, however, extremely precarious in the wake of the war of 1972 and before the imminent reversion to authoritarian rule.

3. Sudan, 1986-8. The institutions of liberal democracy rule in Khartoum failed to prevent a disastrous famine in the war-affected South and a mild famine in western Sudan.

4. Ireland, 1845-9. The great Irish famines of these years occurred despite the existence of a parliamentary system and a free press.

These cases can all be taken as exceptions that prove the rule. In case one, severe famine was prevented, but undernutrition and poverty were not—as is the case for independent India as a whole. This compels us to analyse the different positions of 'famine' and 'poverty' in Indian political discourse. In case two, the institutions were democratic and liberal in name only. In cases three and four, the affected populace was not regarded as full citizens of the country by the government and also by the most vocal and influential citizens. The affected people were not only in no position to defend their own rights, but they were regarded as undeserving by their rulers. But this begs the question: what are 'real' democratic institutions?

An interesting parallel here is the argument that democracies do not go to war with one another. While this may be true of mature, capitalist liberal democracies, the generalisation holds much less for new or transitional democracies. In countries in which a newly elected civilian government is endeavouring to secure its power, it may be tempted to play the nationalist card, and provoke national or ethnic conflict. It is arguable that it is new, insecure transitional democracies that are most vulnerable to armed conflict.[4]

By a similar argument, it could be claimed that insecure or immature democracies may be more vulnerable to famine than stable authoritarian governments. This could come about because an insecure parliamentary government feels compelled to respond to the most vocal constituencies, ignoring more marginal ones. Thus in the case of Sudan, the authoritarian regime of President Jaafar Nimeiri could afford to ignore the most traditionally powerful constituencies in Sudan during the drought of the early 1970s, and respond to the needs of the remoter rural areas. But the parliamentary government of Prime Minister Sadiq el Mahdi in the late 1980s,

while being acutely sensitive to the demands of the urban populace, ignored the needs of rural people and especially Southerners-
against whom a vicious war was being fought. Thus in 1988 the
Sudan Government was so accountable to the people of Khartoum
that it had to forgo a major agreement with the IMF in order to
maintain a subsidy on wheat for urban consumption, but could
wholly ignore the starving people of Bahr el Ghazal in the South.[5]

While Sudan is an extreme case, this analysis points to a general problem that can occur with representative systems of government: certain groups have louder voices than others, and minorities can be excluded completely.

WHY SHOULD DEMOCRACY PREVENT FAMINE?

The assumption behind the claim that democracy prevents famine
is that civil and political rights—to free speech, to free association, to elect representatives of one's choice, contribute to the protection of social and economic rights—the right to food and livelihood. Certainly, one of the major uses of civil and political liberties has been to promote social, economic and cultural rights. Those
engaged in the women's suffrage movement, the anti-colonial independence movements, and the civil rights movement, did not
claim their civil and political rights solely for their own sake. They
also believed that achieving these liberties would help them to at-
tain better livelihoods, economic advancement, improved education, and more respect for their cultures and societies. The struggles
for the different categories of rights were indivisible. In mature
capitalist democracies, politicians appeal to voters' economic self-
interest, and many people cast their votes because they hope they
can better their economic position. It would seem logical that citizens of a democracy would use their civil and political liberties to
ensure that they are protected against famine.

But it is not so simple. Gross abuses of social, economic and
cultural rights can exist in democracies. Homelessness in the US
and chronic poverty and undernutrition in India are two examples.
In these cases, it seems that citizens have failed to use their civil
and political liberties successfully to achieve basic social and economic rights. Why is famine different? Is it that famine is a more
profound abuse than poverty or homelessness? That it affects the
entire society and not just certain unfortunate sections? Both these

seem implausible as complete answers. More likely, it seems that historically, famine has become a salient political issue in certain countries in a way that these other deprivations have not. Meanwhile, other issues—lack of political independence, racial discrimination, land alienation—have often achieved a comparable salience.

The basic reason why a government prevents famine is because its interests—the power of its leaders—depends on it. Elected politicians fear the retribution of their constituents in the polling booths, and hope for the electoral reward of successfully delivering famine prevention. Civil servants fear disgrace or demotion of their failure to prevent famine is exposed, while hoping that they can use the opportunities of a famine emergency to prove their capabilities and win promotion.

What mechanisms can make this work? Here we can distinguish between a variety of processes. There is a fundamental distinction to be made between 'primary' and 'secondary' mobilisation in pursuit of rights.

• Primary mobilisation. This is when people mobilise in pursuit of their own interests. These are mass movements. Their aims may be expressed in a rights idiom, or not. Cases include the women's movement, the labour movement, the US civil rights movement, the anti-colonial movements in various countries under imperial rule.

• Secondary activism. This is the activities of specialist institutions to promote human rights, democracy and other goals. Organisations such as Amnesty International, Human Rights Watch, Oxfam, etc., do not mobilise a mass constituency as much as use the skills of professionals and the power of the media to put pressure on politicians. This has been called 'mobilising shame.'

As a general rule, effective political action against famine requires both primary and secondary mobilisation. Primary mobilisation is essential because politicians heed the logic of numbers. Under any competitive electoral system, representatives cannot afford to ignore the complaints of large numbers. Famines—particularly when they involve large numbers of destitute people converging on towns—are also a major threat to security, and governments must take heed. But primary mobilisation alone is insufficient, because those simply seeking food can be provided with handouts, which does not amount to an anti-famine measure. Secondary activism, in the form of articulate leadership that can identify the issues and link them politically, is also essential.

Famine must be made an issue of legitimate political concern. This means disarming those who like to present it as purely a natural disaster and those who prefer to see it just as a challenge to charity. The issue of famine needs to be sustained politically even when there is no famine, and complex measures need to be instituted well in advance of any future crises. Economic, nutritional, epidemiological, agricultural and other expertise is necessary to change famine from being merely a charitable demand into a political cause. This is not easy. However, the issue of famine is also a case in which a farsighted political leadership can link the basic material interests of large numbers of people to other political agendas, such as national independence or major economic reform. Coalition building is central to creating an anti-famine politics. The hungry rarely organise themselves, and their hunger is rarely of direct interest to other social groups except philanthropists who are notoriously resistant to political mobilisation of any kind. Those who take up the issue of famine must be ready to enter the political arena directly and make famine and related issues an electoral question; they must be ready to push to make commissions of inquiry and other mechanisms of accountability into a reality.

Successful anti-famine coalitions have often linked fighting famine with other goals. In colonial India, the nationalist leaders of Congress were at least as interested in political independence as in the conquest of famine, but the strategic alliance they struck with the masses on the issue of famine benefited both. In Botswana, relatively wealthy farmers and herders have derived substantial benefits from the drought relief programme.

One of the most unfortunate byproducts of the international humanitarian industry has been the way in which mobilisation around famine has been undermined. Much of the international media (especially television) and most specialist international institutions have endeavoured to depoliticise famine. This will be discussed more below.

Mobilisation against famine has several interlinked goals. If achieved together, they amount to a 'political contract' against famine.

1. To ensure a timely response to the threat of famine. In many countries there are various forms of famine early warning systems, but there needs to be a political trigger to action if these are to work effectively. A coalition of affected people plus professional groups (including journalists, trade unions, farmers' associations, academics, civil servants etc) can help provide that political trigger.

2. To help create effective anti-famine mechanisms. Having the political will to prevent famine is essential but not sufficient. It must be augmented by a sound economic understanding of the causes of famine, combined with sound nutritional, public health, agricultural, environmental, migration, and other policies. This requires investment in technical expertise.

3. To educate the public. It is important that political mobilisation does not become widely separated from the more technical debates. It would be rather ironically pointless to have sophisticated famine prevention systems in place, but a popular demand for just free food distribution. Therefore the public must be well informed. This must begin with a well-informed press and legislature. The regrettable tendency for the international media and western legislatures to confuse famine prevention with the provision of international relief is the sort of error that should be avoided.

4. To ensure that all citizens and residents are entitled to protection against famine. One of the recurrent problems in many democratic systems is that majoritarian democracy creates permanently disenfranchised minorities who may be the first in line to suffer from famine. One of the dangers of equating 'democracy' with just free elections and the dominance of a majority (often an ethnic majority), is that a state can claim to be 'democratic' but still fail to provide the basis for human rights including protection against famine. A political mobilisation against famine must ensure that, just

as all are equal before the law, all must be equally entitled to protection against famine.

5. To enforce accountability. This can be done in various ways.

• Preferably, all should be employed.

• Electoral accountability of members of parliament, parties and governments to their electors, including all citizens with voting rights, and also organised groups such as trade unions, farmers' associations, etc.

• Wider democratic accountability, represented by public opinion, letters and editorials in newspapers, etc. A free and informed press is important for educating the public and politicians, acting as an early-warning system, and evaluating performance. A wide and well-informed public debate at various levels is essential. There must be a demand for good information about famine, creating mechanisms for supplying that information.

• Legal accountability, especially relevant where there are laws and codes of practice to establish effective measures against famine, which can be made real through the courts or through commissions of inquiry. The possibility of enacting legislation to criminalise aspects of famine creation deserves close attention, though it is probably more important and relevant to try and ensure the thorough use of existing sanctions relating to negligence etc.

• Professional accountability of public officials, health workers, planners and managers, and the technical accountability of the anti-famine system itself. Lessons must be learned and lesson learning must be enforced. Whatever the political will, famine will only be defeated if the right economic and managerial measures are implemented. Accountability on this front can be exercised through formal evaluations or through peer pressure. There must be political pressure to find the right economic and other measures necessary for famine prevention, and pressure to ensure that they are correctly implemented and evaluated. In non-democratic systems, professionals may be able to identify good anti-famine measures, but they will not necessarily be the political pressure to implement them. In a poorly informed democratic system, there will be pressure to respond, but not necessarily in a truly effective way.

In conclusion, more than just 'democracy' is required to prevent famine. In fact, liberal political institutions and popular mobilisation appear to be more important than simple electoral democracy. Famine must be politicised in a democratic manner, but there are also technical and educational requirements that need to be met for an effective famine prevention system, and a political or even legal obligation to prevent famine afflicting all citizens. The above paragraphs outline a particular set of mechanisms, processes and pressures which amount to an 'anti-famine political contract.' The idea of an 'anti-famine political contract' refers to the specific mechanisms that can exist, usually within a democratic state, to prevent famine. The remainder of this chapter is concerned with a series of questions about how such a political contract can be created and enforced.

CAN THERE BE ANTI-FAMINE POLITICAL CONTRACTS WITHOUT DEMOCRACY?
Are there variants of anti-famine contracts that are not dependent upon electoral democracy, or even on peace? There are interesting examples of effective anti-famine measures that suggest this possibility, and also its shortcomings:

1. Communist China. The 1940s famine in Hunan was one of the events that helped discredit the nationalist government in China and bring the Communists to power. During the subsequent decades, the Communist government achieved remarkable success in combating rural poverty and undernutrition, so that life expectancy in China rose rapidly to near-western levels. However this otherwise excellent record was marred by the worst famine of the 20th century, during 1959-62, when as many as thirty million people perished.

2. In the early 1970s, a number of authoritarian governments in northeast Africa all implemented effective anti-famine measures.

Sudan withstood the 1970s 'Sahelian' drought without suffering famine. The new revolutionary government in Ethiopia introduced far-reaching land reform measures in 1975 and set up the Relief and Rehabilitation Commission. The military government in Somalia responded energetically to the drought of 1974-5. In each of these cases, a combination of idealistic mass mobilisation and professional commitment by civil servants briefly created efficient anti-famine systems. But within a few years all had collapsed, and all three countries suffered severe famine in later years.

3. The Kenyan government responded rapidly and effectively to the drought of 1984, using rural relief distributions as an opportunity to rebuild the mass base of the ruling party KANU. Despite a greater proportional food deficit than either Ethiopia or Sudan at that time, famine was avoided. But the commitment to famine prevention was both uneven (pastoral groups continued to suffer severe famine) and circumstantial (the government has been markedly less energetic in responding to subsequent food crises).

4. Tigray, northern Ethiopia, during the war against the Dergue in the mid-1980s. In the face of a war directed against the civilian population that involved the creation of severe famine, the Tigrayan People's Liberation Front (TPLF) made famine relief and prevention its strategic priority. This helped gain the adherence of the great mass of the Tigrayan peasantry and thereby ensure victory. Since then, the ruling TPLF has invested much in the economic development of Tigray, and the struggle against poverty has figured high in the government's agenda. However, the weakness of democratic institutions nationally and the absence of a free press or competitive elections within Tigray region make the durability of this anti-famine contract open to question.

The first three cases all illustrate the basic point that any government can, if it so desires, take effective measures to combat famine and poverty. Most governments, if secure and stable, or if they are seeking to consolidate a power base among a constituency affected by famine, are likely to take such measures. However, in such cases, anti-famine measures are a privilege rather than a right. The affected people cannot enforce their demands, and if the priorities of the government change, then anti-famine programmes can melt away.

The final case—Tigray—is indicative of a wider phenomenon in which guerrilla armies under enlightened leadership rely on the support of the populace, and hence adopt social and economic programmes that serve the interests of the masses. Another example of this phenomenon is the National Resistance Army under Yoweri Museveni in Uganda. During the struggle, the fact that the guerrillas rely on the support of the people compels them to respond to the demands of the people, and this can make for an effective anti-famine political contract. However, other guerrilla armies have not followed this path. The Sudan People's Liberation Army is a case in point, which has done very little to protect the people of Southern Sudan from famine. In such cases, enlightened leadership, commitment to a social agenda and the development of some forms of representative institutions are key to the possibility of a political contract against famine (and indeed a political contract of any sort).

In conclusion, there can be anti-famine commitments and anti-famine programmes in the absence of democratic accountability, but an anti-famine contract requires the interested party-the people-to have some capacity to enforce the bargain. Liberal political systems provide a number of mechanisms that can help people to do that. In authoritarian systems, the only recourse is protest, either armed or unarmed.

WAR AND FAMINE

At the turn of the 21st century, the commonest cause of famine is war. While war is even more resistant to theorising than famine, it has proved possible to catalogue some of the major means whereby war creates famine. These include:

• Diversion of resources to the warfront;
• Diversion of manpower to the warfront;
• Destruction of food by belligerent forces;
• Requisitioning or looting of food by belligerent forces;
• Destruction or looting of items necessary for food production or

storage, including livestock, farms, seeds, etc;
- Rendering land unusable by use of land mines, poisoning wells, free-fire zones, etc.;
- Blocking or holding-up of food transport, either by outright pre vention and blockade, or by other measures such as strict regula- tion or requiring food transports to move in convoy;
- Prevention of activities by the affected population essential for survival, including marketing livestock, migrating for work, for aging for wild foods, fishing, trading, etc.;
- Destroying marketing systems by strict control, regulation, or threat of attack on markets and traders;
- Forced removal of civilian populations;
- Blocking aid or stealing aid (although this garners most publicity it is usually the least important because of the low proportion of relief food in general consumption).

These various methods of creating famine tend to crystallise into several patterns:

1. Counter-insurgency famine. A government seeking to combat a rural insurgency commonly seeks to establish tight control over the rural population. Methods include relocation of scattered farms to protected villages, control over trade and movement, control over food stores, destruction of farms and food stocks in remote areas where they may be used by guerrillas, etc. These measures can all amount to the creation of famine.

2. Destabilisation famine. A guerrilla force or government army may seek to destroy the social base of its adversary by so destablising the community that people can no longer live normal lives. In some wars, whole areas are ravaged in order to undermine the social base, economic power and authority of the adversary. Famine results.

3. Blockade famine. Guerrilla armies routinely besiege government- held towns, reducing them to starvation. The reverse occasionally occurs. Governments may also seek to isolate and blockade whole rebellious provinces. In inter-state wars, it is common for one coun-

try to try to cut off the shipping and overland trade routes of the other.

4. Ethnic cleansing famine. Starvation is one method used by ethnic cleansors, who pursue a strategy that is a mix of the above, with the aim of forcing an entire civil populace to relocate.

These categories are not wholly distinct and tend to overlap. For example, population removal for ethnic cleansing is commonly justified as a counter-insurgency measure.

Indirectly, war also contributes to famine. War tends to undermine democracy and the rule of law. By creating authoritarian or military governments, it thereby undermines the possibility of democratic action against famine.

We cannot ignore the stopping of war if we are concerned with the prevention of famine. Yet strategies for dealing with the two are usually disconnected. Some of the major economic components of war-affected societies that warrant attention include the following:

1. The self-reinforcing cycle of famine creation in war-stricken environments, in which certain groups seek to achieve security or even relative prosperity at the expense of others. The economics of primary accumulation and asset transfer in famine-stricken societies has recently received some attention. Private and public interests often coincide in famine creation. Where a government aims to create famine, it commonly encourages its servants to pursue their own interests at the same time. Famines create major opportunities for self-enrichment by those in positions of power. Military officers may collaborate with merchants—or become merchants themselves—to profit from the inflated prices of foodstuffs in besieged towns. They may also profit from the resale of looted goods, or become engaged in protection rackets and other black market and profiteering activities. In extreme cases, war has become a highly profitable business, with the military and commercial sectors becoming highly integrated.

Major donors have long been concerned with military-commercial linkages. For example, the World Bank was highly critical of the Military Economic Board in Sudan. But such complexes tend to move underground when they have been formally abolished. Economic policies, especially for post-conflict societies, need to pay special attention to how to disengage warfare and trade, and dismantle military-commercial complexes.

2. The destabilising implications of poorly coordinated or poorly sequenced post-conflict transitions in which the hardships of an economic transition destabilise a political transition, or vice versa. Famine is intrinsically destabilising to a political order, so that it is tempting for a transitional government and its donors to seek a quick fix to a food shortage, simply to get it out of the way. However, this tends to store up problems in the long term. If handled in a more sensitive manner, a famine relief programme can be an opportunity for public education about famine prevention and the need for a democratic politics of food.

3. The economics of disarmament and demobilisation. Without effective post-conflict demobilisation and the reintegration of former combatants, the probability of a country returning to armed conflict is high. During times of food shortage and famine, the incentives for former combatants to take up banditry or return to organised rebellion are much increased. Famine prevention and relief programmes therefore need to be especially robust during post-conflict transitions, and should pay special attention to this category of recipients, who may be less needy by objective criteria, but whose potential for causing profound problems is disturbingly high.

4. The realities of cross-border destabilisation. One country cannot be expected to achieve a lasting peace if its neighbours are still embroiled in a conflict. Flows of refugees, the need to maintain armed forces on a state of alert, the need to prevent infiltration or destabilisation, are all major pressures on a transitional government. As a result, a country-by-country approach to post-conflict transitions is likely to be insufficient.

Detailed examination of these factors is beyond the scope of this chapter. However they point to the additional difficulties of achieving a political contract against famine in a country emerging from war.

THE POLITICAL ROLE OF AID

History demonstrates that famine is conquered primarily by internal political processes in the affected countries. Aid can have an ancillary role but should not aspire to be the principal factor. The grand claims for aid made in the media, in relief agencies' commercials, and in the legislatures of western governments, are rather far away from the more modest claims made by specialist evaluations. Simple arithmetic alone indicates that in recent African famines, relief supplies rarely account for more than 10-15% of overall food consumption by the affected populace.

There is a large literature on the unintended economic consequences of aid, especially relief food distributions. These will not be repeated here. Instead this section will examine how relief aid programmes impact politically on recipient countries. The major political problems with aid include the following:

1. The tendency of large high-profile humanitarian operations to backfire. Most major high-publicity famine relief programmes have had extremely serious negative unintended consequences. These include the massive diversion of resources to belligerent forces and authoritarian governments, and the sustaining of war efforts and attempts at socio-economic transformation. This seems to be a particular feature of very large-scale operations, with smaller relief activities less prone to these problems. This may arise because a high media profile creates a political and funding imperative for major UN agencies and NGOs to maintain a presence, rendering them more vulnerable to manipulation, because the sheer scale of activity makes monitoring and control less effective, and because a high level of media attention attracts less scrupulous NGOs that are ready to make unethical compromises.

2. External dependency and orientation of accountability towards external donors. The economic dependency of recipient countries inevitably creates internal political problems in those countries. Recipient and debtor governments become highly sensitive and responsive to their creditors and financiers, and less sensitive and responsive to their recipients. The best government personnel are deputed to negotiate aid and credit agreements. Government fi-

nancing and policy decisions are coordinated with donor schedules. Local institutions including local governments, NGOs etc also become oriented towards external donors rather than local constituents. Less concretely but equally significantly, governments abdicate responsibility for fighting famine, by putting responsibility on aid donors and blaming them when things go wrong.

3. Weakening of national capacity. In intensively aided countries, many of the most educated personnel are either attracted to employment in aid institutions, or become engaged in aid-related tasks on behalf of the government and local institutions.

4. Cultural and informational factors. A protracted aid encounter creates an important if subtle cultural shift in the recipient country. External aid donors increasingly come to define the problems and solutions of the recipient country. Their dominant position in major policy debates undermines the possibility of the recipient country conducting its own domestic debates on these issues. National journalists and opinion formers (academics, political leaders, etc) may take the lead in being overly-influenced by western perceptions and prescriptions, and thus over-inflating the role of aid and the charitable approach at the expense of local policy-related and political solutions . The end result may be that the citizens themselves come to believe that solutions lie in the hands of aid agencies, not their own actions. This level of demoralisation and dependency is perhaps the most difficult obstacle to overcome.

5. Lack of transparency in the aid encounter itself. All major aid programmes now aim to promote democracy and good governance. However, the aid encounter is not a good model for this. Negotiations over aid contracts and modalities are conducted in private between representatives of donor and recipient governments. There is little or no opportunity for democratic participation. Many elements of the aid relationship are in fact not in the public realm at all. In the aid encounter, the donor has arbitrary power, and there is no right of appeal by the recipient. This is not a good model for democratic politics. It encourages secretive and elitist decision-making and discourages accountability to the recipient population.

Overall, relief aid appears not to contribute to the development of a form of governance that is likely to promote the struggle against famine. The basic elements of a political contract against famine are simply not there in the aid encounter. On the contrary, aid can be an obstacle to the development of the political awareness and political processes needed for such a contract to emerge.

Where a contract already exists, however, aid can achieve its humanitarian goals without adverse political impacts. For example, the Botswanan drought relief programme is essentially an indigenous relief and rehabilitation programme based upon a national political contract, but it often utilises aid resources to implement its commitments. This experience is in line with the general assessment of poverty alleviation and social welfare programmes: aid can support pre-existing sound policy, but can rarely achieve the same goals in the absence of such good policy, and aid donors cannot create or dictate good policy.

One of the major challenges for aid donors genuinely concerned about famine prevention is to find ways in which to minimise the risks of adverse political outcomes. The major means for doing this appear to lie in the direction of making the aid encounter more democratic and transparent. This will not only help to reduce the possibilities for abuse, but will be an exercise in public education (in both donor and recipient countries) and can help initiate processes of open debate in the recipient country that will promote democracy.

PROSPECTS FOR ANTI-FAMINE POLITICAL CONTRACTS IN AFRICA

Many in the humanitarian international will argue that the prospects for any form of an anti-famine political contract in Africa are so remote that considerations relating to it should not influence their decision-making, and that the adverse side-effects of relief programmes can therefore be disregarded largely or totally.

There is no doubt that Africa faces a number of special problems:

1. The characteristics of most African famines. Most African famines are associated with war, or are agrarian or pastoral famines,

which are slow-onset and low visibility, with limited political impact. It is harder to generate a political coalition around such famines than the rapid-onset high visibility famines characteristic of Asia.

2. A modern history in which famine has rarely been an effective and enduring political issue. This is compounded by the fact that some anti-famine measures, such as environmental protection projects, have an unfortunate history of being ill-conceived and brutally implemented, helping to discredit them.

3. Historically, most anti-hunger political contracts in Africa have been based on towns. Since colonial days, governments have felt keenly obliged to provide cheap food to townspeople-because this is where their power can be threatened. Unfortunately, the obligation to guarantee urban food security has rarely been extended to rural areas, and in fact cheap food for cities has often been provided to the detriment of rural areas.

4. Weakness of contemporary democratic systems. Many democratically elected governments have yet to secure their power bases, and many are based on ethnic or regional coalitions that exclude certain groups.

5. Lack of high quality public debate about the nature of an effective anti-famine policy. For many journalists and public figures, famine is either not a subject of serious interest, or it is a problem to be solved by international charitable action.

6. Weakness of contemporary human rights activism, which is largely focussed on secondary activism rather than primary mobilisation, and which concentrates on civil and political liberties and tends to neglect social and economic rights.

7. The prevalence of war.

8. The numerous other pressing challenges for politicians and electorates in Africa including conflicts, breakdown of governmental services, corruption, etc.

9. Protracted and intense nature of the aid encounter, which has led to demoralisation and dependency among wide swaths of those who should be taking responsibility for famine prevention.

Certainly, if one is seeking a single formula for an anti-famine political contract, that formula will be elusive. But this is not the challenge. African countries are vulnerable to famine for markedly different reasons, and the measures needed to ensure protection from famine vary enormously from one country to the next. The experience of famine in, say, Mali is markedly different to the experience in highland Ethiopia, which is different again from Tanzania.

Anti-famine measures will also change over time. The immediate priority in one country may be the end to a war and the end to the exploitative and predatory relationships associated with it, but later the main requirement may be a sound food security policy to protect marginal areas against deprivations caused by harvest failures.

A focus on famine itself may not necessarily be the most productive approach. In some areas, famine is closely related to war, in others, to the vulnerability of pastoral livelihoods to rainfall fluctuations, and in yet another, to market failures. In some cases, the most pressing issue is the underlying cause of impoverishment (perhaps land alienation), and in others, the outcomes of cyclical food shortages (perhaps epidemic diseases and health crises). In each case, a different constituency will need to be mobilised and different political idiom developed to tackle the most pressing issues.

It is also necessary to be alert to some of the dangers that may arise with an attempt to construct a democratic politics of food.

1. The main danger is of populist over-simplification of the issue, especially with regard to urban populations. A democratic politics of food does not mean cheap food for the towns.[6] It was this kind of politically-motivated distortion to the food market that contributed to much of Africa's food insecurity in the first place.

2. A second danger is that over-concentration on food issues may be counter-productive. Famine is not just a food shortage, so that a

policy that focuses over-much on food availability may fail to do its job, and divert attention and resources away from the policies that would actually be more effective.

However, on balance, the dangers of not beginning to develop a democratic politics of food are far greater than these risks.

There are also some positive aspects to the current situation in Africa.

1. States are here to stay: the extreme neo-liberal view that African states are unsustainable appears to be withering away. As it is only possible to achieve democracy in the context of statehood, this lays the foundation for the creation of democratic anti-famine political contracts.

2. There is a consensus on democracy and pluralism as the only acceptable forms of government in Africa.

3. There is a rapid development of African civil society and expansion of free exchange of information. Governments can no longer exercise tight censorship and prevent their citizens from knowing what is going on in the rest of the world-or the rest of the world from knowing what is happening within their borders. African citizens are better informed and more sophisticated than ever before.

4. The considerable accumulated expertise about effective food security is such that any stable, peaceable African country should be able to design and implement a food security policy that safeguards against all but the most extreme disasters.

5. Increasing recognition of past policy errors in food security by both African governments and international financial institutions and donors.

6. Acknowledgment of the need to give special treatment to post-conflict transitions.

7. Minority rights are increasingly a subject of concern, and all governments recognise that the interests and needs of minorities cannot be ignored in the name of majoritarian rule.

In conclusion, while the challenges are considerable, there is no justification for discarding the possibility of democratisation in Africa. On the contrary, the severity of Africa's current crises demonstrate the bankruptcy of existing practices and the need to search for policies and programmes that also address the long-term needs of the region. It is probable that an approach to famine prevention that prioritises the requisite components of democracy will not only be more successful at attaining food security, but will also simultaneously strengthen the prospects for democracy as well.

The first steps to take concern debate and public education. The issue of the politics of food is famine prevention is paradoxical: there is extremely low awareness among most African publics and also policymakers about the importance of the issue, but also a tremendous receptivity to the ideas once they have been floated. It follows that a vigorous public debate across the African continent on these issues may be able to begin to move policy.

NOTES

1. A. K. Sen, 'Individual freedom as a social commitment,' *New York Review of Books*, 14 June 1990
2. A. K. Sen, *Poverty and Famine: An Essay on Entitlement and Deprivation*, Oxford, 1981.
3. J. Rivers et al., 'Lessons for epidemiology from the Ethiopian famines,' *Annales Societe Belge de Medecine Tropicale*, 56, 1976.
4. Edward Mansfield and Jack Snyder, 'Democratization and War,' *Foreign Affairs*, May/June 1995, 79-97.
5. African Rights, *Food and Power in Sudan: A critique of humanitarianism*, London, 1997.
6. English demonstrators in the early 19th century once took to the streets demanding a 'provisional government' in the belief that this would supply them with provisions.

6

HUMANITARIAN CAPACITIES AND INSTITUTIONS

INSTITUTIONS FOR HUMANITARIAN RESPONSE

Even in the most crisis-ridden of African countries, such as Somalia, citizens have shown that they can organise highly successful business ventures. African generals are among the ablest military commanders in the world. There is a record of successful African humanitarian ventures carried out under some of the most difficult conditions imaginable, such as war-stricken Ethiopia and Eritrea during the 1980s. There is certainly no absence of African voluntary action and private contributions to help the needy. Why is it then that humanitarian action in Africa lies so overwhelmingly in the hands of foreign organisations?

Part of the reason lies in resources. Most African governments lack the tax bases to implement major relief programmes, and most African citizens, when they give to help the poor, prefer to do it directly to the needy family or individual rather than through institutions.

A second reason lies in the intellectual paradigms that exist. When there are successful African humanitarian enterprises, they do not get the recognition they deserve. For example, in Ethiopia in the 1980s, there were two parallel relief operations. On the government side, there was a UN and international NGO managed operation, which largely failed. On the rebel side there was an operation exclusively managed by local people, which succeeded. But the model of aid that has been widely adopted has been the

UN-INGO model—failed but not discredited. Comparable problems exist throughout the continent. Under donor pressure, Zimbabwe was forced to abandon its successful food security policies.

A third reason is that, when African institutions are developed, they are often just imitations of western ones. Western donors like to assist 'local NGOs' but will only do so when those NGOs faithfully copy the western model and follow western agendas. When Africa develops its trans-national institutions, there is strong pressure for them to be just pale shadows of their UN counterparts. African peacekeeping is criticised when it is unlike western models of intervention—as if those models were successful. But if a system is failing, it is not prudent to copy it. Africa needs to innovate its own institutions relevant to African realities.

This chapter examines some options for institutions for humanitarian assistance in peacetime crises such as droughts, in situations of conflict, and for refugees and displaced people. It examines the role of information systems and early warning. The final section is concerned with donor conditionalities and aid sanctions. Most of the focus is not on the institutions themselves, but the legal and humanitarian rationale and context for institutions. By creating the right legal and political context, the right sorts of institutions are likely to emerge. Or rather, some existing institutions will stay, others will be reformed, and others will disappear. And some new ones may emerge.

This chapter does not address food security policies as such, including marketing structures, strategic reserves, employment and food-for-work schemes, support to livestock markets in times of drought, etc. However, it is important to underline that all experience indicates that some state intervention in the food and labour markets is important to guarantee basic food security. Governments must provide a safety net of last resort, and guarantee citizens' right to basic relief.

These suggestions will disappoint those who want immediate solutions to immediate problems. International humanitarian agencies often dismiss more radical reform measures on the grounds that they will not bear results tomorrow. But it is only by adopting a slightly longer term approach than the short-term panic horizon characteristic of international humanitarianism that results can be achieved. In addition, the expectations on humanitarian relief must not be too high. Relief aid cannot prevent conflicts or build peace. It can mitigate refugee flows, but only in very particular circumstances. It is important, but cannot replace other forms of action. Nor should it impede other forms of action.

LOCAL AND INTERNATIONAL INSTITUTIONS

Many international aid workers are motivated by a genuine humanitarianism and sense of solidarity with the poor and oppressed. Even the harshest critics of the international aid system are ready to concede this, and to acknowledge that such people can play an important role in the struggle for basic material welfare for all. The questions are, why does a system that is staffed by so many capable and well-intentioned people often function so badly, and what can be done to harness the genuine altruism and skill of many humanitarian workers to the best effect?

The operations of the major multilateral humanitarian institutions in Africa—specifically the UN specialised agencies—pose a particular challenge for Africa. The UN and its agencies have wide mandates, but it is only in Africa that their full mandates are exercised, including development, humanitarian relief, human rights, democracy and governance, peacekeeping, environmental protection, and a host of other activities. In an important sense, international humanitarian organisations need Africa, because it is there that they can fulfil their mandates, and their staff can have their careers. This is an opportunity for African countries: how are they to utilise this international engagement with Africa to best effect?

Compared to other continents, Africa has few sophisticated national relief and development organisations that can challenge and compete with international agencies. The lack of local competition means that it is possible for international agencies to get away with lower standards than would be permissible in, for example, south Asia. When Africa develops a more professional, institutionalised and competitive voluntary sector, then the performance of international agencies will also improve.

African humanitarian institutions will be disadvantaged for the forseeable future because of the imbalance of resources between Africa and Europe and North America. This is seen most dramatically by comparing the international responses to crises in Europe compared to Africa. For example, refugees from Kosovo in 1999 received approximately sixty times as much international assistance as refugees in Africa. International agencies even installed street lighting in Kosovar camps in Macedonia. Meanwhile, the international NGO world is dominated by a relatively small number of agencies. Just the top ten agencies control about 60 per cent of the resources of the entire international development and relief voluntary sector.

While creating more equality in access to resources is a longer term aim, in the short term the priorities must be to promote African engagement in the international debate on humanitarianism, and to improve the accountability of the international aid system to its intended beneficiaries.

CONTEXTS FOR HUMANITARIAN ACTION

This chapter distinguishes four contexts in which humanitarian action takes place. These are not hard-and-fast categories, but they are indicative of the different kinds of constraints that humanitarian action faces.

1. Peacetime relief assistance. This is, for example, 'normal' drought relief in which there is no civil unrest or conflict, and government institutions are present, functioning more or less well.

2. Major conventional or semi-conventional war, either between states or between well-organised centrally commanded adversaries within a single state. In these circumstances, the provisions of international humanitarian law (IHL) are relevant.

3. Assistance to civilians under the control of an anti-government force, in circumstances where the government is refusing free access. In this situation, according to IHL, a humanitarian agency can only work by forsaking neutrality, and acting in solidarity with the people of this area.

4. Assistance in circumstances where there is no effective state authority at all. There may be no government of any sort (Somalia)

or the government's exercise of sovereign power may be almost wholly fictional (D.R. Congo).

This chapter argues that the four situations demand different responses. Further, it argues that it most humanitarian organisations will have to make choices about which of the situations fits their mandate, and which do not. For example, an agency operational in normal peacetime relief will find itself in frequent conflicts of interest if it also tries to operate under IHL provisions in that same country. The different contexts demand different relationships with governing authorities, different skills and different attitudes among humanitarian staff.

The categorisation does not imply that 'development' assistance can only be provided in certain circumstances (e.g. where there is a functioning government) and cannot be provided in others. For example, in situations such as much of Somalia or parts of eastern DRC, development interventions can play a key role in mitigating resource conflicts that underpin ongoing violence. National and international NGOs can function in the absence of a state authority, although they need to pay close attention to their precise roles.

It is important to note that the above categorisations break down in the context of genocide: this calls for different rules. In some cases, the legal framework is an issue of political dispute. From one side, a programme may be seen as an act of solidarity that promotes democracy and long-term development; from the other side, it may be seen as an act of illegal subversion. Some of the best humanitarian programmes are 'illegal' in this way-for example the cross-border assistance to Eritrea and Tigray in the 1980s. In such cases, where the issue of legality is disputed, moral choices must be made.

RATIONALE FOR SEPARATING PEACETIME AND WARTIME INSTITUTIONS

The rationale for insisting on separate relief institutions for normal peacetime operations and for activities during conflict is founded in the fundamental distinction between the legal regime governing peacetime and wartime. During peace, sovereign governments are constrained by the requirements of human rights law. During conflict, belligerents are obliged to conform to international humanitarian law. This fundamental distinction should be upheld.

In recent years, some jurists and many international institutions have tried to blur this distinction. This is very unfortunate. It leads to legal uncertainty and conflict of interests between different humanitarian organisations and even within the same organisation.

Another consequence, very relevant to Africa, is that it complicates the relations between host governments, supposedly independent relief agencies, and donors. In normal peacetime circumstances, the relationship between an international relief agency and a host government is clear: the agency abides by domestic law and regulations and acts in conformity with government policy. In wartime, in theory, an agency acts in accordance with the procedures and standards laid down in IHL, with the consent of the belligerents.

But blurring the distinction between peace and war gives foreign agencies uncertain legal standing. Are they working in accordance with domestic legislation or under the very different requirements of IHL? Often, in practice, the agency staff simply do not know. This applies to NGOs and disturbingly often to UN specialised agencies as well. Not knowing their legal standing and hence their proper channels of communication and negotiation, agencies instead run to their western donors and get the donors to intercede on their behalf. Instead of a relationship based on law and 'partnership' the relationship becomes a simple power struggle. Mutual distrust is the inevitable consequence.

This situation can only be resolved by clarifying the legal standing of relief agencies. In peacetime they must operate in a normal, legal and proper manner; in conflict they should be governed by the requirements of IHL. There should be as little ambiguity as possible.

PEACETIME RELIEF INSTITUTIONS
Most relief operations in Africa are undertaken during peacetime, or where there are civil disturbances but no anti-state belligerent that can effectively administer territory. Thus, relief operations in countries such as Mali and Zimbabwe fall into this category. So do relief operations in parts of northern Sudan where there is no insurgency (e.g. northern Kordofan) and in Uganda, where there are insurgents (the Lord's Resistance Army) but they are incapable of administering any territory.

Overall, relief institutions for peacetime operations should be consonant with two major policy aims of African governments. (1) They should be subject to democratic oversight—that is, they should be transparent and accountable. (2) They should be commercially competitive—that is, they should not receive unfair advantages vis-à-vis other service providers. This applies to all institutions, national and international, concerned with public policy or public funds. (A third aim, that they should be compatible with development objectives, will not be discussed here.) This chapter assumes that all African governments are in broad agreement with these aims.

CREATING A DEMOCRATIC HUMANITARIANISM

The rationale for a democratic humanitarianism is based on the following argument. Famine and similar crises can be prevented when the political will exists. Political will is most effectively created, maintained and enforced when the people who have a direct material interest in famine prevention are involved themselves. These people are the farmers, herders, labourers and others most at risk from food shortages. Therefore it follows that any institutions and procedures concerned with famine prevention should be open and accessible to the wider public and their representatives.

In addition, in poor and famine-prone countries, disaster response institutions play a large part in government and public policy. Like other aspects of government and the civil service, they should be subject to democratic control.

This is not to rule out citizens' direct action, for example self-help groups and the like. On the contrary, freedom to organise in pursuit of legitimate material interest is an essential democratic right, and obtaining food and health are basic rights. Soliciting and giving assistance is a right for citizens. It is also a right for citizens' organisations and local NGOs to solicit voluntary contributions and expertise from outside the country, and to work with international networks (subject to the requirements of transparency, national security, principles of religious tolerance etc).

For foreign NGOs coming with their own money (raised directly from citizens, not from donor governments), the situation is more complicated. The NGOs clearly have the right to dispose of these funds subject to the law, but they have no right to be operational in another country: for them it is a privilege. It therefore comes down to the inclination and interests of host governments how to regulate such activities.

But any institutions that use public money (from national or foreign taxpayers) must be subject to democratic scrutiny and regulation. It goes without saying that they must be subject to the rule of law.[1]

A democratic humanitarianism might mean most or all of the following:

• local decision making, to the extent possible;
• transparency (budgets should be published and decision-making procedures made public);
• being subject to professional standards laid down by national professional bodies;
• institutions and policies should be subject to parliamentary over sight;
• encouraging public debate over food policy and humanitarian assistance policy;
• mechanisms for hearing and adjudicating complaints should be established;
• commissions of inquiry should be set up after major operations to investigate what went wrong and what went right an what procedures should be changed for the future.

Such measures can contribute to the creation of political contracts against famine and other extreme hardship.

COMPETITIVE SERVICE DELIVERY

Public policy should be decided by democratic means. But the delivery of public services is subject to considerations of efficiency and effectiveness. In the field of relief action, western donors have privatised most service delivery. They should now cooperate with African governments to make it competitive.

Most relief action involves public money. So-called international 'NGOs' and 'PVOs' in reality get the great majority of their funds for relief work from western donors.[2] In some cases this is 90% or more. These relief institutions play a major role in the economies of African countries. For example, the entire health and foodgrain sectors of the economies can be dominated or strongly influenced by relief activities. NGOs can also have a big impact on the labour market for professionals (doctors, lawyers, accountants). Almost all African countries have agreed on the need to develop market based economies based on free competition. This goal can only be achieved if all major sectors are open to free competition, and some are not closed off. But, if international relief agencies are able to operate in the food sector with subsidies, tax-breaks or monopolies, important distortions will enter the national economy. It follows that the implementation of public policy in the relief sector, as a public service sector, should also be subject to the requirements of competition.

This does not of course preclude citizens' voluntary action using resources freely donated by citizens. Such assistance is relatively minor and is not a significant part of service delivery. But any public money, from national or foreign taxpayers, must be subject to market constraints.

Currently, western donors have privatised most relief assistance (putting it through NGOs) but not made it commercially competitive. Contracts for service delivery in African countries are often awarded by donors without free and fair procedures for competitive tendering. On the contrary they are often awarded by subjective and secretive processes of evaluating proposals, subject to pressure from lobbyists, and even subject to legislative constraint that in any other economic sector would constitute an unfair restriction on trading. In addition, donors often insist on tax privileges for their selected implementing organisations, further distorting the possibilities for free competition.

This implies:

- free competitive tendering for service delivery contracts (i.e. international NGOs, national NGOs, commercial companies, government departments can all bid);
- service delivery organisations should not enjoy tax privileges not enjoyed by commercial companies;
- contracts should have penalty clauses for non-fulfilment;
- recipients/beneficiaries should have the legal right to sue if contracts are not fulfilled;
- independent monitoring of contractual obligations.

One of the aims of these measures is to let the market decide, rather than the bureaucracy. These measures should therefore cut down bureaucracy. It will probably be necessary to implement these conditions in full for large contracts: for small programmes of (for example) less than $250,000 per year, simplified and expedited procedures may be preferable.

The rationale of 'urgency' is often used to bypass normal contracting procedures. This can be justified in exceptional cases. But very often, emergency systems are set up well in advance of crises or evolve more slowly. In all but a few very exceptional cases, there are ample opportunities for establishing procedures for normal competitive procedures for contracting out services.

This should ensure that taxpayers obtain the best value for their money, distortions in the economy are minimised, and above all that the needs of the recipients are met most efficiently.

CONCLUSION

Currently there is a profusion of poorly-regulated and poorly-coordinated humanitarian organisations. Africa needs its own indigenous organisations, governmental, non-governmental and intergovernmental. But rather than setting up new institutions that will simply be competitors and imitations of the existing ones, it is better to change the rules of the entire business, and let the kinds of necessary organisations and processes emerge organically from African realities. The above suggestions are based on the supposition that African nations are committed to democratisation and to economic competitiveness. If these sorts of reforms are followed, then the existing institutions, which are mostly international, will be forced to adapt, or they will die. In their place, other institutions will emerge: democratic organisations, commercial companies, national NGOs, government departments, etc. These will emerge from the political and economic realities of Africa and not the institutional models of a failed model of international humanitarian relief, so they will be appropriate and sustainable. Some international agencies will remain, but only if they are compatible with these realities.

NEUTRAL AND IMPARTIAL HUMANITARIAN ACTION IN CONFLICT
International humanitarian law provides for two models of relief

assistance: neutral and impartial assistance and assistance provided by one belligerent or in close cooperation with it. This section is concerned with neutral and impartial assistance, and the following one with solidarity assistance.

Neutral and impartial assistance is subject to extremely strict conditionalities laid down in international humanitarian law. If a belligerent has reason to suppose that any relief is being diverted or abused by the other, or turned to military advantage in any manner, or the other belligerent party or the humanitarian agency is refusing to allow third-party inspection or monitoring of the supplies, then that belligerent can withdraw consent for the relief operation to continue. (The Federal Government of Nigeria insisted on this with respect to the ICRC operation in Biafra, and when the Biafrans refused to agree to these terms, the ICRC was obliged to close down its programme.)

This section will examine the ICRC, UN agencies and international NGOs, and the question of monitoring. For humanitarianism in wartime, the law is all important. IHL is founded on the principle of neutrality, which means maintaining the legal fiction that both sides in a war are morally equivalent. The succeeding section will examine the options to pursue when it is not desirable to remain neutral.

THE ICRC

The ICRC is in theory built on the elaborate rules of IHL. In law, the neutrality of the ICRC is theoretically akin to the neutrality of a state that is (a) non-belligerent and (b) not leaning towards one side in the conflict. However it is questionable whether the ICRC has fully succeeded in fulfilling this mandate. Occasionally, ICRC delegates or lawyers assert that an operation is neutral simply because it is the ICRC implementing it.

The ICRC's mandate cannot cope with genocide. The organisation's biggest ever historical crisis occurred when it obtained evidence of the Nazi genocide of European Jewry but declined to publicise it, for fear of jeopardising its neutrality. Arguably, in such extreme situations the principles of neutrality break down and the organisation should be obliged to break its own rules for the sake of a greater humanity. Questions have also been asked about whether the ICRC should have acted differently in Rwanda.

The role of the ICRC in conflicts is, in theory, unique and invaluable. But it depends crucially on the confidence that governments and belligerents have in the organisation. It is the responsibility of the ICRC to maintain that confidence and to rebuild it where it has broken down. But African governments should also indicate to the ICRC that they recognise the principles of its mission, and would welcome it sticking to them.

UN SPECIALISED AGENCIES

For other international humanitarian organisations, the picture is different. UN organisations have mandates that make them, in theory, accountable to governments and to the law. There is much opportunity for clarifying their mandates, which are often very broad—so broad in fact as to create considerable potential for confusion. Only in Africa does the UN enjoy the capacity to act according to its full range of mandates.

Currently, only UNICEF has a clear mandate that enables it to operate in a conflict situation independently of a host government. This makes it similar to the ICRC. Its mandate to protect children means that it is automatically dealing with people 'protected' under IHL.[3] It is important for UNICEF to clarify how it can operate under the regime of IHL: it should not be content with simply stating that the Rights of the Child are paramount and inviolable.

Other UN agencies may also find themselves operating in a conflict situation. WFP may be a provider of food to UNHCR, governmental or other relief programmes. UNDP has taken on the role of emergency coordination, irrespec tive of whether it is a peacetime or a wartime emergency. WHO has a specific health mandate that may make it operate in such a situation. Similarly the Desert Locust Control organisation and others.

There is an important potential contradiction between these UN agencies' accountability to their host government and their need to respect IHL in a war zone. This has created problems in a number of cases.

For example, in Sudan, UNICEF is the co-ordinator for Operation Lifeline Sudan (Southern Sector) in SPLA-controlled areas; where its operations are subject to fairly strict rules of conduct broadly derived from IHL. (They need refinement but the principle has been established.) Meanwhile in the Northern Sector of the same operation, UNDP is the coordinator, but operates under a standard country agreement drawn up by the Sudan Government. UNDP also has interests in peacetime development programmes in northern Sudan. This creates a situation where UNDP is implementing government relief and development policies in the war zone, and insofar as these policies are integral to the government's counter-insurgency, UNDP has itself forsaken neutrality in the war. In fact it is operating in violation of IHL and the SPLA should be entitled to ask it to cease operations (as it would do in the case of the ICRC). (The situation is a mirror image of the situation in which the ICRC closed down its Biafran operation.)

More broadly, UN specialised agencies suffer the recurring problem of coordination and management in situations of conflict. In peacetime the situation does not arise because all are supposed to work according to country agreements, putting the ultimate responsibility for coordination with the host government. In conflicts where the government is a belligerent or is not exercising full control over its territory, full government coordination is not appropriate. Sometimes this is addressed by having a 'lead agency'. This rarely works effectively because UN agencies (not to mention INGOs) are jealous guardians of their autonomy. In addition, in almost all cases, no UN agency has the appropriate legal mandate to operate in a fully legal manner. UNICEF is the most flexible, but it is unlikely that other UN agencies would agree to be coordinated by it. The Department of Humanitarian Affairs was supposed to resolve this question, but it merely added another competing organisation to an already confused situation. (Its subsequent change in status to the Office Coordinating Humanitarian Affairs may have helped in some situations.)

Experience has shown that in practice it is impossible for a UN agency accustomed to dealing with a host government according to a normal country agreement to adjust to the different and more independent working relationships required during a conflict. (UNDP in Sudan is a good example.) Equally, UN agencies that have become accustomed to working in an independent way, because of the lack of a strong government or any government at all, do not find it easy to adopt normal working relations when a new government comes and peace returns. They may even end up openly challenging the legitimacy of that government. (This problem occurred in Rwanda and is likely elsewhere.)

This situation has arisen because UN agencies have come to operate in conflicts in a piecemeal manner without acknowledging the legal and other issues that arise. Despite the number of long and expensive consultants' reports commissioned by the UN and donors on the subject of 'coordination' in 'complex emergencies', the situation cannot be resolved by tinkering with the present arrangements. It requires more radical change, namely the complete institutional separation of peacetime and wartime operations.

UN organisations can only work effectively in war zones if they are ready to submit to an entirely new legal and managerial order. The obligations of IHL and the practical requirements of a conflict zone are so different from the normal working relationships of a peacetime country agreement that one organisation cannot do both. There are two basic options.

(a) UN agencies' conflict-area programmes could be managed by another 'protecting' agency for the duration of the conflict.

(b) Arrangements could be made by setting up a special UN or OAU coordination and monitoring office, to ensure the independence of UN programmes in the war zone and their adherence to IHL. A monitoring capacity will be needed. This could be either the UN Humanitarian Fact Finding Commission (set up in 1991 but never utilised to date) or an independent monitoring commission.

Neither of these proposals will be popular among the UN agencies, which are never ready to limit their programmes or freedom of action. However a step in this direction will be important in clearing up the confusion that currently exists and helping to build better regulated and more accountable humanitarian institutions.

DONOR AGENCIES

A number of donors have begun to be more directly active in emergencies. The US Office of Foreign Disaster Assistance, the European Commission Humanitarian Office and other emergency desks of European governmental donors have become directly engaged in administering humanitarian programmes in the Balkans, and to a lesser extent in Africa. This is a development with far-reaching consequences. Most of these offices have been recently established and are not well versed in IHL. It makes the effective regulation of international humanitarian activity much more difficult.

All major western donors are party to the main instruments of IHL and therefore should be bound by them in any directly administered programmes.

INTERNATIONAL NGOs

For international NGOs, the legal regime in a situation of conflict is the same as for the ICRC (insofar as they aspire to be neutral), while the relationship with government is more akin to the UN agencies.

For an NGO already operating in a country when a conflict breaks out, the dilemmas are comparable to those for UN agencies as outlined above. An international NGO has the right to offer services in a conflict zone and for this not to be seen as a hostile act by belligerents. But NGOs do not have the right to operate with the privileges of neutral status if either belligerent makes a legitimate objection, or if they fail to fulfil the rather onerous obligations laid on them by IHL. There is no room for enjoying the privileges of a neutral organisation without fulfilling the corresponding obligations. It is also not possible for an NGO to reject the principle of neutrality but still claim humanitarian privileges, except in the case of the fight against genocide.

For an NGO, if it acts in accordance with IHL, then it becomes a 'protected' organisation and its staff also enjoy 'protection', in the sense of the belligerents being legally obliged not to attack them. If a belligerent makes a legitimate objection, then the NGO has the option of acting in solidarity with one side or the other, but without the protection of neutral and impartial humanitarian status under IHL.

It is worth examining what 'solidarity' means in practice. In the case of the cross-border assistance to ERA and REST during the war against the Mengistu regime, humanitarianism entailed solidarity with the people of Eritrea and Tigray, subjected to a near-genocidal war and man-made famine. Some NGOs operating in non-government held areas of Sudan have made similar choices. In the case of many NGO programmes for Rwandese in eastern

Zaire in 1994-6, they had forsaken impartiality for the moral choice of solidarity with the Hutu Power forces. It was a straightforward moral choice, though most preferred not to acknowledge it.

SOLIDARITY ASSISTANCE

'Solidarity assistance' is here used simply to mean any assistance provided by any organisation that does not conform to the strict requirements of neutrality and impartiality. Such assistance can be humanitarian, but it cannot enjoy the protection of IHL. Moral arguments in this area are more complex and may be somewhat subjective (as moral arguments tend to be). At its worst, solidarity assistance can mean giving practical aid to combatants or helping promote extremist ideologies. There are plenty of examples of this. At its best, solidarity assistance can mean preventing or punishing genocide, or helping democratic forces in their political mobilisation of the people. IHL is founded on the necessary fiction that the belligerents in a war are morally equal (or the more workable formulation that their justification for fighting should not affect their actions during wartime). Sometimes this principle does not hold, and in such situations it is morally quite justifiable to enter into a solidarity relationship with the more progressive side. But the price to be paid is abandoning neutral status. One organisation cannot both operate as a solidarity agency and also claim to be neutral and impartial under IHL. In Southern Sudan, a number of NGOs have in practice managed to get away with this practice, operating both inside OLS and outside it in solidarity with the SPLA, but this practice could endanger OLS.

This section will examine the humanitarian roles of armies themselves and other assistance organisations.

ARMIES

According to IHL, the primary responsibility for the material welfare of a civilian population in a conflict zone falls upon the military forces in control of the area. This is often forgotten by commanders and humanitarian workers alike. Armies have the first and the greatest responsibility to ensure that people have food, health care, decent living conditions, etc. This applies to governmental and non-state belligerents.

Assistance provided by a military force, or a special section attached to it, can hardly be described as 'neutral'. But it has an obligation to provide for the basics for all civilians under its control. This assistance is quite legitimate and cannot be dismissed as 'non-humanitarian' by relief agencies. There is however a case for independent monitoring of any such assistance programmes.

In Africa, the option of assistance provided by armies does not usually arise because the armies or the states or movements behind them do not have enough resources. Western donors are unlikely to want to use this channel of assistance because, no matter how good the monitoring, the suspicion will always remain that assistance is being used by the military itself.

But African militaries might consider setting up their own humanitarian assistance departments, using national resources, to provide essential humanitarian assistance in conflict zones. They could invite independent monitoring commissions to be present.

ASSISTANCE ORGANISATIONS

Citizens or organisations acting in solidarity with one belligerent in a conflict cannot be said to be neutral. But they can still be humanitarian. There are many examples of this. In the Ethiopian and Eritrean liberation war, most relief organisations were active on one side or the other, rarely on both. The extent to which they were genuinely humanitarian depended solely on how much they met actual needs, and the position they adopted vis-à-vis unacceptable political and human rights realities. Similarly in Southern Sudan, Biafra, and southern African liberation struggles.

An organisation can start off as neutral and take the decision to abandon that status. In Biafra, after the Federal Government challenged the relief agencies to abide by IHL and allow Federal inspection of their flights, and the Biafran forces refused, most relief agencies continued their assistance. They did so under the implicit understanding that they had forfeited neutral status and had now become a legitimate target of attack. Their work was humanitarian (largely) but no longer neutral.

The decision to stay in Biafra was facilitated by the fact that most agencies already had an investment of programmes there, and staff could see the practical benefits of the assistance they were providing. It is a common reality that aid agencies tend to stick to programmes that they have started-they have raised the funds, made the necessary agreements, set up the administrative and logistical structures, and above all made the decision to be present. Reversing a position tends to require much stronger arguments than adopting a position in the first place.

Non-neutral humanitarian aid should still be impartial (that is, given according to need) and professional, and can be accountable. In principle, non-neutral humanitarian assistance could be monitored by an independent commission to ensure that it is still impartial and is not being diverted to military forces.

One of the advantages of non-neutral assistance is that it can be developmental. IHL in practice prohibits development assistance in a war zone, because it will bring military advantage to one party. (Which means that the other party will legitimately object, making it unlawful to proceed.) But by forsaking neutrality, organisations can take on much wider briefs for development, capacity building, etc.

There is an important role for non-neutral humanitarian assistance. Where a government is committing genocide or comparable large-scale crimes against humanity, neutrality no longer makes sense. In addition, where there is a conflict between democratic and anti-democratic adversaries, there will be roles for both neutral and non-neutral assistance. (Struggling for democracy is in itself no guarantee that forces will respect IHL, while non-democratic forces may, in the circumstances of war, respect IHL.)

ASSISTANCE AND PROTECTION FOR
REFUGEES AND INTERNALLY DISPLACED PERSONS

Africa has more than its share of refugees and internally displaced persons (IDPs). It also has externally-displaced persons (EDPs): people who have crossed an international frontier during conflict but do not qualify for refugee status (such as the Rwandese civilian populations of the former camps in eastern Zaire).

REFUGEES

The legal regime governing refugees and EDPs in Africa was laid down in the 1969 OAU Convention and other documents (notably the 1951 UN Convention). This has not changed. However, many

African governments have failed to fulfil their obligations under the law (although they are generally more generous than western countries with their 'fortress Europe' and 'fortress America' approaches). In addition, in some circumstances the UNHCR and other international agencies have chosen to act without regard to the law. African governments have rarely tried to demand more lawful action from UNHCR.

UNHCR has allowed the implementation of its protection mandate to be driven by the demands of its assistance programmes. This is unfortunate and is calling into question the very rationale of the organisation. The greatest challenge on this front was its assistance programme to Rwandese EDPs in Zaire in 1994-6, a programme that was unlawful on several counts. In fact, in many locations UNHCR is becoming little more than an emergency assistance agency for people in conflict, and is losing its special focus on refugees. Other agencies, national and international, can provide assistance, but only UNHCR has the legal mandate to protect and represent refugees according to the relevant international law. Recent developments are a disservice to genuine refugees and asylum seekers and create conflicts of interest within UNHCR.

This presents a challenge to Africa. If UNHCR does not improve on its mandate accountability then African measures to ensure it respects the law are required. African governments could insist on this in their country agreements with UNHCR—but this would not help in situations where there is little governmental authority. The OAU Commission of 21 could expand its office and monitor the performance and mandate accountability of UNHCR.

INTERNALLY DISPLACED PERSONS (IDPs)

There has been much debate on assistance and protection for IDPs in Africa. The nub of the argument is that (a) IDPs need assistance because they have been forced to move and (b) they are often victims of abuses perpetrated by their own governments, which therefore have little interest in protecting them. Among international agencies there have been repeated calls for UNHCR or another international organisation to have the mandate to intervene to provide them with assistance and protection, disregarding the attitude of the host government. Such a mandate and mode of operation is not likely to meet with much practical success, which is why there has not been any progress.

In fact, there are legal instruments that give protection (in theory) to most if not all of the rights of IDPs. There is a need to reaffirm these instruments and to collect them together in a single document. (These recommendations have been made before.)

Discussion of IDPs has been confused by the way in which they have been lumped together with refugees, as 'internal refugees' or as 'almost refugees' who may be about to cross an international border if they are not assisted where they are. Clarity can be introduced by a different approach, asking the questions:

1. Do the IDPs remain within a conflict zone, or have they fled away from the conflict zone?
2. Who is the de facto authority in the place where the IDPs are?
3. Are the IDPs subject to systematic discrimination and/or abuse, on the basis that they represent an 'enemy' populace?

If IDPs are in a peaceful zone, then respect for human rights is the responsibility of the governing authority (usually the government). In this case assistance can be provided through normal country channels. There is certainly a case for a human rights monitoring mechanism to ensure that the IDPs are respected.

If the IDPs are in a zone of conflict, then IHL takes over, and the IDPs are entitled to assistance and protection in common with other civilians in the war zone (see above). If the government refuses impartial humanitarian access to IDPs in a non-government zone, there is a strong case for solidarity assistance. Again, there is a strong case for monitoring compliance with IHL.

IDPs in a peaceful zone may require special protection, in a manner parallel to enemy nationals during an international war, because the government may consider them a subversive element or security threat. In these circumstances, human rights monitoring is especially important.

ASSISTANCE DURING PARTIAL OR COMPLETE STATE COLLAPSE

In cases of actual or potential state collapse, there is no conventional model of action. In such cases, more judgement calls are needed, and rules are harder to identify and follow. It is unfortunate that some international humanitarian agencies have rather relished the autonomy and freedom of action that exists in such situations, encouraging them to emphasise 'anarchy' and play down what elements of real authority do exist.

The danger in such situations is that assistance can help fuel conflict, maintain military forces, and undermine local civil authority. But in other situations there is an opportunity for assistance to have the opposite impact, namely to sustain and underwrite peace processes, and help stabilise civil authority.

Complex judgments are needed, in which IHL is not always useful. It is partly in response to such situations that the Red Cross and NGOs have developed 'humanitarian principles'. These are a potentially useful exercise, but their relevance and effectiveness is undermined by:

(a)The general ignorance of IHL among humanitarian staff;
(b)The tendency for humanitarian principles to supersede IHL rather than augment it;
(c)The stress on the privileges of aid agencies and their staff in the documents;
(d)A process of developing the principles that excludes the full involvement of African governments and political and military authorities;
(e)The attempt to make the principles universally valid, rather than just applicable to exceptional cases of state collapse.

The project of 'humanitarian principles' was initiated by UNICEF in Southern Sudan—a case of near-collapse. The programme was good at identifying general principles, but less good at helping relief agencies address practical dilemmas they faced in their work. It was hampered by the fact that while the SPLM was ready to enter into a dialogue, the Sudan Government was not—so that the different sectors of the operation were run according to different principles. In addition, the relief agencies appeared to believe that 'humanitarian principles' laid down the SPLA's obligations towards them, without corresponding obligations by the agencies towards the SPLA and local authorities. For example, international aid staff who are accused of corruption are not brought before local courts, but (at most) reassigned elsewhere.

In this situation, a better approach might have been to clarify mutual obligations under IHL, and to negotiate with both sides how development and capacity-building assistance could be provided under mutually-agreed terms, subject to some form of independent monitoring.

The D.R. Congo is a more complex and fluid case, but there are lessons that could be drawn from Sudan and applied.

(a)IHL remains a valid framework for humanitarian activity.

(b)This is complicated in the case of DRC because the DRC government has a duty to prevent and punish genocide, which entails disarming the former Rwandese Armed Forces present in the country and handing their leaders over to either Rwanda or the International Criminal Tribunal.

(c)There is a need for rehabilitation, development and capacity-building assistance in large parts of the country, in areas under government and rebel control. Such forms of assistance will be important in ensuring peace and stability, because local resource conflicts are a major contributor to national-level conflict. The capacity for international organisations to implement such programmes should be negotiated between the parties to the conflict.

In Somalia, not only is there no state, but attempts at rebuilding the state from the top have clearly failed. The alternative is approach is building from below, attempting a resource-driven solution. A detailed examination of this approach cannot be presented here.

EARLY WARNING

Information is power. The humanitarian information systems that exist reflect dominant paradigms of thinking and power relations. In addition, we cannot separate the information we want, and how we want it, from what sort of response is called for.

Information systems are essential for preventing and managing humanitarian crises. Accurate, timely and appropriate information can help prevent crises, while information flows during relief operations are essential to the efficiency and effectiveness of those operations. But from these obvious observations it does not follow that more information is necessarily better. Still less is it true that existing information systems perform their ostensible tasks.

This section will look at several different kinds of 'early warning systems' for drought, food shortage and conflict-related crisis.

'FAMINE EARLY WARNING' IN PEACETIME:
1. TECHNICALLY-BASED SYSTEMS

Since the droughts of the mid 1980s, there has been a proliferation of 'famine early warning' systems. The rationale for these systems is based on the proposal that if 'we' (i.e. western donors and the UN) had 'known' about the droughts in Sudan, Ethiopia, etc., earlier, something would have been done to prevent them. Lack of knowledge was blamed for the poor responses. In fact, this rationale is historically incorrect: enough information was available, but for political reasons governments, donors and the UN chose to interpret it in a certain way that precluded effective action. Early warning is something of a red herring: the issue is less one of information than the political trigger to action. However, early warning systems serve the important institutional purposes of allowing implementing agencies to cover their backs: in case of a crisis, they can say to donors 'I told you so'. One could argue that this is the real reason why they are maintained at such expense.

But, despite these criticisms, in principle the point is self-evident: for any sort of famine-prevention response, information is needed. The 'early warning' systems that have been established are based on the monitoring of the weather, areas planted, crop production, market prices, and other signs of distress such as malnutrition rates and displacement. There are two principal international large scale agricultural-information based systems, run by the FAO and the US Department of Agriculture, and others run by agencies such as USAID utilising market information as well. Most drought-prone countries have their own systems.

These systems have become extremely complex and sophisticated, and provide banks of data for statisticians. They have become well integrated with the annual round of national food needs assessments and food aid supply from major donors, and thus serve their basic purpose reasonably well. Several issues arise with them:

(i) They often replicate other capacity in government departments, such as agriculture, statistics, trade and health. Governments have to maintain the informational sections of these departments anyway, so an additional capacity purely for famine early warning introduces an element of redundancy, and consumes resources that could have been more efficiently utilised in upgrading existing capacities.

(ii) There is the problem of 'calibration'. Are the systems oriented towards big crises or little ones? For a major nationwide drought crisis, it is arguable that the routine agricultural statistics collected by agricultural departments, however unreliable and slow, will serve well enough. For small crises, more skill is needed, but it is arguable that such highly centralised and sophisticated systems are unnecessary.

(iii) The system is geared towards a certain kind of response, namely a big external supply of food aid. One of the reasons why donors need early warning is that delivering large quantities of food takes a very long time, so advance warning is needed. If alternative models of response are given priority, then the demands of the system can be changed. For example, if most of the food is to be purchased in-country, then a much shorter lead time is needed. Similarly if the country has developed a national food security policy that involves grain banks for emergency supplies.

(iv) Similarly, if 'normal' or 'peacetime' relief is to be institutionally integrated into development strategies and governmental institutions, then a different set of procedures is called for. Rather than a parallel system specifically geared to the needs of food-aid suppliers, a system integrated within the relevant ministries could be developed which initiates sector-specific responses. For example, for public health planning for emergencies, the key question is not 'when will the crisis occur?' but 'where will it occur and who will it affect?' If this is known, then basic public health infrastructure can be established with the aim of (a) serving needs in ordinary times and (b) being on hand for emergency response. This is similar for ministries of agriculture, public works, etc, who can have stand by labour-intensive programmes prepared for such eventualities.

(v)The biggest question with technically-based early warning systems is the trigger to action. This is the 'missing link' between good information and famine prevention. All early warning systems are based in technical departments that do not have the political clout to initiate responses themselves. They may work reasonably well within a routinised process of national food needs assessment and donor provision, but once that routine breaks down (e.g. in the case of a major crisis—just when it is most needed), political action is needed. The early warning system will absolve the technical departments of blame for having failed to inform their political masters, but will not solve the problem. Solving this problem requires a political commitment to fighting famine.

2. MEDIA AND PUBLIC REPORTING

A parallel and complementary system for famine early warning can be provided by the press. If there are press reports of imminent food shortages, the information of an impending crisis can be accurately assessed and widely known. This may not be as rapid as a technical system that has access to satellite monitoring of weather patterns, but it is more likely to be accurate on the ground (farmers know the prospects for their crops better than any satellites or any outside experts). Moreover, because the information is in the public domain, it can provide the missing political trigger to action. In the history of famine prevention in India, the Indian press has played a key role in initiating timely and effective responses. This does not replace a technical early warning system, but it augments it and provides a means of monitoring it that is, in principle, open to democratic scrutiny.

In India, this works because of the entrenched liberal values in large sections of the independent national press, and the pluralist political system. In particular, the newspapers and radio are responsive to their readers and listeners, who are themselves residents of areas likely to be affected by any food shortages. The press has become a democratic watchdog. It is not likely to work so well in many African countries, without such developed traditions of a free press, and without the same public awareness of the politics of food. Other civic organisations like farmers associations, rural councils, traders associations and the like should be encouraged to take up campaigning on issues of food and hunger as their democratic right.

The international media does not play this role. Occasionally, the international media 'discovers' a famine (such as Jonathan Dimbleby in Ethiopia in 1973) but this is not exactly an early warning and such situations are exceptional. On the contrary, the tendency for the international media to sensationalise, exaggerate and distort has become one of the problems in developing sound public policy towards famine prevention and relief.

The domestic media in any country cannot be expected to provide a timely and unbiased view of humanitarian crises in wartime. In peacetime, however, the capacity is there. This requires greater expertise and sensitivity among correspondents to the issues, and also a demand from readers and listeners to investigate¾in short, the beginnings of a democratic politics of food. Journalists' sources of information should be both technical early warning systems and the citizens themselves. With a government responsive to democratic pressure, this should help to solve the problem of the lack of a 'trigger'. This can assist in creating a genuine anti-famine political contract.

CONCLUSION

There has been much technical progress in famine early-warning in peacetime over the last fifteen years. However, the systems that exist are (1) geared to the institutional needs of food aid donor organisations and (2) are often not well-integrated into the democratic development of the host countries. There are important areas for both policy and democratic improvement, including (1) integrating early warning systems into wider national health and developmental planning and (2) developing the capacity of citizens groups and national media to investigate the issue.

EARLY WARNING FOR HUMANITARIAN
CRISES RELATED TO CONFLICT

The challenges of conflict-related humanitarian crises are much greater. Currently there are three main sources of 'early warning' information: (1) systems set up by the UN and international agencies; (2) internal government systems; and (3) public systems (the media). None of these operate in a way that meets the requirements for timely and appropriate humanitarian action in conflict.

It is intrinsically difficult to set up an early warning system for conflict. One reason for this is that those who start conflicts aim to exploit the element of surprise-or at any rate, keep their intentions secret. If someone had ever succeeded in building an effective system, perhaps most of the world's conflicts would have been prevented. As a result, most information systems for conflict zones tend to be means of keeping up to date on developments, rather than providing advance warning of what may happen next.

1.INTERNATIONAL CONFLICT-RELATED INFORMATION SYSTEMS
An example of such a system is the Integrated Regional Information Network (IRIN) system run out of the UN in Nairobi which covers central and north-east Africa. It is not an early warning system, but more in the way of a wire news service. Similar examples include the OLS information system in Sudan and ad hoc UN-based systems for Somalia. Some private consultancies have also set themselves up in business by providing analyses and security-related information (e.g. the London-based Control Risks Group).

Separately or jointly, international agencies have their methods of assessing humanitarian needs (numbers of people in need, malnutrition levels, food availability, etc). These are necessary, though subject to some legitimate criticisms, including (a) that numbers of refugees and 'in need' people are commonly exaggerated, and (b) that initial analyses of local food systems are poor. However, the key aspects of the information systems are the collection, interpretation and use of political information.

Apart from the technical and survey information, these information systems tend in either of two directions, or both.

(i)They are simply news-coordination networks, receiving public reports from journalists (especially Reuters, AP and AFP) and international NGOs and UN agencies, and recycling them to subscribers. This seems a slender rationale for the expenditure of such substantial resources: subscribers could instead just read the newspapers and listen to the BBC 'Focus on Africa.'

(ii)They are a form of military intelligence. Relying on unattributable information and analyses, they provide confidential information and analysis to international organisations about what they believe will be the political and military developments in the region concerned.

In reality, the distinction between the two may not be clear cut. It is possible for a system to be ostensibly a public news-coordination network and privately an intelligence gathering and advisory service for international agencies. These agencies may then take on a security-related role, for example by calling for military intervention by former colonial powers.

Several aspects of these information systems warrant comment.

(i)They are exclusively oriented towards international agencies and their emergency departments. They do not serve the requirements of national institutions.

(ii)Although initially modelled on peacetime 'early warning systems' and deriving one of their justifications from this parallel, these are not early warning systems at all. There is no formal process of prediction, and analysis is left up to the reader (influenced by the editorial processes of the service editor, who may concentrate on alarmist or pessimistic reports).

(iii)There is no formal trigger to action. While a peacetime early warning system can have a threshold of alarm built into it, this is not so for a conflict-related information system.

(iv)They are needed because international humanitarian agencies are not ready to rely on the information produced by national authorities. They demand their own sources of information. To date, African governments and inter-governmental institutions have failed to generate credible information about the nature and extent of humanitarian crises. Humanitarian institutions cannot work in an informational vacuum.

(v)The international agencies feel a strong sense of threat from the political environment in which they work. They believe that they are working in a situation of disorder in which anything can happen, and that they are threatened by any organised forces in the region. Therefore they collect, overtly and covertly, political and security information. The paradigm of 'post-modern wars' (related to 'anarchy', 'neo-barbarism', 'neo-medievalism' etc) provides the ideological justification for believing that they cannot obtain guarantees of security from governmental structures, and instead must develop their own security and intelligence systems.

(vi)While international agencies continue to operate in their current manner, they will demand these sorts of informational and intelligence services. While there are fundamental problems with this working relationship, most of the time, the information services do not cause undue problems. But at times, the implications for national security can be disturbing.

For example, at the time of the planned international military intervention in Zaire in November 1996, the UN information systems in the region acted as the de facto 'intelligence' arm of the UN agencies which were calling for the intervention. The publicly available information provided by the information offices of the UN agencies and by IRIN provided no early warning information to support the claims by several international agencies (UN and NGO) that 'a million refugees will die before Christmas' which were used to justify calling for intervention. However, the agencies still made these claims, and called for troops.

Thereafter, the international agencies played a 'numbers game' to manufacture the claim that 200,000 so-called refugees had 'disappeared', presumed murdered, in Zaire. This claim overlooked (a) the failure to count the refugees in the camps before the war of November 1996, (b) the universal tendency for refugee numbers to be inflated, so that the missing 200,000 could largely be put down to an over-estimate of these numbers, and (c)the fact that many 'refugees' were an army, militia and camp followers. Some agencies (e.g. Oxfam) spoke of the missing refugees being 'airbrushed from history' and compared this episode to the US bombing of south-east Asia. Furthermore, we may note that in (a) the failure to count the refugees in the camps before the war of November 1996, (b) the universal tendency for refugee numbers to be inflated, so that the missing 200,000 could largely be put down to an over-estimate of these numbers, and (c) the fact that many 'refugees' were an army, militia and camp followers. Some agencies (e.g. Oxfam) spoke of the missing refugees being 'airbrushed from history' and compared this episode to the US bombing of south-east Asia. Furthermore, we may note that in April 1999 the UN suddenly 'discovered' between 110,000 and 170,000 refugees in eastern Zaire. This episode is a dramatic demonstration of the political way in which information can be manipulated.

These systems can be changed only if the institutional responses to emergencies are changed. While they may intermittently abuse their information systems, international agencies have genuine reasons for demanding them, under current conditions. Therefore the problems caused by abuse of information systems cannot be addressed in isolation from the wider problems of humanitarian responses to conflict situations.

4. INTERNAL GOVERNMENTAL INTELLIGENCE SYSTEMS

All governments, African and non-African, have their internal sources of information on conflicts in Africa. For such political emergencies, governments are the best informed, and the host government and its neighbours are best informed of all.

For obvious reasons, these systems do not work in a public manner. The information is not public. Nor is the analysis. There is no public political trigger to act on the basis of the information provided.

The intelligence systems of western governments cannot openly be used by neutral humanitarian agencies. But there is usually a discreet exchange of information and analysis between these agencies and their governments. This sometimes leads to friction when international NGOs seem to be privileged recipients of confidential information from western governments. The intelligence systems of host governments and their neighbours are not utilised as a resource for humanitarian response. For obvious reasons, African governments are not willing to share their information with international agencies. This situation seems unlikely to change.

5. THE MEDIA IN WARTIME

The media in wartime are a mixed blessing. International humanitarian law and human rights law all provide for some media access to war zones, and most armies have considered it in their interests to facilitate some access. One of the reasons for this is that some information about conflicts always comes out, and when journalists are denied access they assume the worst, and may take the propaganda claims of the other side more seriously than they deserve. The allegations over large massacres by the alliance forces in Zaire are a case in point. Protecting journalists is also in commanders' interests, as a dead journalist is by definition bad news. The Geneva Conventions provide for special insignia and special protection to journalists in war zones, but do not guarantee their right to obtain information¾some censorship is a military necessity.

But the international media also distorts its presentation of conflict in Africa. This is particularly the case for television. Journalists are under pressure to shorten, simplify and dramatise, and in the case of TV, to get dramatic pictures. They will fall back upon shorthand terms that their readers and viewers will understand (notably 'anarchy' and 'tribalism') which distort the realities. Political analysis is sacrificed for immediacy and the 'human angle'. They will cover bad news and not good. This contributes to the paradigms of 'post-modern' conflict and the belief that Africa cannot achieve legitimate governmental systems.

Also, foreign correspondents often team up with international humanitarian agencies: the journalists focus on the work of the international agencies, while the latter provide logistics, accommodation and analysis. This often means that the 'story' is the work of a foreign relief agency, told from their point of view. In extreme cases, 'news' and 'international NGO commercials' become almost the same thing. A claim by a relief agency ('agency x claims a million face starvation') is often a news story in itself. Thus the international agencies become a crucial intermediary in how Africa is presented to Europe and north America¾and indeed other parts of Africa, given the dominance of international news corporations in the African continent itself.

The international media can be a direct stimulus to action by western governments. When fundamental national interests are at stake, a western government will be able to ignore media reports of mass human suffering. But when they are not, or when governments are particularly sensitive to the public mood on humanitarian issues (commonly just before Christmas), then they may be impelled to act. A western government may even be forced by a combination of media and NGO lobbying to act against its better judgement. (For example the US government reversed its position on military intervention in Zaire in November 1996 under such pressure, and changed from opposition to reluctant support.)

It is neither possible nor desirable for African governments to exercise total control over information concerning conflicts. Some information will always come out, and if one side is preventing any media access, the other will take advantage of it. While the African media remains in such a weak position vis-à-vis the main European and American networks, Africa will have to tolerate being simplified and distorted to fit non-African agendas. And while international relief agencies remain as central intermediaries in the presentation of Africa outside, their interests will be generally well-served by the media presentation of crises.

There are some more positive trends. There is a growing African media. Some journalists have always been honest and have struggled to present complicated realities in a truthful way. Some journalists have become, through experience, sceptical of the claims by international relief agencies, and can sometimes present more objective analyses. These can be important allies. They can be encouraged by providing more access for them, and thereby reducing journalists' reliance on relief agencies.

The global dominance of non-African news corporations has far-reaching consequences for the capacity of Africa to develop the intellectual capital and legitimate discourse for addressing its own problems. For this discussion, the problem lies with the prominent role of international relief agencies: if the negative implications of their high profile role can be overcome, then the distortions of the media will be less significant.

IMPLICATIONS

Establishing a conflict early warning system is an intrinsically difficult exercise. Perhaps the basic problem lies in the idea of 'early' warning, and a more productive approach would be to identify potential issues that might lead to conflict, and link them with potential institutional responses. This would imply a process of:

1. Building a database of all actual or potential sources of conflict in a subregion, including undemarcated borders, shared natural resources, religious or ethnic differences, high levels of smuggling, etc.

2. Create fora and training programmes so that officials in foreign ministries, security services, inter-governmental organisations etc., are aware of these issues and have channels of communication and a common framework of understanding.

The emphasis would then fall upon pre-emptive capacity building in existing institutions, so that conflict prevention can be facilitated, and rapid response to imminent conflict becomes easier.

No system aimed at conflict prevention, early warning or rapid response can be foolproof. Those who have an interest in sparking conflict will seek ways to maximise their use of surprise, outwitting whatever institutions exist. But this lack of perfection should not cause us to be fatalistic.

DONOR AID CONDITIONALITIES

Donor aid conditionalities ostensibly try to achieve political and human rights goals that are secondary to the aid itself. In principle, the tying of aid to human rights, democracy and lack of corruption could mean many things, including rewarding compliant states with extra aid, financing long-term programmes for instilling human rights, democracy etc., alongside restricting aid in response to violations. In practice, donors have found it extremely difficult to strike the right balance.

• There is a natural tendency for an aid programme, once it is underway, to continue even when there is evidence that it is not working, and there is evidence of human rights abuses that might warrant its closure. The aid business is governed by a basic demand to preserve jobs, spend budgets and maintain influence. As a result, there is a tendency for established aid programmes to resist investigating human rights concerns that might jeopardise their existence.

• When donors do invoke some form of sanctioning, by far the largest element is punitive conditionality: withdrawing aid in response to alleged violations. In order to overcome the institutional conservatism in any aid programme, a high-level political decision is needed—and this usually entails a blunt or clumsy intervention, i.e. punitive sanctioning. An aid donor clearly has the right under international law to impose conditions. In fact, because aid is limited it is rationed, and if conditionalities are not explicit, they are implicit. Aid is an instrument of foreign policy and it is the privilege of a sovereign donor government to use it as it thinks fit. But if a donor genuinely believes that it is promoting human rights and democracy through aid conditionalities, it is almost certainly mistaken.

Donor conditionalities on aid are thus commonly caught between the institutional interests of self-preservation in the aid industry, and the clumsiness of the instrument of sanctioning.

PROBLEMS WITH HUMAN RIGHTS CONDITIONALITIES
There are many problems with human rights and related conditionalities for aid. In fact, few conditionalities prove effective, for various reasons.

(i) Donor double standards. Donors tend to apply these conditions to countries that are far away and have little strategic or commercial importance to them, or which do not have a vocal diaspora among their domestic constituents. This is inevitable. States have interests which are more important than protecting non-citizens in far away countries.

(ii) Changing fashions. Because the ethical element in donor foreign policies is so closely tied to their domestic concerns, and the domestic constituencies that are vocal on ethical issues are very volatile, and because most conditionalities do not work, policies change. One year it is human rights, the next it is democratisation, and the year after eliminating corruption. This inconsistency makes it very difficult for recipient countries to plan their policies accordingly, making it simpler to try and evade the sanctioning by other means.

(iii) Conditionality overload. The sheer number of legal conditions imposed by legislatures on many western donors foreign assistance makes it almost impossible to have an aid programme at all. Aid may be tied to release of political prisoners, competitive elections, gender policies, anti-abortion laws, environmental policies, minority rights, religious freedoms, etc. In practice most donors ignore most of these conditions most of the time, and most recipient countries are not even aware of the conditions until they may be suddenly invoked.

(iv) Conditionalities usually mean punitive sanctions. This is a cost-free way of making a political statement. In fact it can be an apparently principled way of cutting back an aid budget: a clever ruse to disarm a domestic aid lobby. Unfortunately there is rarely a corresponding reward or positive engagement by the donor. If a donor cuts off assistance to a police training programme because of alleged abuses by the police, it is rarely if ever linked to a commitment to restore or even increase the aid if the abuses are halted.

(v) Punitive sanctions are selectively imposed on the poorest and most aid-dependent countries. This is simply because that is where they are most likely to work. Cutting back on aid to a strong country (such as China) will have no effect and may even damage the donor. But if the recipient is Burundi, it may have some effect and the donor can get away with it.

(vi) Recipients facing high expectations that are not quite fulfilled suffer, while those with long-standing poor records may benefit from modest improvements. So for example, in his very first days in office, President Kabila was penalised for not being a perfect democrat, while President Mobutu had earlier earned aid benefits from his modest moves away from dictatorship.

(vii) There is a tendency to link human rights and economic doctrine. For most western donors it is an article of faith that political liberalisation and economic liberalisation go hand in hand. *Any* governmental intrusion into society is condemned as a human rights abuse when it may be a legitimate regulation of economic activity.

(viii) They often confuse governmental *inability* to ensure respect for human rights (e.g. when a government has inherited a country ravaged by years of misrule) with a government's *deliberate abuse* of human rights. This is a symptom of the wider problem that most African governments are simply too poor to operate good judicial systems, to have well-trained police forces and good quality prisons (etc.). And donor-dictated economic policies do not always make matters easier.

(ix) There is no right of appeal. Although punitive sanctions are imposed in the name of human rights they are not themselves subject to any due process at all. Donors do not have transparent decision-making procedures; there is no independent investigation of whether the initial charge was warranted; the sanctioned recipient has no right of appeal; and there are no independent means of establishing whether the abuse (if it occurred) has been corrected. This is a fundamental point.

If the aim of aid conditionalities are to develop human rights, the rule of law and democracy, they do not provide a good model themselves. They can only encourage cynicism among recipients, and therefore act counter to their stated intention.

In addition, the concept of 'human rights' cannot bear this huge and arbitrary burden. They have become 'overinflated' with unrealistic expectations, and used in an arbitrary way to justify policies that serve other ends.

IS THERE A ROLE FOR AID CONDITIONALITIES?

Links between aid and human rights are essential. But they should not be the haphazard kind outlined above and currently practised.

(i) Aid itself should be subject to the rule of law. Aid institutions should be subject to democratic processes. This is a condition that *recipients* should insist on. Donors, if they are serious about wanting to promote human rights etc, should also insist on it.

(ii) Similarly, in conflicts, assistance should be governed by the relevant provisions of IHL.

(iii) Positive engagement is important for donors. Countries in Africa, especially those emerging from decades of misrule, need law and order institutions: judicial systems, police forces, prisons, human rights education, etc. Donors can assist.

(iv) Protest withdrawal is an effective instrument for an aid agency, in extremis. For example, development or relief programmes may become pointless in an environment of extreme abuses of human rights, leaving development agencies with no option but to withdraw. The act of withdrawal can also have the effect of drawing public attention to the human rights situation. (MSF's withdrawal from Ethiopia in 1985 over the resettlement issue and Community Aid Abroad's from Somalia in 1989 over the war in the north are examples.) The force of these cases derives partly from their exceptional nature: this is a weapon easily misused or over-used.

Given the highly heterogeneous and often competitive nature of the aid business, it is unlikely that donors will be ready or able to coordinate strategies on these difficult issues. This strengthens the position of the recipient country, which can use this advantage either positively or negatively.

RECIPIENT AID CONDITIONALITIES

Based on long-standing and intimate experiences of the aid encounter, Africans can make some constructive proposals for how to democratise the aid process: by recipient aid conditionalities.

The aim of these conditionalities would be to make the whole process of sanctioning and imposing conditionalities more transparent, predictable and fair.

The ideal is some sort of mechanism for examination of conditionalities and aid sanctions, that would allow for independent assessment and monitoring of what the conditionalities are, whether the aims are being met, and whether the process of imposing conditionalities or aid sanctions has been through a due process. If donors are unready to cooperate with such a mechanism—which is probable—then a citizens' group from across the continent could take on this task, in an informal manner, using international public opinion to expose and embarrass.

CONCLUSIONS

This chapter has made few suggestions for specific institutions that can be created. Instead it has concentrated on the regulatory and legal frameworks that could make humanitarian assistance (most of it internationally-financed) more effective and compatible with the goals of democratisation, competitiveness and observance of IHL. By changing these frameworks¾a project that will take several years¾it is hoped that a conducive environment will be created for appropriate humanitarian institutions to grow, while those that are not well suited to African realities will disappear.

The main (tentative) recommendations are, for peacetime relief:

• A variety of mechanisms for democratising the aid process.
• Subjecting emergency service delivery to the constraints of commercial competition.

For humanitarianism in conflict:

• Asserting the primacy of IHL.
• Institutionally separating wartime and peacetime programmes, and considering options for the administration of UN programmes in war areas.
• Giving a monitoring role to the UN Humanitarian Fact Finding Commission or an appropriate OAU mechanism.

The issue of information and 'early warning' in situations of conflict cannot be distinguished form the institutional mechanisms for humanitarian response, and the political interests at work in those institutions. In the long term, Africa needs to develop its own media, its own intellectual and academic paradigms, its own institutions for humanitarian action etc. In the meantime, more effective use of national media is perhaps the most important issue.

NOTES

1. There is a grey area where private donations receive tax relief, resulting in a semi-private fund.
2. Note that this discussion is concerned with relief and basic welfare only, not development and activities such as promoting human rights, which have their own constraints.
3. There are some contradictions between the Declaration on the Rights of the Child, a human rights document, and the provisions of IHL, which require clarification. For example, 'children' in the age group 16-17 may bear arms and thus be combatants under IHL, but still appear to be fully entitled to the protection of the Rights of the Child.

7

International Humanitarian Law

'The road to international hell is paved with "good" conventions.'
— Bert Röling, international jurist

Overview of International Humanitarian Law

International humanitarian law (IHL), also known as 'the laws of war', are a necessary paradox. They seek to regulate and humanise the most unregulated and inhuman of all activities, namely warfare. Historically, all societies have recognised the concept of warriors' honour and the need to keep warfare within bounds. The laws of war are thus an older legal tradition than human rights law. The respect they have earned is founded on their realism and practicability. They recognise legitimate military objectives in a way that almost all military commanders will find acceptable. They do not pass judgement on the right to wage armed struggle, neither do they appeal for peace at any cost nor pronounce one belligerent to be inherently 'just' and the other not.

Since 1945, IHL has been developed and gained unprecedented international recognition. The conventions adopted in the period 1948-51 mark the high point of international humanitarian legislation: instruments that are tough, workable and fair. The Conventions adopted in that period are the foundation of IHL:

- The Genocide Convention of 1948.
- The four Geneva Conventions of 1949.

• The UN Refugee Convention of 1951.

These fundamental documents of IHL were all drafted in the six years following the end of World War II in Europe/North Africa and East Asia. The main European and North American powers and many lesser powers (excluding the defeated Germans and Japanese) were well-represented in a series of diplomatic conferences. The motives of the lawyers, diplomats and generals who drafted the laws were to avoid the horrors of genocide, total war and mass displacement that they had recently endured, while recognising the reality that conflicts would continue in future, and that the interests of states as belligerent parties needed to be recognised. The basic instruments of IHL are therefore a pragmatic compromise between the necessities of war and statecraft, and the desire to limit inhumanity and absolutely prevent its worst manifestation, namely genocide. As for preventing war, that is the role of the United Nations itself.

The Geneva Conventions may be criticised as the work of imperial powers, still determined to exercise force as they saw fit. Major weapons used by the victorious WW2 Allies, such as aerial bombardment of cities and use of nuclear weapons, are notable by their absence. But this realism, while a cause for some cynicism, is also a strength: IHL is not idealistic, it cannot be criticised for being impossible to implement.

More recent developments have been a mixed blessing. The refinements of refugee law in the 1960s and 1980s were necessary. The Additional Protocols to the Geneva Conventions, agreed in 1977, filled some important gaps in their predecessors, but also blurred some important distinctions and were written in a legalistic manner that made them more remote from the realities of war. One authoritative commentator (Prof. Geoffrey Best) has concluded that their impact was to make IHL 'overinflated.' That comment was made before a flurry of ad hoc legislation by the UN Security Council in the 1990s, prompted in turn by its leading western members, who were themselves pressured by humanitarian agencies. A succession of Security Council resolutions has introduced the right of humanitarian intervention and changed the focus of much IHL from the legal protection of non-combatants to the physical protection of aid givers. Combined with the blurring of legal mandates of humanitarian organisations, notably UNHCR, this has grossly overinflated contemporary IHL and brought it to a state of crisis.

The Genocide Convention—the simplest and strongest of all instruments of international law—is discussed in issue chapter 2. The 'Hague laws' which seek to limit the kinds of weapons used are a variant of IHL which will be discussed in this chapter. The most famous of these conventions are the 1925 prohibition on chemical weapons and the 1997 Ottawa Convention on the prohibition of anti-personnel land mines.

This chapter examines the rationale of IHL and its relevance to contemporary Africa, with particular focus on the rights of civilians and the roles of humanitarian organisations. It argues that IHL as developed between the 1940s and the 1980s has limitations, some of them quite severe, but that should not be considered sufficient reason to embrace the developments of the 1990s. On the contrary, it is argued that the basic tenets of IHL retain lasting relevance and should be reaffirmed. On the other hand, most recent innovations in IHL adopted by the UN Security Council and international humanitarian agencies have proved regressive and should be rejected. There is also room for some cautious reform.

IHL concerns humanity during conflict. This necessarily limits the scope for democratic accountability. However, the issues of legality and legal accountability, humanity and appropriateness are all highly relevant.

THE GENEVA CONVENTIONS:
PRINCIPLES AND OPPORTUNITIES
The Geneva Conventions of 1949 are notable in that they go much further than previous instruments of IHL in extending protection to civilians caught up in conflicts. This reflected the realities of WW2 and was to prove highly relevant to subsequent conflicts. However, compared with previous instruments of IHL, there are many continuities. Six elements of the Geneva Conventions are notably relevant to this chapter:

1. Although adopted shortly after the UN passed the Universal Declaration of Human Rights, the Geneva Conventions are not hu-

man rights documents. IHL is an older and more pragmatic tradition than human rights law, which is often not well suited to the realities of warfare. The Geneva Conventions do make reference to the rights of individuals (notably in Common Article 3), but essentially they deal with a situation outside human rights law, namely the obligations of states, as belligerents, to individuals who are not their citizens. With the gradual extension of IHL to cover internal conflicts (especially with the Second Additional Protocol of 1977) this distinction became blurred even further, but a fundamental distinction remains between IHL and human rights law. Under IHL it is legitimate to kill and injure enemy combatants, and it is permissible to attack legitimate military targets. Under human rights law, the right to life is paramount and non-derogable.

The recent tendency for fusing human rights law with IHL is therefore fraught with dangers. It invites bringing both IHL and human rights law into disrepute, because armed conflicts inevitably involve violations of rights (thus inviting belligerents to disregard human rights entirely, even in peacetime), and if rights violations are seen as violations of IHL, then IHL will come to be seen as impracticable and irrelevant. Instead, is seems to be more appropriate, practical and humane to maintain the separation between IHL and human rights law.

2. The term 'protection' is central to IHL. 'Protection' is a legal term of art. It does not refer to the actual legal capacity to protect an individual, still less the physical ability or right to do so. A 'protected' individual is one whom a combatant should try not to kill or injure. As in many aspects of IHL, this modest but realistic measure has been inflated by commentators with little knowledge to imply a legal duty not to harm 'protected' persons under any circumstances (not correct: 'imperative military necessity' overrides) or even further to imply a legal right to intervene to provide physical protection for non-combatants (an option never even considered in the Geneva Conventions).

There are many steps that can be taken to give practical meaning to 'protection'. These include: greater awareness of IHL among soldiers, officers and politicians; more internal and independent investigations into allegations of breaches of IHL, and more measures against those responsible for them; more mechanisms for monitoring adherence to IHL and for providing avenues for civilians to complain.

It is not appropriate to try and give meaning to 'protection' by awarding the right to intervene militarily to external powers, above all not former colonial powers.

3. IHL is concerned with the 'protection' of non-combatants, namely the injured and others hors de combat, prisoners of war, the shipwrecked, civilians in the zone of conflict, and non-nationals in the territory of a party to a conflict. It is secondarily concerned with the provision of essential medical and other supplies. The drafters of the 1949 Conventions had assumed that most wars would be between states and that the states themselves would be the providers of assistance. The Conventions make reference to the ICRC and, in passing, to other impartial providers of assistance, but very little protection is afforded to them. The 1977 Protocols extended this protection somewhat, but it remained essentially secondary to the main purpose of IHL.

The drafters of the Geneva Conventions were well aware that relief supplies could be abused, and placed very strict conditions on impartial assistance for it to qualify for any form of (legal) protection. It must be agreed by the belligerents, subject to their inspection, and there must be no reason to doubt that it is being used for military advantage in any way.

These elements of the Geneva Conventions are strong and can be reaffirmed. Aspects of the 1977 Protocols need to be clarified to underline that they are not a license for international organisations to act with impunity. The idea that international organisations are the privileged subjects of IHL should be rejected.

4. IHL is built around a recognition of military necessity. Article 52 of Additional Protocol I provides the following definition:

> Military objectives are limited to those objects which by their nature, location, purpose or use make an effective contribution to military action and whose total or partial destruction, capture or neutralisation, in the circumstances ruling at the time, offers a definite military advantage.

Characteristically, IHL is worded in terms of *preventing* or limiting military action, but the effect is to *permit* military actio Related to this is a central concept in IHL: proportionality: the degree of force used by a belligerent should be proportionate to the military objective to be attained. The use of excessive force may cause civilian casualties or damage disproportionate to the military objective. Proportionality is necessarily an indeterminate concept and can only be applied subjectively by a military commander in the field, but is a determining principle nonetheless.

The concepts of military necessity and proportionality are relevant and valid and should be retained. In current circumstances where many international organisations appear to believe that IHL is about preventing all state violence, these concepts need to be reaffirmed.

5. IHL is essentially about the obligations on soldiers. But in the circumstances of modern wars, both conventional and guerrilla, civilians are often present in large numbers in zones of combat. Obligations on civilians must be read between the lines of the Conventions rather than being directly stated. The principal factor here is that the presence of civilians does not render a place immune from attack, implying that there is an obligation on civilians not to allow themselves to be used in this way.

Particularly in the 1977 Additional Protocols, which were drafted in the light of wars of national liberation, there is no satisfactory resolution of the status of civilians who may also be an integral part of a war-fighting capacity. The law tries to hold a firm line, providing legal protection to civilians, in their capacity as civilians, even though they may be part-time guerrillas. But this is clearly incompatible with the acknowledgement of military necessity.

This area of IHL is a prime instance of 'overinflation': it invites abuses and therefore awaits clarification. This is an area where the legal advisers to African governments should consider reform.

6. Respect for the provisions of IHL makes the construction of peace easier. Although this principle is nowhere stated in any text of IHL, the retention of humanity in warfare is an important foundation for peace negotiation and post-war reconciliation. Belligerents that

respect IHL are thereby respecting the humanity of the enemy, and earning that respect in return.

IMPLEMENTATION OF IHL

The overwhelming responsibility for implementing the Geneva Conventions falls upon the belligerents themselves, assisted by either a neutral 'protecting power' (a third country that takes on this role) or the ICRC. The 'protecting power' provision has been rarely used and instead the ICRC has taken the prime role. This carries with it very heavy obligations for preserving not only neutrality but the appearance of neutrality. The principal responsibility for enforcement and dissemination (i.e. public education) is domestic.

Enforcement of IHL has always been problematic. The Nuremburg and Tokyo International Military Tribunals set a precedent for the criminal prosecution of those charged with war crimes and crimes against humanity. It was only in the late 1980s that the UN began to follow this up, first with investigations into violations of IHL in the Iraq-Iran war and subsequently in other conflicts (Iraq-Kuwait, Former Yugoslavia and Rwanda). The last two cases have seen the creation of International Criminal Tribunals. A standing International Criminal Court was agreed at the 1998 Rome Conference and will be established in the coming years. Cases brought under the domestic law of individual countries, such as the charges brought against General Augusto Pinochet, are also increasing, and the principle of extra-territorial jurisdiction for crimes against humanity is more widely accepted. The 1977 Protocols also envisaged an international humanitarian fact finding commission, which was set up in 1991 but which has been inactive. The UN's involvement in this area has created a conflict of interest with the UN's other activities, notably negotiating to establish peace. This has been especially marked in Former Yugoslavia, and is an issue that will handicap further development of mechanisms to enforce IHL.

In Africa, there is wide experience of trying to bring accountability for war crimes and crimes against humanity. These include the Special Prosecutor's Office in Ethiopia, the Truth and Reconciliation Commission in South Africa, the current prosecutions in Rwanda, and, among others, similar exercises in Uganda and Namibia. Establishing either a standing African court for crimes against humanity, or common standards for accountability for such crimes, should be considered.

One of the main themes of this chapter is that ambitious attempts to enforce a particular understanding of IHL have clashed with realities on the ground (notably in Central Africa), creating the danger of discrediting IHL altogether. This leads us to a general rule: any mechanisms for enforcement of IHL, such as criminal courts, should be based upon a wide consensus about what is ethical and what is not, that includes politicians and military commanders. The process of generating this wide consensus, through diplomatic conferences and the like, is therefore an integral part of building an effective enforcement mechanism. Similarly, the priority in Africa is not new and more refined law, but the dissemination and implementation of existing law.

IHL AND CONTEMPORARY AFRICA

The 1990s has seen two major developments relevant to IHL (and also refugee law) in Africa. The first is the changing nature of warfare, state power and population displacement. The second is the overinflation of some concepts derived from IHL, which have undermined the law itself.

There is no doubt that the 1990s have seen changes in the nature of conflict in Africa, related to the erosion of the power of central governments, the widespread availability of armaments, and economic liberalisation and globalisation. This has been accompanied by many grave violations of IHL. However, contrary to some European and American theorists, this does not amount to the demise of the legitimate African government and its replacement with 'warlords' and 'post-adjustment rulers' whose political projects do not require territorial control or any form of popular consent. Conventional IHL remains highly relevant to wars in Africa.

However, in the 1990s, IHL has been brought into disrepute in Africa. This began in Somalia (and to a lesser extent, Liberia) but reached a crisis in former Zaire in 1996. This happened because the United Nations itself undermined the very principles on which IHL is based. It came about through extreme over-inflation of some concepts of humanitarianism. This has profound consequences for the future of IHL and indeed the future of the African continent.

The Fundamental Challenge:
Improving Soldiers' Behaviour

By far the most important challenge facing IHL is to improve soldiers' respect for it. This does not require new legislation but the dissemination of the existing corpus of law. There is a tendency in the international community, also found in Africa, to have lower standards with respect to Africa, and to allow African armies to get away with poor levels of respect for IHL, on the spurious grounds that nothing better should be expected in Africa. This is not acceptable: the standards of IHL apply everywhere. The challenges of bringing African soldiers' respect for IHL up to the required standard includes the following:

1. Promoting discipline and self-esteem among soldiers. A good army requires its troops to show moral qualities including restraint, readiness to follow orders, good behaviour, etc. Wearing the uniform should be a matter of pride. IHL is only enforceable if armies are sufficiently organised to have coherent command structures, discipline etc. It is also interesting to note that effective disarmament and demobilisation depends upon a high level of discipline and effective command in the forces to be demobilised—or the demobbees are likely to turn to banditry or insurrection. Ironically, the first task of a demobilisation programme may be to train the troops to be more disciplined!

2. Dissemination of the Geneva Conventions and promoting understanding of them among soldiers and commanders. The concept of the 'warrior's honour' is found among all armies and is a sound basis for developing education on humanitarian law. But most soldiers, commanders and civilians in Africa do not know about IHL. (The same is true in Europe and America.) This means that they tend either to believe that there is no attempt to introduce humanity into warfare, or that only the 'humanitarian principles' of international agencies exist. It is important that African governments take seriously the task of public education about IHL. This education should be targetted in particular at soldiers, commanders, civil servants and political leaders, for it is they who take the key decisions, and authorise or permit the violations that are so regrettably common.

3. Development of domestic measures for enforcement of IHL. The primary responsibility for implementing IHL falls upon armies themselves and national governments. Internal disciplinary procedures within armed forces need to be strengthened and brought into line with IHL where appropriate. Also, the appropriate elements of IHL can be introduced into domestic law.

4. Bringing armies under civilian control. Although this is not a strict requirement for IHL to be workable, armies under civilian control have greater potential for respecting IHL. They are less likely to act with impunity. In this way, the implementation of IHL is linked to the democratisation process.

THE 'RIGHT OF INTERVENTION' AND HUMANITARIAN POLITICS

The right of intervention has a long and disputed history. This is not the place to discuss the arguments. However, it does appear to be an accepted norm that one state can intervene militarily in another in order to protect its own citizens if they are at dire risk, or to forestall a major crime such as genocide. Fundamentally, it is a principle in international law (the law regulating relations between states and the right to wage war) rather than IHL (regulating conflict once it has begun and rights in war).

Recent problems with humanitarian intervention in Africa have not arisen because of the invalidity of the concept, but with the manner in which it has been applied. This in turn has arisen because, in the US, the UN and among international agencies, humanitarian sentiment has become a camoflage for other interests, and those interests have in turn manipulated humanitarian law. This reflects the weakness of Africa as much as the power of the US and Europe.

IHL is founded on realism: it acknowledges political realities and the necessities of war-fighting. In the 1940s, the realities were the power interests of states and armies, which were partly influenced by public opinion. In the 1970s, liberation politics had an appreciable influence on IHL. But by the 1990s, a new political player had emerged: international humanitarian agencies. A complex alliance emerged of the 'humanitarian international' (UN agencies, relief NGOs, human rights organisations, journalists) with western governments, which were simultaneously responding to the public mood at home and trying not to become politically entangled themselves.

The assertive international humanitarians have under their command an army of lawyers, journalists, lobbyists, diplomats, public relations specialists, etc. African political leaders and military commanders who actually fight wars in Africa have no such weapons, though it is ultimately their responsibility to ensure respect for IHL. The political balance between war-fighters and 'humanitarians' has always been essential to the realism of IHL. This balance was now lost.

The outcome was the 'right of intervention' and indeed the 'duty of intervention'. It is no surprise that the strongest advocates of this doctrine have been French organisations with a strong commitment to symbolic and theatrical action rather than patient problem-solving. The ultimate outcome of this approach is the doctrine of 'humanitarian impunity': humanitarian organisations can do no wrong; they are above the law. Unsurprisingly, humanitarian institutions vigorously dispute this interpretation. But Africans who have experienced the humanitarian international in full force are more sceptical about the motives and likely outcomes of interventions.

One of the main weapons of the advocates of this approach has been a lazy reading of IHL. They have inferred from the idea that civilians in war are 'protected' that there is a duty to provide them with physical protection. At a simplistic moral level this makes sense, but it is wholly unsupported by IHL. Nonetheless, the political clout of the advocates of this approach have been such that, given the right circumstances, they have been able to reformulate IHL. They did not need a diplomatic conference (as in 1949 or 1973-7). In fact, such a conference would have blocked their vague but radical 'humanitarian' legal agenda. So, instead, to placate public opinion in the west, the UN Security Council passed a series of ad hoc but far-reaching resolutions (Iraqi Kurdistan, Somalia, Former Yugoslavia).

In November-December 1992, the UN authorised United States military intervention in Somalia. The context was the conflict and famine in Somalia, which ironically were at that moment taking a marked turn for the better. There is little doubt that the reasons for the intervention had more to do with the US's need to develop a new tool for international politics and the relief agencies' need for more funds. (Reluctant to intervene in Bosnia, one senior US general told President Bush: 'we do deserts; we don't do mountains').

These political interests were reflected in the legal mandate of Operation Restore Hope: this was to 'create a secure environment for the delivery of humanitarian relief.' I.e. the subjects of the intervention were the relief agencies, not the Somalis. By these means, the international legal precept of humanitarian intervention was becoming mixed up in the principles of IHL. The end result was that one undermined the other.

In May 1993, the UN authorised 'all necessary measures' for the capture of General Mohamed Farah Aidid. The UN forces themselves violated the Geneva Conventions in their battles in Mogadishu, justifying this on the grounds that they had been authorised by the world's highest legal authority, the UN Security Council. This was 'humanitarian impunity' par excellence. Only in 1999 did the UN formally instruct peacekeeping forces that they should be bound by IHL.

The 'right of intervention' was also invoked in Zaire in November 1996 by France and leading international humanitarian agencies. A French minister, when challenged with the point that 'humanitarian intervention' should mean at the very least enforcing the Genocide Convention and thus apprehending and punishing those guilty of genocide, replied that the humanitarianism of the French government went no further than delivering food and enforcing a ceasefire. Thus a very simplistic (and politically coloured) interpretation of 'humanitarianism' was being used to undermine some fundamental precepts of IHL.

It is pointless to argue whether these recent developments in IHL are 'legal' or 'illegal'. Though contrary to the spirit of the Geneva Conventions and other instruments of IHL, they have been approved by the UN Security Council (albeit casually, without even a fraction of the consideration that went into the Geneva Conventions). The point is that they are unworkable: they have over-inflated IHL to a point where the law has been brought into disrepute.

The core values and basic instruments of IHL need to be preserved. To do this requires reversing some of the recent innovations in 'humanitarian' action. This is not a simple process. It has legal, political and diplomatic elements. These might include:

• African governments, under the auspices of the OAU, reaffirming the basic documents of IHL. This could be done by convening a special diplomatic conference to consider specific aspects of IHL relevant to the African continent.

• African governments, through such a conference, rejecting the doctrine of humanitarian impunity and the privileges awarded to international humanitarian agencies.

• African governments, through such a conference, clarifying that 'humanitarian intervention' should it be carried out for whatever reason, must in its implementation (by both armed forces and humanitarian agencies) be subject to IHL.

• The United Nations reasserting the need for humanitarian agencies to be accountable within the framework of both international law and IHL.

• African governments reducing the influence of international humanitarian agencies by developing local alternative forms of humanitarian action.

It must be stressed that Africa does not need more instruments of IHL. There is a danger that diplomatic conferences end up by adopting new laws. The existing laws, with one or two exceptions, are quite enough.

'HUMANITARIAN PRINCIPLES' IN CENTRAL AFRICA

For understandable reasons, international humanitarian agencies are not content with IHL as enshrined in the Geneva Conventions. It places obligations on them that they may find onerous or inappropriate (impartiality, accountability to host governments), while giving them little freedom of action. Instead they have promoted 'humanitarian principles', which can mean different things:

1. 'Ground rules' for how humanitarian agencies and belligerent parties should behave in particular situations. These take the form of supplementary rules to IHL to enable humanitarian agencies and belligerents to define their obligations to one another. In this form, humanitarian principles are negotiated between the agencies and the belligerent forces for a specific situation.

2. An alternative body of law to IHL, which elevates certain elements of humanitarian action (specifically the delivery of relief commodities and the protection of international agencies) to become overriding principles. In this form, humanitarian principles tend to be a set of ideals categorically stated by an agency or agencies. Such principles can become a set of vague, generally laudable, but negotiable ideas of how humanitarian agencies and belligerents should behave.

These two forms of 'humanitarian principles' are distinct and should not be confused. The chief problems with type 1 'humanitarian principles' are that belligerent forces are constantly tempted to find open or secret means of violating the ground rules in order to advance their military and political interests. In such situations, monitoring is both essential and difficult-and often dangerous too. Mechanisms for adjudication of disputes and enforcement of rules are extremely difficult. The major instrument in the hands of the humanitarian agencies is withdrawal, a threat they are understandably reluctant to use too readily.

Major difficulties also arise with the second type. Type 2 'humanitarian principles' or hybrid forms have some virtues. They are an educational exercise. Humanitarian assistance needs some form of regulation. If the agencies can succeed in regulating themselves effectively then this means that others do not need to do it. They are an implicit acknowledgement that the morality of humanitarian agencies is open to question and needs some codification. They may succeed in dampening some of the aid donors' political manipulations of relief. (Then again, they may not—for example they are ill-suited to dealing with the major distortion whereby refugees in the Balkans receive far more assistance than those in Africa).

However, type 2 'humanitarian principles' suffer from a number of disabling defects. They have been negotiated by the agencies among themselves, rather than with governments and belligerents. There is no diplomatic forum in which governments and the UN can discuss them, and amend, adopt or ratify them. It is not clear what accepting them actually means.

Similarly there are no legally accepted norms and procedures for evaluation or enforcement. There can be widely differing interpretations of what they mean. They may be contradictory, and in such cases there are no clear guidelines for which principles should take priority.

They are negotiable: they are statements of intent rather than law. They are 'soft law.' When they are put on a par with the authentic instruments of IHL, such as the Geneva Conventions, they therefore undermine the latter, by making these negotiable too.

They confuse human rights law, IHL, international law, the 'soft law' of humanitarian aspiration, and professional standards. Despite their claims to universality, they are grounded in the specific historical experience of western humanitarian agencies, and are not rooted in African traditions and historical realities to the same extent. They are very 'overinflated'. For example they disclaim any conditionality on assistance, saying that agencies should treat all suffering people alike and that humanitarianism means that no conditions at all should be considered. Relief assistance is never enough: it is not a free good: hence in practice it is always rationed, and the agencies' conditionalities are merely unspoken.

As a result of this, they are open to abuse. Violation of a 'humanitarian principle' can lead, without due process of investigation, to a 'humanitarian' response that is wildly inappropriate and subject to abuse.

Type 2 humanitarian principles can become indistinguishable from internal regulatory schemes and statements of principle from international agencies. The Red Cross's ten-point 'Code of Conduct', drawn up in 1994 and 'approved' by governments and NGOs in 1995, consists principally of abstract statements about the aims of humanitarian relief, and concrete demands from host governments and belligerents to respect and privilege relief agencies. A professor of international relations commented:[1]

Not one of the ten points addressed in any way the critical issue of how to protect vulnerable populations and aid activities, nor how impartial relief work could be combined with human-rights advocacy, sanctions or other coercive measures. [Donor] governments and NGOs appeared to be addressing humanitarian issues in a pious and abstract manner far removed from the harsh dilemmas resulting from wars.

The men and women who drafted the Geneva Conventions would have been shocked by such naivete. The SPHERE Humanitarian Charter is comparable: the principles laid down, such as neutrality, impartiality and independence, seek to guide the actions of agencies in general, rather than providing concrete guidelines for action when faced with particular situations.

A particular problem with type 2 humanitarian principles is that they may seek to do too much. Humanitarian agencies are typically also development agencies, committed to support for local organisations, capacity building, advocacy on behalf of the poor and oppressed etc. These are all tasks that are needed in war situations. But an agency that starts down the road of implementing developmental-type programming in a war situation will inevitably end up acting as a solidarity-type agency, supporting one or other belligerent party. This assistance can be genuinely humanitarian-but it can also be incompatible with neutrality.

More widely, type 2 humanitarian principles provide much leeway for differing interpretations by different agencies. Arguably it would be better to have a minimal set of requirements that are required for assistance to count as 'humanitarian', and leave the remainder to discretion. Responding to real human need would be essential, but neutrality and independence would be optional.

Turning to abuse of humanitarian principles, a striking example is the call by leading agencies for military intervention to protect the UNHCR camps in eastern Zaire in November 1996. The agencies claimed that major violations of humanitarian principles were being perpetrated. These included: forcing international agencies to withdraw; attacking UNHCR camps with armed forces; and the prospect of mass deaths from starvation. They spoke of the violation of 'humanitarian space', a concept without either legal or practical force—or indeed any definition at all—as though it were a crime against humanity. Assuming that 'humanitarian principles' were equivalent to international law and IHL, several relief agencies claimed that the military assault on the camps by the Rwandese army and the AFDL was illegal under both international law and IHL. They therefore called for a foreign military force to be sent to protect the refugees and enforce humanitarian law (though, as noted above, the French interpretation of this extended only to delivering food and enforcing a ceasefire). All these counts were incorrect:

1. The camps were not refugee camps and the people in them were not refugees (see below).
2. The concept of 'protection' in IHL does not refer to physical protection.
3. International law does not prohibit military action against insurgent military forces based in a neighbouring country, when the neighbour's own forces have failed to contain them.
4. IHL does not prohibit attacks on populated areas including 'refugee' camps when they contain legitimate military targets, as these camps did.
5. The population was not at risk from immediate mass starvation.

On five counts (at least) therefore the humanitarian agencies were themselves misinterpreting IHL and the situation on the ground, and therefore undermining IHL and bringing it into disrepute. Their position had a certain mass appeal to an ill-informed audience and was indeed endorsed, in part, by the UN Security Council, which itself thereby further undermined IHL.

The legality of 'humanitarian principles' and the confusion between different aspects of law needs to be challenged. IHL is too valuable to be discarded in this way.

African governments should make it clear that while they welcome international agencies' commitments to self-imposed codes of humanitarian principle, these should in no way replace, alter or impinge upon the requirements of international law and IHL. 'Humanitarian principles' cannot be the basis for challenging other requirements of law. In addition, they should in no way lessen the onerous obligations that IHL places upon those who try to provide humanitarian assistance during conflict.

OTHER WEAKNESSES OF IHL

IHL suffers from a number of weaknesses that are relevant to contemporary Africa. These are not recent developments but are rooted in the Geneva Conventions and the Additional Protocols. Among them are:

1. The definition of 'civilian' in the Additional Protocols. Given that many fighting forces in Africa are irregular and are closely integrated with certain civilian sectors, the very strong definition of 'civilian' in IHL is impractical. A notion of different categories of 'innocence' among civilians is widespread: for example infants are more 'innocent' than political cadres. This needs to be reflected in IHL.

2. There is a contradiction between IHL's preference for international wars and international law's preference for internal wars. Under IHL, the provisions are much stronger for international conflicts: there are more guarantees for the protection of civilians when one state is fighting another than in an internal conflict. But international law is very strongly against international conflicts (save in exceptional circumstances, of which the Rwandese attack on the military camps on its border should have been one). This creates the double standard whereby a state that is being destabilised by a neighbour is obliged to sponsor internal opposition forces in that country instead of dealing with the problem directly, a fact that gives less protection to civilians of that country.

3. Additional Protocol I gives 'international' status to members of national liberation movements, but provides no clear definition of what a national liberation movement is. At the time, it was intended to apply to anti-colonial wars, but this historic circumstance has passed, and it is unclear whether it could apply to other wars for self-determination or against oppressive regimes (for example in Southern Sudan).

4. The prevalence of internal conflicts and the development of more and more 'humanitarian' and human rights instruments has led to

considerable confusion and a lack of clarity of application of IHL. As has been argued, IHL is more suited to conflicts than human rights law because its focus is not the state but the belligerent party and because it is more practical. This warrants clarification.

5. The legal sophistication of much IHL means that it is inaccessible to those who are actually fighting wars and, as a result, impractical. The idea of 'customary humanitarian law' is widely used to stigmatise nasty behaviour, without any process of actually negotiating with belligerents and states. This process of 'overinflation' runs the risk of provoking belligerents to abandon IHL altogether. It is important to redress this balance. The sophistication of legal argument counts for very little when contrasted with the practical realities on the ground. African politicians and commanders do not have the political clout to challenge humanitarian lawyers in New York and Paris (and would be caricatured as dictators and human rights abusers if they did), but at least symbolic action is needed.

6. The measures in IHL to prohibit the creation of famine are weak. This is an important area because the great majority of casualties that arise in most African conflicts do so because of war-created famine, rather than the immediate consequences of war. The 1977 Additional Protocols introduced measures that specifically prohibited the destruction of items necessary for the survival of the civilian population (even if these items also had military uses) and stressed the obligation to permit neutral and impartial humanitarian relief. But the provisions in the second Protocol, which apply to internal conflicts, are much weaker than those in the first. Additional Protocol II only prohibits acts that have the specific aim of creating starvation. A second shortcoming is that the Protocols make no mention of prohibiting the prevention of *activities* necessary for the survival of the civilian population. In some circumstances it is essential for civilians to be able to move, to go to market or tend livestock, but prohibitions on movement in such cases are not prohibited. Given that one of the most devastating aspects of African warfare is the tendency to create famine, this omission is important.

These drawbacks are not sufficiently grave to invalidate the basic instruments of IHL. They are enough to give serious consideration to an African diplomatic conference to adopt a Protocol on specific aspects of IHL relevant to Africa. Most of such a Protocol would consist of reaffirming the fundamentals of IHL, but elaboration in specific areas such as the creation of famine would be in order.

THE REFUGEE CONVENTIONS: BACKGROUND

The 1951 UN Refugee Convention derived from the experience of Europe in the 1930s and '40s. It was based on the hope that the refugee phenomenon was a product of these particular historical circumstances and that as a result, would be temporary. The mandate of UNHCR was therefore only awarded for a few years, to be renewed if necessary.

The central definition is that of a refugee, as someone who has fled 'a well-founded fear of persecution'. War criminals are to be denied refugee status. The host government is given the right of awarding refugee status, but the office of the UNHCR was set up to provide legal representation for asylum seekers and refugees.

In the 1960s, with the growth of the problem of mass refugee exoduses, particularly in Africa, the UN adopted a second Protocol and the OAU adopted its own Convention. These provided more generous terms. Communities could be provided with refugee status en masse, rather than each individual having to prove his or her claim. The criteria for claiming refugee status were broadened to include flight from 'external aggression, occupation, foreign domination, or events seriously disturbing public order.' The main motive behind this broadening of the scope of the law was the large number of refugees generated by anti-colonial struggles in Southern Africa, but the flight of refugees from Burundi and Rwanda in the 1960s was also significant. Further elements introduced then and subsequently were the imperative of demilitarising refugee camps (militarised camps remaining liable to military attack) and the need to relocate camps some distance from the border.

But the central elements of refugee law remained intact: the refugee is someone compelled to leave his or her country because of threats arising from political circumstances, and refugee status should be confined to people generally regarded as civilians under IHL.

In 1984, in response to the relief needs of refugees from Ethiopia and Eritrea in Sudan, the UNHCR's mandate was broadened to include a new category: 'persons of concern to UNHCR'. This was essentially a way of enabling the agency to provide for people who might not fit the legal definition of refugee. It has become the hinge on which the UNHCR has transformed itself from a primarily legal organisation (a high commission, in fact) into primarily a relief organisation.

UNHCR lawyers have generally resisted the idea that its mandate should be broadened to include all internally-displaced people, on the grounds that these people are still governed by human rights law and that the consent of the host government is required for any actions on behalf of IDPs. But in Former Yugoslavia, the UN awarded UNHCR a similar role in the ambiguous circumstances of the break-up of that state.

REFUGEE LAW IN CONTEMPORARY AFRICA

For various reasons, refugee law as developed in the 1950s and '60s is less relevant to Africa today. However, that is not a reason for discarding it altogether: the core values expressed in the existing legislation remain valid and should be kept and defended against erosion.

Several developments have called refugee law into question.

1. 'Fortress Europe' and North America. Developed countries have led the way in closing their borders and spurning asylum seekers. The burden of assisting refugees has thus fallen overwhelmingly on poorer countries.

2. Globalisation, human mobility and multiple reasons for flight. Forced displacement is a complex phenomenon and even the broader definition of refugee introduced in the 1969 OAU Convention misses out many people who have been forced to leave their homes.

3. The phenomenon of internally displaced persons (IDPs). The numbers of refugees (who have crossed international borders) is consistently matched or exceeded by numbers of IDPs. These people often have comparable needs in terms of assistance and protection. Given that host governments often fail to respect the rights of these people, humanitarian agencies have often sought an international role for protecting them.

4. Cases of state collapse or fragmentation. Countries such as Somalia and Liberia have been unable to discharge their obligations towards either refugees or IDPs. Former Zaire had neither the wish nor the capacity to do so. In Former Yugoslavia and the former Soviet Republics of the Trans-Caucasus and Central Asia the situation has been if anything more complicated. These cases have preoccupied the energies of many humanitarian agencies, notably UNHCR, with the unfortunate result that they have come to see such cases as typical rather than exceptional.

The main contentious application or misapplication of refugee law in Africa has concerned the fugitives and externally-displaced people who fled Rwanda in 1994, erroneously but commonly referred to as 'refugees.' It appears that UNHCR interpreted events in the early 1990s to mean that its legal mandate had become irrelevant, and that it needed to cope with a world in which state authority had become meaningless, and hence in which it needed to establish its own, non-state, political-humanitarian order. The logical end point of this would have been the creation of a de facto UNHCR extra-territorial jurisdiction in refugee camps, protected by international troops.

In Former Yugoslavia, UNHCR provided assistance and relocation to civilian victims of war, in a way largely incompatible with its original legal mandate. This has brought the organisation under serious question for apparently assisting in ethnic cleansing.

In Central Africa, UNHCR sought to play a similar role, again forsaking its mandate in terms of being an all-purpose relief agency. At least in Former Yugoslavia the UN had a force that was supposedly to provide some physical protection: in Central Africa UNHCR had no such counterpart. This led to an 'overinflation' of the concept of refugee, which was extended to people who had no such claim under the 1951 and 1969 Conventions. The results of this included:

• Extending assistance and protection to people who were war criminals and belligerents.
• Providing assistance to militarised camps. The presence of civilians in these camps did not bestow a civilian character on them.
• Objecting to the compulsory repatriation of Rwandese in neighbouring countries on the incorrect grounds that these were 'refugees'.Calling for external military intervention to provide physical protection.

UNHCR thereby brought its mandate-and indeed refugee law in general-into disrepute. This chapter argues that UNHCR has made a major error in forsaking the foundations of its legal mandate. It is not the 'UN Refugee Agency' (as its press officers like to describe it), it is the UN High Commission for Refugees. No-one would want to deny that it has been forced to handle extremely complicated situations that do not fit well with its mandate, and that these have been very large and expensive operations. But these must be regarded as exceptional circumstances, not the general rule.

A much more appropriate response to these exceptional cases would have been to create ad hoc international structures, with case-specific rules and time-limited mandates, to provide humanitarian assistance. The established specialised agencies, notably UNHCR, would have been better advised to retain their independence from these essentially political arrangements, and should have pursued their mandates.

This is a case to be pursued at the OAU. In its 1969 Convention, the OAU provided the world's most generous refugee law. African states remain outstandingly generous to refugees, especially in comparison with developed nations. But this hospitality can only prevail if UNHCR (and indeed western donors and the UN Security Council) respect the need for a balanced approach. UNHCR should be primarily an organisation concerned with the legal protection of bona fide refugees. Where there are no other assistance agencies present (e.g. for the relatively small numbers of urban refugees in countries without a large scale refugee programme), then a modest assistance programme should be in order. But massive assistance programmes in situations of legal and moral uncertainty are extremely hazardous and have threatened the integrity of the organisation. It would be advisable for UNHCR to return to a much more cautious interpretation of its mandate, with an emphasis on protection.

There are some encouraging signs in 1998-9 that the UNHCR Executive Committee has acknowledged many of the problems that arose concerning the security and exclusively civilian and humanitarian character of refugee camps in Central Africa. This is an important first step towards a realistic and principled approach to tackling them.

LIMITATIONS ON WEAPONRY

International law restricting certain types of weapons is more heterogeneous than IHL as such. Strictly speaking it belongs to a different tradition of international law-the 'Hague Conventions.' Key measures include:

- The 1925 convention prohibiting the use of chemical weapons;
- The 1980 protocol on certain weapon types that cause excessive suffering;
- The 1997 convention on the prohibition of anti-personnel land mines;
- The 1998 ECOWAS moratorium on the import, export, transfer and manufacture of small arms and the 1999 Hague Appeal on small arms.

These are widely signed and ratified by African countries. Few countries possess chemical weapons capabilities. Landmines are still used in several conflicts, and many countries have a very serious problem of mines left from earlier wars. In addition, Africa has a convention prohibiting the use of mercenaries (the only one of its kind in force).[2] The continent is a de facto nuclear weapons-free zone, though this has not been affirmed by any formal treaty or convention. The OAU could consider a treaty that declares Africa a weapons of mass destruction free continent.

SUMMARY OF CONCLUSIONS
The basic instruments of humanitarian law are highly relevant to Africa. They are just and practical. This final section will examine how the valuable elements can be retrieved, while problematic elements can be discarded.

THE GENEVA CONVENTIONS
While the Geneva Conventions of 1949 remain relevant to circumstances in Africa today, more recent innovations in IHL have moved steadily away from the essential aim of practicability. IHL has become hostage to the political and institutional opportunism of the UN Security Council and its members, and international humanitarian agencies. This has brought it into disrepute.

There is no need for new instruments of IHL. The Geneva Conventions will do as they stand. The Additional Protocols have some unsatisfactory elements but they are, on balance, strong and appropriate. By contrast, almost all developments in the 1990s are inappropriate.

An African diplomatic conference on aspects of IHL relevant to the situation in Africa would be one course of action. Alternatively, the OAU Council of Ministers could simply:

- reiterate the commitment to the basic instruments of IHL;
- reject the doctrine that IHL gives privileged protection to aid givers;
- lay down the principle that further lawmaking in IHL cannot considered legitimate unless agreed by all interested parties.

This would allow Africa to lead through IHL rather than following in the area of humanitarian principles.

REFUGEE LAW
The solution to the crises of mass displacement in Africa lie in the political sphere. This is not the task of UNHCR or refugee law. But the legal protection of refugees remains important.

The first steps at an institutional and legal level are straightforward. The UN and OAU should reaffirm that UNHCR is bound by the 1951 and 1969 Conventions. UNHCR should be stripped of its role as a provider and coordinator of material assistance to large-scale communities, and should resume its former role as the legal representative of refugees and bona fide asylum seekers and the provider of modest assistance to individual cases. This is not a simple role, but it is an important one.

If the UNHCR prefers to continue in its current extra-legal role as the 'UN Refugee Agency', then it might be appropriate for the OAU to set up an African High Commission for Refugees with a legal mandate under the 1951 and 1969 Conventions. Separate ad hoc arrangements may need to be made for exceptional cases in which state authority has collapsed or states are conspicuously incapable of meeting their basic obligations. UNHCR should be independent of those arrangements.

MECHANISMS FOR ENFORCEMENT

Enforcement is always the problem for any institutions dealing with violations of international humanitarian law. The institutions may need the consent of states or belligerent parties to gain access, they may not have the judicial powers to subpoena witnesses, and of course they may lack any powers to enforce their sanctions. This means that, to be effective, any mechanisms must be agreed multilaterally, based on a strong degree of mutual consent.

This chapter has suggested several possibilities for institutions and processes:

• An International African Criminal Court.

• A committee set up by the OAU to monitor IHL and investigate allegations of abuses by both belligerent parties and humanitarian agencies.

• A diplomatic conference at the OAU to reaffirm the African commitment to the basic instruments and principles of IHL, namely the Geneva Conventions and their Additional Protoocols. Some specific clarifications could be made, for example on the prohibition of famine as a weapon of war. This conference could also state that while the Geneva Conventions are law and should be enforced, recent statements of 'humanitarian principles' are no more than statements of aim and cannot be considered on the same level.

• A demand by the OAU and its member states that UNHCR should conform to its legal mandate.

• A commitment to the dissemination of IHL and promoting IHL within armed forces by African governments.

Enforcement must always be taken seriously. But the nature of IHL is such that its success is to be found not in documents and courts, but in a developing moral consensus about what is acceptable and what is not. It would therefore be a mistake if mechanisms for enforcement were to run too far ahead of the ethical consensus among politicians and military commanders. Imposing such mechanisms may create a serious mismatch between principle and pragmatism that it may threaten to bring the whole enterprise into disrepute.

NOTES

1. Adam Roberts, 'Humanitarian Action in War: Aid, protection and impartiality in a policy vacuum,' London, IISS, Adelphi Paper no 305, 1996, pp. 60-1.
2. Abdel-Fatau Musa and J. 'Kayode Fayemi, (eds.) *Merceneries: An African Security Dilemma*, London, Pluto Press, 1999.

8

HUMANITARIAN ACCOUNTABILITY

INTRODUCTION

This book has developed the idea that accountability is essential for effective action against famine and comparable humanitarian disasters. The history of effective famine prevention has suggested that four major areas of accountability are important:

1. Electoral accountability: the opportunity for an electorate to take the ultimate sanction against those in power who have failed to provide protection from famine.

2. Wider public accountability: the opportunity for a full public debate on all aspects of famine prevention, food policy, humanitarian action etc. This refers to discussions in the media, the chance for trade unions and other associations to press their case, commissions of inquiry, and academic freedom to debate and investigate.

3. Legal accountability: institutions should be accountable to the law and their mandates, and there should be procedures for investigation and redress.

4. Professional accountability: there should be professional standards which can be established and enforced, including professional standards for evaluations of programmes.

These kinds of accountability apply to governments, governmental and inter-governmental institutions and NGOs (both national and international) alike. They apply in peacetime and wartime. However, for different institutions and different circumstances, different procedures and mechanisms will be needed. The basic principles for humanitarian action should be that it is humane, impartial efficient, effective, democratic and legal. If an aid programme aims to promote democracy, it should also be democratic and transparent itself. Some humanitarian action in wartime should also be neutral. It should try to minimise negative unintended consequences, according to the maxim 'do no harm.'

For a long time it was customary for international NGOs and UN agencies to dismiss any examination of the past with the riposte that they are only concerned with the future. This is outrageous, and the international agencies have belatedly come to acknowledge that there must be some mechanisms for examining the past, so as not to continue the saga of blunders and misdeeds. However, internal mechanisms for evaluation and accountability, such as many of the studies by the experts who visit Africa as consultants, are not adequate. First, they do not meet the full requirements for accountability. Second, reports sit on shelves and there are no means for enforcing the 'lessons learned'. Accountability without sanctions is meaningless. Third, some of these reports are unprofessional.

The 1996 'Joint Evaluation of Emergency Assistance to Rwanda' is a case in point. There are no strong reasons to doubt the professionalism and sincerity of the researchers and authors of the report. But what purpose did it serve? It was rather coy in naming the names of agencies and individuals who performed in a substandard way or told untruths, and so no penalties were meted out. On the contrary, agencies which received faint praise subsequently basked in this endorsement and used it to try and fend off any criticisms. No aid official was sacked, no agencies went out of business and no apologies were even offered—leave alone compensation—after what was, by universal consent, one of the most disastrous humanitarian adventures ever in Africa. In addition, when critics asked questions about the humanitarian programmes, agencies replied by saying that an evaluation had been done, so there was no purpose in further criticism, not even public shame. The report pointed out that many of the numerical claims (e.g. for people 'saved') were exaggerated and incorrect, but did not attempt its own investigation into numbers of people who had died. In short: the evaluation did not compel any substantial changes in the institutional status quo. The proof of this was barely six months after the completion of the report, when many of the agencies made exactly the same mistakes—or worse—with respect to the conflict in eastern Zaire. Evaluations have now been commissioned and carried out of the humanitarian activities in Zaire/D.R. Congo in 1996-7 in rather the same manner.

Mechanisms for accountability must be democratic, founded in law and must have real sanctions and penalties to impose. They can only be democratic if they are embedded in African political structures, including the OAU, national legislatures and local civic organisations.

The OAU's Panel of Eminent Persons to examine the genocide in Rwanda and surrounding events is the most important initiative in this area ever undertaken in Africa. It is vitally important that it succeeds, and that it sets a precedent for frank and comprehensive institutions for accountability, with, hopefully, sanctions to match.

MEASURES FOR ACCOUNTABILITY IN PEACETIME
African countries are aspiring to democracy, freedom of information, the rule of law, the elimination of corruption, and economic competitiveness. In all these areas, humanitarian action in normal, peaceful circumstances must seek to be accountable. This also entails mechanisms for hearing and arbitrating on complaints, independent mechanisms for maintaining professional standards, and the question of penalties.

A DEMOCRATIC HUMANITARIANISM
Humanitarianism should always strive to be more democratic than the wider political context in which it operates. There can be no justification for humanitarian workers being less democratic than, or even only as democratic as, politicians. The humanitarians should lead the way. They should therefore volunteer to place themselves under the constraints of a democratic system. If they have not yet thought of this, then they should welcome with open arms the ini-

tiatives of politicians who propose to democratise humanitarianism, and if they have any criticisms, it should be that the democratic proposals do not go far enough.

If the national government is not democratic, the choices for international agencies are more difficult. But at the minimum, donor agencies and NGOs should make the terms of their aid transactions and agreements public, should evaluate their programmes publicly, and should endeavour to create public fora for open discussion of aid issues. Such measures can minimise the accusation that the aid industry is colluding with undemocratic governments.

There are four elements proposed in a basic national democratic framework, supplemented by additional measures for international organisations (discussed later).

1. Legislative oversight. Parliaments and other legislatures (national and local) should take an active interest in all aspects of relief and development programmes. They should have parliamentary committees dedicated to the issue and should summon aid workers and citizens to testify before them, and make proposals to them.

2. Public inquiries. When a relief operation is needed, something has gone wrong. It may be entirely a natural disaster-but this can never be known without inquiry. And in any case, responses to a natural disaster will vary in their competence, energy and honesty. The public and their representatives need to know. This entails routine public inquiries with quasi-judicial powers at a local or national level into the causes and nature of crises and the responses to them. In exceptional circumstances, a special national commission of inquiry could be convened. This will allow the civil servants, aid workers and citizens who performed selflessly and well to get the credit they deserve, those who failed to be exposed, shamed and if necessary sanctioned, and for lessons to be learned. It will also be an educational exercise for the general public.

3. Food, shelter and health care are basic rights for citizens. Meeting these needs is not a question of charity but entitlement. It is the citizens' responsibility to ensure that their political leaders do not violate these rights with impunity. This implies that a mass

mobilisation around the politics of food will be the key. Citizens will establish political contracts with their leaders, and, should the latter fail to fulfil their side of the bargain, they will use the electoral system or other forms of protest to sanction them.

4. Freedom of information and association. Historically, civil and political rights-notably the freedoms of speech and association for citizens-have been used to pursue the goals of social and economic rights, such as freedom from hunger. For citizens, therefore, it is a basic right to form organisations such as local assistance agencies, or political parties or pressure groups to campaign for practical measures such as food security and health care.

TRANSPARENCY AND FREEDOM OF INFORMATION

Humanitarian activities and food and health policies affect the basic welfare and rights of citizens. They therefore have a right to know about them: to demand information and documents and summon the relevant officials to answer questions. The mechanisms outlined in the preceding section should suffice for national institutions. But for international agencies, further additional measures are called for.

Aid donors and international agencies involved in a country must submit to the same freedom of information requirements. They should: Publish their country programme and overall accounts and budgets; Make their decision-making procedures open to public scrutiny; Allow the right of access to all relevant documents held by the organisation; Conform to all national procedures for inquiry and evaluation.

Some of these measures (such as a right to information) have already been established for the World Bank, so NGOs and UN agencies should have no difficulty in following this lead. An additional element is the need for full public discussion about the rationale, ethics and philosophy of aid programmes. Too often, debates about the rationale of aid are held behind closed doors, with little or no participation from those affected by the aid process. Many academic paradigms about aid-and indeed about Africa in general-are constructed and adopted in international institutions without any serious discussion in Africa at all.

THE RULE OF LAW

Were it not for the remarkable fact that some NGO staff have claimed that they need not be bound by the laws of their host country, it would not be necessary to repeat that it is an absolute precondition that foreign aid workers and organisations act in conformity with the laws of the country where they work.

Giving and receiving assistance is a right. The victims of a disaster have a right to receive essential humanitarian assistance. The minimum rights of a donor are to decide whether to give aid or not, and how much, and to monitor whether that aid has been disbursed correctly. But for a foreign agency to operate in an African country is a privilege.

Many African countries are not democratic, and one of the ways in which they abuse their power is by manipulating foreign aid, selectively giving access to certain agencies, restricting and channelling their work, and expelling those they disagree with. The agencies' correct response to such abuses is not to claim that they have a right to be present and to operate, or to argue that they represent the victims (which they do not). Rather, if they have acted in a transparent and democratic manner, then their decision about how to respond will be strongly influenced by the demands of their recipient community.

A second aspect to the rule of law is mandate accountability. Many agencies have legal or quasi-legal mandates. UNHCR is (supposedly) governed by the refugee conventions, UNICEF by the Rights of the Child, etc. Other agencies such as NGOs have mission statements that have legal implications. These mandates and mission statements should be taken into account in national and local evaluations and inquiries into humanitarian activities.

FINANCIAL PROBITY AND COMPETITIVENESS

Again, were it not for the fact that some NGOs have declined to publish accounts or submit them to audit, it would go without saying that for any organisation above a certain size, accounts should be independently audited. (Laws commonly provide for very small local organisations to be able to function in a more-or-less informal manner with simplified auditing procedures or none at all.)

There is a wider context for financial accountability. Many international aid organisations get most or even all of their programme finance from donor governments. They are therefore using taxpayers money for public service programmes. They should therefore operate consistently with wider economic policies adopted by the national government (often on the instructions of the IMF and other donors). These policies mean free and open competition for contracts.

It follows that legislation on monopoly trading, closed bidding for contracts, fair and unfair competition, equal treatment in taxation, should apply to international aid organisations. Foreign agencies that bring their own money (raised directly from their individual supporters) may have exemptions from some of the rules on economic activity. But they should not be entitled to undercut national service providers, nor should their presence in the country be changed from a privilege to a right.

MECHANISMS FOR HEARING AND ARBITRATING COMPLAINTS

Some international humanitarian agencies—notably the Federation of Red Cross and Red Crescent Societies—have proposed the creation of the office of an ombudsman, to hear and arbitrate complaints. This is an excellent idea.

The model of a ombudsman for the relief and development sector can be taken up by national and local governments. Its mandate can then be determined according to law, with appropriate procedures and sanctions. It could have a range of powers ranging from abuses of administrative procedure and employment law to investigating unfair economic practices. It could have the power to impose minor sanctions, and would have the right to refer cases to the public prosecutor or another higher authority if appropriate.

PROFESSIONAL STANDARDS

Relief and development is an area with few professional standards. In some areas (health professionals for example) it is not difficult to find and enforce the appropriate professional standards. In others (administration, rural development) it is more difficult.

Employment law in many countries has mechanisms for ensuring that qualified nationals are given preference when posts arise. These procedures could be harmonised across different African countries. A particular challenge is employment in regional offices. For example many organisations have offices in Kenya that cover the whole of north-east Africa, and use the fact that staff have jobs that cover the entire sub-region as an excuse for preferentially employing non-Africans. A common sub-regional approach would solve this problem.

Another means of helping to establish and enforce standards would be to set up relief and development workers' professional associations. Like medical associations and bar associations, such organisations—run by national professionals themselves—could help enforce standards and ethics, scrutinise methods of hiring and firing and, campaign on other professional issues such as pay, working conditions, training etc.

STANDARDS FOR EVALUATIONS

A vitally important area for establishing professional standards lies in the area of evaluations themselves. Many assessments of humanitarian programmes are incomplete or partial. Clearly, an agency or a donor can ask for an evaluation of any single aspect of a programme that it has been involved with. But there should be agreed standards for a programme evaluation to be considered comprehensive and impartial.

Among the suggested requirements for a comprehensive and impartial evaluation are the following:

1. The evaluation should have access to the internal records of governments, aid agencies and donors. Where access has been denied, the evaluation should state this.

2. The evaluation should cover impact as well as efficiency and management. In particular, evaluations should include an attempt to assess mortality rates, to put an end to the current practice of making unsubstantiated claims about lives lost, saved and at risk. (It is shocking that students of famine mortality find far superior statistics for 19th century India than they do for contemporary Africa.)

3. The authors of the evaluation should be required to present and debate their findings in public in the affected country.

SANCTIONS AND COMPENSATION

The corollary of a mandate or legal privilege is obligation enforceable in law. Codes of conduct and the like will be meaningless if there are no penalties. All mechanisms for accountability should be established with built-in penalties.

For governmental institutions, civil service codes should be drafted with accountability for relief programmes in mind. For non-governmental institutions, an appropriate regimen will be required. Sanctions could begin with reprimands matched by apologies from the organisations. At a higher level, there could be fines. At the highest level, expulsion (for foreign organisations) and closure (for local ones). All of these procedures require some due process. None of these penalties should exclude the possibilities of legal redress through the courts and payment of compensation. It is a commonplace that many relief and development programmes do more harm than good: it follows that if they do harm, then the victims should be entitled to compensation. Entitlement to compensation should not depend on proof of an intention to commit harm (often there is none) but rather on proof that harm has been inflicted. Procedures for determining actual harm and determining compensation can be established in administrative law.

Enforcement of sanctions may be a problem for international agencies. Moral pressure is important and may go a long way, but agencies found guilty may be ready to launch counter-offensives using the media and their donor governments, accusing the African governments of abuses of human rights etc. For UN agencies and donors, bound by country agreements, there are possibilities of enforcing legal redress (though the donors and agencies will complain). For NGOs, there is the possibility that the agency will simply leave the country and avoid paying its bills. To minimise this possibility, African countries can adopt common standards and procedures, to allow the 'extradition' of an NGO from one country to another-the agency would then be left with the option of abandoning Africa altogether.

MEASURES FOR ACCOUNTABILITY IN CONFLICT

It is much more difficult to establish procedures for accountability in situations of conflict because of the absence of functioning democratic and judicial structures and the constraints of security. However, more modest structures and mechanisms are workable.

THE OBLIGATIONS ON BELLIGERENTS NOT TO CREATE STARVATION

For the belligerent parties, international humanitarian law provides a clear framework that lays out their obligations. The belligerents are required:

• Not to conduct wars of starvation, not to destroy objects indispensable to the survival of the civilian population and not to relocate populations by force except for imperative military necessity or for the benefit of the population.

• To provide essential material relief themselves to the population.

• Where this relief is insufficient, to permit relief activities by impartial humanitarian organisations, subject to their security needs and guarantees that relief is not being diverted or misused.

The UN Humanitarian Fact Finding Commission can, in principle, investigate the extent to which belligerents are observing these obligations. The OAU Commission of 21 could also undertake this task. Given the principle that regional organisations should take primary responsibility, there is no conflict of interest here. The OAU Commission of 21 could set up a special committee mandated with this task.

NEUTRAL HUMANITARIAN ASSISTANCE

For relief agencies, the framework of international humanitarian law is appropriate as a foundation for four kinds of accountability.

1. Accountability to the parties to the conflict. IHL lays responsibilities on the belligerents not to conduct wars of starvation and to allow relief, but also gives them the right to scrutinise relief operations and, under certain circumstances, terminate them.

2. Mandate accountability. Some humanitarian agencies have legal mandates and others have mission statements. These, along

with voluntary codes of conduct, should regulate relief agencies' activities. This is largely a question of self-regulation.

3. Independent monitoring of humanitarian action. Given that both the above sorts of accountability are likely to be inadequate, an independent monitor is called for to investigate and evaluate observance of IHL by belligerents and humanitarian agencies. The UN Humanitarian Fact Finding Commission and the OAU Commission of 21 both have this mandate.

4. Ad hoc independent international inquiries after the event. The OAU Panel of Eminent Persons to investigate the genocide in Rwanda is a model for how such inquiries should be set up. After the Panel completes its work, the OAU should utilise this precedent and build upon its strengths, while trying to eliminate any weaknesses that have been revealed in the mechanism. Either there could be a standing OAU Panel to investigate humanitarian emergencies, or a succession of case-specific inquiries.

The experience of other, broadly comparable inquiries suggests that the OAU Panel may meet several significant obstacles, including:

• Lack of judicial power to subpoena witnesses, meaning that individuals can refuse to testify, and governments may even try to evade the inquiry;

• Some witnesses may be too afraid to come forward to testify in a public manner, or even in a confidential manner, given the high profile of the Panel;

• The recommendations may not be followed up;

• The general public and citizens' organisations may not be actively engaged in the process or informed about it.

However, it is the responsibility of citizens and civil organisations to ensure that they engage with this important initiative, and to press for the recommendations to be implemented. A parallel Independent African Forum where citizens and civil organisations can participate will help this process.

NON-NEUTRAL HUMANITARIAN ASSISTANCE

Assistance in conflict may lose its neutrality and yet remain humanitarian, particularly when it is supporting a democratic or anti-genocidal cause. In such a case, different forms of accountability are required. These may include:

• Accountability to the belligerent party under whose authority the assistance is provided. If the assistance is justifiable, then the belligerent party should have some human rights credentials and a democratic programme;

• Accountability to international legal instruments such as the Genocide Convention or a UN or OAU decision to remove an undemocratic regime;

• Mandate accountability;

• Independent monitoring of assistance to ensure impartiality, professionalism and effectiveness;

• Ad hoc commissions of inquiry after the event.

However, formal mechanisms of accountability in such a situation are always likely to be incomplete, and much depends on the integrity of the humanitarian institutions themselves and their staff.

CONCLUSION: A PAN-AFRICAN AGENDA

Many African countries have experienced famines and other humanitarian tragedies. They have a common interest in preventing such disasters in the future. They also know that it is essential to face the past honestly and openly.

One of Africa's tragedies is that the moral high ground of relieving these disasters has been taken by international institutions that have a rather mixed record of delivering on their promises. These organisations also need to face their past honestly and openly.

But many of them are reluctant to do so, and will need encouragement.

This chapter has suggested a range of measures for accountability for both peacetime and wartime relief operations. They must be implemented by national governments and also, if possible, at a local level, to bring the process of evaluation down to the people as much as possible. The measures will also have more moral force and greater effectiveness if implemented across the continent. Common principles, standards and procedures will be extremely helpful.

There is no one single formula for creating and enforcing accountability, and no mechanism can be created that can be appropriate for all situations. The positive side of the confusion and plurality of the NGO world is that humanitarian disasters are confused, varied and unpredictable. Moral and political judgement will always be required for some exceptional cases.

INDEX